When
People
Unite

ISBN: 978-1-7327849-0-1

Printed in the United States of America

For the people.

When! Before the present epocha, had three millions of people full power and a fair opportunity to form and establish the wisest and happiest government that human wisdom can contrive?

Such regulations, however, may be better made in times of greater tranquility than the present, and they will spring up of themselves naturally, when all the powers of government come to be in the hands of the people's friends. At present it will be safest to proceed in all established modes to which the people have been familiarised by habit.

— JOHN ADAMS, *THOUGHTS ON GOVERNMENT*, APRIL 1776

Table of Contents

A Short Introduction

I've had the great opportunity to spend some time with people from across the political spectrum, in person locally and by phone nationally, in the last couple of years. I've been struck by how much we agree, despite what our politicians and media insist.

We made some real progress working out just what it is we want (government of, for, and by the people, for starters). We've defined what it is, what is preventing it from working, and what some alternative approaches to government by the people might be. We've even discussed ways we can reduce the need (perceived or actual) for government engagement in the economy, after first agreeing just what we expect from an economy.

The groups featured people from polar-opposite views on the last two presidential administrations, yet we had no trouble agreeing that what we have now isn't working and even on ideas on how it should be working. The groups featured people absolutely devoted to free-market Capitalism and people who were just as profoundly skeptical that it works in the interest of the common good, yet we had no trouble agreeing on what we expect from an economic model for it to be considered good.

The very fundamentals of our society are not working. The systems we rely on to help us get along and solve complex issues and resolve differences are failing. Practically all of us agree on this point. Yet we keep fighting on those complex issues instead of working together on fixing the fundamentals so we have tools and institutions available to us to work through the complex issues.

If "We the People" unite together to discuss and work through the fundamentals, I'm convinced we can develop political and economic systems that we can all believe in. We've seen what happens when the people lose faith in these systems, but there is no one with sufficient motivation and trust from the people to advance new ideas that work for the people. It has to be us (the people) that step up to show how working together works.

What follows is an exploration of what could happen if the people united, after an exploration of the history of the people's attempts to achieve control over their own lives and destinies. The purpose is not to suggest a solution but merely to suggest what is possible when the people unite.

Prologue

There have been a handful of instances in United States history when the people (in contrast to its leaders) have been broadly skeptical about whether the government truly operates in the best interests of the governed. At these times, people sensed that the system was focused on the interests and the needs of a tiny minority who benefited disproportionately from control over land, wealth, or connections to the right people (referred to as the "elite" throughout this book). Throughout most of history, the government would offer benefits to the people only when doing so also benefited those at the top. This doubt that the government truly served the people existed at the founding of the country. It was there at the beginning of the 1900s. It was back again in the 1960s. And there is serious skepticism now again in the 2010s.

Despite all the apparent divides between the left and the right today, however, there has rarely been greater agreement on fundamental principles. Both sides want people who are willing to work hard to have opportunity and be rewarded for that work. Both sides want to live in a country and world where they feel safe to believe what they want to believe and live how they want to live. To put it succinctly, most of us want freedom, opportunity, and the pursuit of happiness. Few people want someone else to monopolize or limit opportunities, to take more than their fair share.

The main difference, then, is in who each group thinks is the most significant threat to their values and freedoms. The left focuses on the privileges and powers—both inside and outside the government—afforded to corporations and the economically elite. They call for more transparent and honest government working for the people instead of for the wealthy. But they also see the government as the best and only tool to balance out the enormous structural advantages enjoyed by wealth in the country and world's economic system. Those on the left, then, are, therefore, willing to tolerate some in government taking advantage of their position in order to have, with government, a mechanism to regulate abuses in the economy. In contrast, the movement on the right is encouraged by the wealthy, pushing people to fear and distrust the government hoping to achieve greater freedom to exploit the country's people and resources. Those on the right highlight the obvious inconsistencies and flaws in our political model to make clear the risks the government poses. As a result, many on the right want to shrink government, while many on the left want to increase the size of government and regulation as the only apparent check on the power and privilege of the wealthy—imperfect as government is.

Actually both are right in their pointing to abuses by elite. There are people who benefit disproportionately from their connections and positions. These elite not only take opportunities away from others but also shrink the total size of the "pie" (total prosperity) available for everyone. Conventional wisdom appears to be that we have to choose between ceding more freedom to exploit to the wealthy and permitting a governing elite to take hold. Yet there are—there must be—other options that we have been heretofore unable to see clearly through the fog created by current elite-dominated economic and political systems desperate to stay relevant despite pressure from the people for greater fair play and freedom.

In this book, I hope to break through into those new realms and possibilities. But first, we must come to terms with the historical scale of the problem. We must take another look at the history of the United States to understand how the country and its current form of government have not lived up to their promise. This better understanding may be our best hope to shake us all free from our current rigid mindsets and circular debates. Then—and only then—we can imagine how a clever and resourceful people, "yearning to be free" and fed up with elitism, could bring to light the promise and potential of the nation.

PART 1

A BRIEF HISTORY OF THE UNITED STATES

It certainly seems that the United States was ideally suited to usher in a better, more humane world. Utopia was in the country's makeup since the early colonies, even if it was not always evident from its leaders. The US is often referred to, after all, as the Land of the Free and the Land of Opportunity. It seemed as if the country's DNA would not accept anything less than setting a new global standard for civilization some day.

But if we carefully and critically examine the course of US history, we see more examples of continuity with the past than anything new. Pockets of utopian thinking quickly gave way to elite rule. We see age-old concepts of oppression and exploitation sometimes repackaged to appear new, other times more obvious knock-offs familiar to anyone who has studied history. The people paid dearly in reduced freedom and opportunity so that the country's favored elite could enjoy their privileges. Slavery is the most obvious example of limited freedom, but opportunity was also severely limited by tax, education, and infrastructure policies that supported the wealthy while restricting everyone else. The people paid an even steeper price whenever different elite battled each other, using the people as pawns. Yet through it all, the people regularly fought back, trying desperately to make the country live up to the promises made in political speeches. It was their tenacity and the persistent sense of potential that gave hope for something better to come for the country.

CHAPTER I

Founded under dubious motives

Explorers and settlers invade the continent with utopian ambitions and with demands from European elite for wealth. After suppressing the utopian dreams, a powerful upper class emerges and deflects local resentment to England, leading to war. Then they force a Constitution designed to secure the position of powerful minorities upon an unwilling population.

A new continent for the taking

It is telling that the history of the United States often starts with Christopher Columbus. His exploits are widely and popularly if not always accurately known—his ignorance and disregard for humanity whitewashed for centuries to make it more palatable. Insisting that the Earth was smaller than centuries-old scientific calculations had determined it to be, Columbus ushered in a dramatic change in how Europe would engage with North America. Unlike those who came before him, his motivations were not as simple as discovery or adventure, or vast virgin fishing grounds away from the competitive European waters. He promoted the trip to Europe's elite as a way to reduce expenses and risks involved in trade with Asia and gain a competitive advantage. In exchange for his efforts and the personal risks, he hoped for a modest share in the financial gains from improved trade.

Half of his funding came from private Italian investors, wealthy enough or desperate enough to invest in his mad scheme. The other half came from the monarchs of Spain. Ultimately, they decided to back him not because they believed in his concept but instead in order to prevent any other kingdom from claiming any rewards in case Columbus's theories somehow happened to be true. Desperate to get ahead in a highly competitive Europe, Spain had to borrow from non-discretionary royal accounts to fund their portion of the voyage. Competition between ruling classes often took massive risks with a country's security. Most of the suffering caused by poor decisions would be felt by the kingdom's people, anyway, not its rulers. The troubled thinking of European political and economic systems produced countless examples of horrific inhumanity in Europe. Monarchs and nobles competed with each other to see who could exploit and torture populations of people more. They did this to maintain and support the lifestyle of a few individuals born into the aristocracy.

When the desperation of the European aristocracy spilled over onto a new continent, it was the people of the new continent who paid the price. The financiers back in Europe set rigid profit expectations, but their distance separated them from the reality of the situation. When things didn't go as planned, it wasn't Columbus making decisions about whether acting inhumanely was the best decision. Instead, it was the voice of feudalism and monarchism propelling him to violate fundamental human virtues by enslaving the Natives. On a mandate to return with riches, Columbus (finding no precious metals) first returned with Caribbean Natives—people he had enslaved, all in the name of his Christian sponsors. In his future voyages in Central America, the northern edge of South America, and throughout the Caribbean islands, he continued this tradition of exploiting people, land, and resources. He was acting far from noble, despite his "noble" backing. The course of history on the continent had been built upon an unsettling foundation.

When the colonies in North America were launched, they were funded by wealthy Europeans who expected the colonists to generate more wealth for them. Just as with Columbus, risk and uncertainty were not accounted for in their expectations, and excuses based on real-world challenges posed by the land, the weather, and the original inhabitants did not deter the investors from their demands. Under social and economic pressure themselves, wealthy European sponsors could hardly afford to help confront unexpected challenges, nor could they ease up their demands upon the colonists. This was especially true for the earliest colonies. In Virginia, the unrelenting pressure from investors to generate wealth created enormous difficulty. Colonists eventually hit on tobacco as a viable cash crop for these purposes but only after much unnecessary human suffering coming in the forms of starvation, internal strife, and unfriendly relations with locals.

Things only got worse with each new wave of colonization. Desperate for short-term profit, the challenges the Pilgrims in New England faced were made worse by the constant interference of their backers in distant Europe. Instead of sending additional supplies to help establish the new colony, more settlers came. Charged for the voyage, these people were expected to generate more revenue. The newcomers only added to the food shortages experienced in the struggling colony. Eventually the situation got so dire that the backers were able to hold the colonists hostage for supplies, demanding a greater stake in the eventual output of the colony. Even then, supplies were sparse, and new mouths to feed continued to flow in. The often-maligned Native populations did far more to help and less to harm the efforts of the colonists than the "civilized" financiers back in Europe did. The lives of ordinary citizens proved expendable in the cause of wealth maximization.

Despite the high expectations of the European overseers, most of the early settlers to North America were simply hoping to make a new life for themselves. They were looking for a quiet place where they could make an honest living without being harassed by people born into better circumstances. Part of the country's utopian roots, a few also came expressly to set up new forms of society and government. For example, the Puritans came with ideas of setting up a society with elements of theocracy and democracy. Their aim was a government that was open to anyone who was accepted into and practiced their faith. However, setting such high standards that even the leaders themselves could not reach them made it impossible to sustain.

Rhode Island was founded as a direct response to the Puritans. Their utopian religious tolerance would eventually set the standard—with many colonies modeling their language for religious freedom around the concepts originating there. Rhode Island also stood out for its enlightened view of the Natives. The citizens of Rhode Island felt their tolerance, egalitarianism, and sense of community made the Natives more civilized than their narrow-minded Puritan neighbors.

Traveling further south, we encounter another hopeful utopian experiment, Pennsylvania. William Penn envisioned it as a model colony where settlers would work hard to establish their own livelihoods while leaving Penn with enough prosperity so that he could live with few duties aside from colony management. It never produced the fortune he was hoping for, and in trying so hard to make his own fortune, he alienated and frustrated many of the colony's residents.

In Georgia, at the southern reaches of England's North American colonies, we find yet another example of utopian trial. Georgia was the last charter provided by England, offered to a non-profit enterprise that envisioned a colony of small landowners who worked their own land. Georgia was meant to be a refuge for people pushed out by the consolidation of the landed aristocracy in the other colonies and in England. Here, slavery was forbidden and heavy drinking discouraged. But the venture seemed doomed to failure from the beginning because of its proximity to South Carolina. Georgia settlers, anxious to achieve the privileged lifestyle themselves, smuggled in slaves and rum and began protesting against the colony managers.

These utopian concepts and experiments were challenged with setting up new settlements from scratch. There was no room for people who considered themselves too good to work. Everyone had to chip in to avoid complete failure. Even people who were able to sponsor indentured servants got their hands dirty, making sure the colony succeeded. But once the hard life-and-death work of getting a colony started was over, a colonial elite began to take shape. There were no systems in place to discourage exploitation. Concepts from Europe rewarding those willing to put themselves ahead of the community prevailed. The European virus of social hierarchy was too strong for it to stay contained or to accept any competing ideology to challenge it.

As elitism grew, it became more entrenched. Temporary concepts of class like indentured servants were soon replaced with the more permanent source of privilege in the form of slavery. When people immigrated to the southern colonies from Barbados, bringing with them the tradition and conviction that a large plantation with a massive number of slaves was the only civilized way for a privileged class to live, the practice gained even more popularity. In the North, wealth began to consolidate in the form of a market economy that allowed people to take out more than they put in. A merchant elite with influence and wealth far above that of other citizens took shape, made possible by their connections in trading, a fair amount of luck, and willingness to exploit opportunities.

In Massachusetts and Virginia, elite rule took on disturbing proportions. The Puritans continued and expanded their religious oppression. Complaints to the Crown that the Puritans were violating the rights of British citizens living in the colony came with increasing frequency. Friends the

Puritans had left back in England were embarrassed by how intolerant the Puritans had become. Things finally went too far when the Puritans attempted the common tactic of manufacturing a crisis with the Native populations in the region in order to distract the non-Puritans in the colony from their complaints. The episode undid the attempt by the British to improve relations with the Natives and nearly resulted in the colony being wiped out by Native retaliation. They were saved only by the intervention of interested parties in New York.

In Virginia, society had developed more in line with traditional Europe—a model of landed aristocracy. The governor in Virginia exploited his position to funnel enormous wealth to himself and his friends, including Thomas Jefferson's great grandfather, William Randolph. Falsely claiming that the money was going toward the building of fortifications, he used the Native unrest instigated by Massachusetts as a cover to tax the farmers oppressively. The exploitation and abuse by the landowners in Virginia pushed the colonists to plead with England for relief, complaining that their rights as British citizens were being violated and that British concepts of freedom and benevolent rule were being ignored.

And things were changing in Britain. Eventually the complaints were persistent enough and the offenses egregious enough that Britain felt compelled to take action. They imposed their own leadership in Virginia and Massachusetts to keep exploitation and privilege within more reasonable limits and more in vogue with English practices. It was the end of independence for these colonies, but a win for the people. Colonies like Connecticut and Rhode Island, places with strong traditions of opportunity and meritocracy, continued to enjoy nearly complete independence and self-rule, free from Britain's attention and regulation.

Life for the colonists on the continent slowly began to settle down. On remote farms, people appreciated their freedom and separation from European society. But in the cities and among the southern aristocracy, people desperately wanted to win the acceptance of the European upper classes. The plantation owners invested in the culture of landowners with extravagant mansions and the frivolities of daily life.

The northern cities competed with each other for greatness and made an effort to "catch up" with European cities. International trade had brought in wealth; the question was how best to use it. For the European aristocracy and for the US Capitalists a hundred years later, the way to prove the greatness of a city was to erect monuments and fantastic buildings that expressed the wealth of the city's wealthiest people. But many in the northern colonies considered the way to greatness to be the people themselves—not the buildings. They invested in education and public-infrastructure projects like sewer systems. They prioritized keeping people from falling into poverty, realizing the poor could bring down the positive sense of community in a city. Doctors did their part to ensure healthcare for the less privileged. They were making plenty of money with their wealthy patients that this simple act of charity had little negative impact on their financial status. Cities regulated business to avoid exploitation of labor and consumers, referred to at the time as "oppressing." These measures worked, and many who visited or heard tales of what North American cities were able to do were impressed. Some Europeans were, to some degree, jealous of life in the colonies.

An unintentional war

But the northern colonies were quickly approaching a peak of utopianism. It would a be a long time before so much sincerity was applied to making sure everyone enjoyed the principles of Freedom and Opportunity. The idea of competing with Europe on the quality of cities and the lifestyles of the lowest in them was not sustainable in a society that allowed people to take comfort and security away from each other. People of status became anxious about losing their status to new upstarts and desperate to hold onto it. The upper classes, made up of the wealthy merchants in the North and landowners in the South, were hardening, becoming hereditary instead of simply through consolidation of wealth. Having wealth wasn't enough to ensure opportunities for one's children. One had to be part of the right families. Certain families, therefore, started to see their position and privileges as a birthright, an entitlement. To ensure their position, politics were controlled with increasing leeway from Britain with the best opportunities limited to the select families and their favorites. Anxiety to succeed was made worse in North America because of the Calvinist belief among many that one's financial success on Earth was an indication of the approval of God, with obvious implications for the afterlife. The pressures to produce personal wealth were enormous and difficult to overcome—too much was riding on it. The view that a city and its leaders were best measured by those at the bottom gave way to the European model of exploitation again.

While little stood in the way of these new elite in the colonies, they were still considered second-class citizens back in Britain. Ashamed by their lower standing, they looked for ways to assert their status. Tax policy after another war with France (the Seven Years War, called the French and Indian War in the colonies) gave them their chance.

Traditionally the way Britain covered its expenses in North America was through export duties. These were essentially taxes on goods as they left the colonies. These taxes were built into the prices farmers and artisans could get from traders and merchants when selling goods for foreign markets. That way, people who produced for the global market and therefore needed the support of Britain's global connections and protection would pay their fair share. Merchants were then theoretically responsible for paying the duties to Britain and helping ensure the delivery of those goods. The problem was that many merchants evaded their duty payments, anxious to establish and prove their worth in an increasingly status-conscious society in the colonies. By not paying the duties, they were, in essence, taking taxes others had paid and putting the money into their own pockets. It was a practice that, unsurprisingly, frustrated Britain, especially after Britain had paid out to defend the colonies against aggressions from Natives and French forces struggling to maintain and expand their presence in North America.

Meanwhile the wars necessary to sustain the prestige of the British Empire and avoid encroachments by competing European nobility were putting incredible strains on the British budget. Their most powerful and influential citizens were also unwilling to pay that bill. To cover their expenses, Britain tried to improve their duty collection. They were anxious to find ways to compel the merchants to pay forward the duties they collected. But the merchants stubbornly protected their "extra" incomes garnered by expropriating the duties for themselves. To achieve and maintain their success, comfort, and security, they felt justified in acting like European elite. They, therefore, didn't hesitate to take as much as they could and pay in as little as they could get away with by exploiting connections, loopholes, and the work of others on the continent.

In Britain it eventually became clear that, if they were going to cover expenses, it wasn't going to come from the merchants. They would need to find a way to generate the additional revenue from the people inland directly. For Britain it was a fair request: that the colonists pay for the defense they had just received. But the colonists saw things differently. They felt that they were already paying for British support through duties. To their way of thinking, if Britain wanted to get paid, they should get that money from the merchants. But instead the British hit on a scheme to tax all official papers, introducing a new Stamp Act. In addition to feeling like a double tax to the colonists, the new tax provoked people in two professions who relied heavily on paper and could mount a significant challenge: lawyers and printers. The lawyers raised a legal objection that had made the rounds in Ireland, that taxation without representation was contrary to modern British principles. And printers published newspapers and pamphlets to mobilize a protest movement against the new tax.

At first popular sentiment was rightly directed against the wealthy in the colonies. People realized that the wealthy and well-connected demanded that everyone else pay their fair share of taxes while actively evading taxes themselves. They not only took from taxes illegally by avoiding paying forward duties on exports but also legally by serving as tax collectors. Their connections in the right circles allowed them to place family members in these lucrative roles and take a cut off the top of each tax receipt.

By 1760 there had been 18 separate uprisings against wealthy colonists, movements that aimed to overthrow the colonial governments that favored them. But that was just the beginning. From 1766 to 1771 the "Regulator Movement" in North Carolina conspired for tax reform, to shift the burden off the poor and remove the tax breaks for the wealthy. But they were not successful. More progress was made further north, but it was fleeting. In 1765 artisans and poor in Boston gave up their petty disagreements against each other and turned against the wealthy. They were looking for a more equitable distribution of wealth and argued that those who work hardest and made the greatest contributions should be rewarded for their efforts. They demanded to know how there could be so much suffering next to so much abundance. In an attempt to reform the system, they formed an informal group called the Sons of Liberty. These developments made the wealthy very uneasy, imagining how the mob could easily be leveraged to overthrow their social and economic privileges. Something had to be done to turn events around. Soon Lawyer James Otis and tax collector Samuel Adams infiltrated the Sons of Liberty and skillfully redirected the anger against the colony's royally appointed governor and lieutenant governor. They ransacked their mansions and stoned the governor. The crisis had been diverted, and only the officials of the British government suffered.

The British became paranoid about colonial aspirations for independence and were, therefore, easily provoked into actions that would turn the colonists against them. One such incident occurred after a British attempt to tax imports of commonly used goods (glass, paper, lead, paints, and tea), introduced through the Townshend

Act. People were conditioned against any new tax, seeing them as a way to transfer wealth from themselves to those close to power on both sides of the Atlantic Ocean. Their protests and a vote in the Massachusetts Assembly engineered by Samuel Adams while non-merchant delegates were out of town provoked extreme reactions by the British. The situation eventually escalated to the event that was sensationalized as the "Boston Massacre." A brief period of heightened tension ensued but faded just as quickly after Britain removed almost all the new taxes. The exception was a tax on tea. It was maintained in order to save face and avoid giving the complete win to the hardening power bases in the colonies.

For the next three years there was very little trouble over taxes in the colonies, and it started to look like the worst was over. The tea tax wasn't much of a problem for the colonists because many simply bought tea smuggled in from the Netherlands. This, however, did cause problems for the British tea merchants. Without the sales in North America, British tea started piling up in warehouses. To help improve the flow of tea, the British government lowered the taxes and streamlined transportation requirements, making British tea more affordable to the colonists. It was an attack on the market for smuggled tea, however, that did not sit well with the smugglers. To stir up resentment for the British, the smugglers funded protests and planted the idea that Britain's lowering of the cost of tea was just a ploy to get the colonies to pay their tea tax. The most famous of these sponsored protests was the so-called "Boston Tea Party," but there were many similar protests that demonstrated just how successfully the anger had been redirected toward the British government.

Redirecting anger away from the abuses of the local privileged minority to a larger entity was a common tactic used by desperate "leaders" throughout history. But it frequently came at a very high cost if sustained, as conditions escalated out of control quickly. As the protests against the British became more vocal and violent, the British became more concerned about losing the colonies. They saw the colonies as a valuable asset to the British Empire, one that admittedly added to the empire's prestige more than its wealth. This fear and paranoia quickly turned to desperation and extreme action that created the threat to colonial independence that had previously existed only in the projected imaginations of those engineering the hysteria. The nerves of both the British forces and the colonial militia were wearing thin. The slightest misunderstanding could erupt with passion into a serious incident that would jeopardize the benefits enjoyed by the privileged classes on both sides of the Atlantic.

Just such an incident happened when the British stumbled into the local militia while hunting down the rebel leader Samuel Adams and smuggler John Hancock. Poor discipline and frayed nerves led to shots being fired and casualties for both sides (273 British, 95 colonial). Since the differences between the two sides were constructed to obscure desperate colonial bids to compete with European aristocracy, there was no basis for negotiation, and things quickly escalated to full war. It was yet another war resulting from an elite desperate to maintain and expand their position against another elite.

The colonial elite may have been better off trying to advance their position through more formal channels in British society, but conditions had escalated beyond the point where such was feasible. Instead representatives of the colonial upper classes gathered to discuss and publish a formal Declaration of Independence to rationalize the complaints the colonies had against the British. No one at the time saw it as a philosophy for a new government. In fact few of the signers of the document paid much attention to its preamble. The flowery prose about freedom and equality was just window dressing to add a sense of righteousness to the cause detailed in the main body of the document. It was only later that this preamble came to serve as a powerful foundation for the country's mythology. Nothing highlighted the lack of attention given to the preamble more than the line stating that "all men are created equal" passing with little sense of hypocrisy in a country where slavery was still very common among the signers and backers of the document. The delegates then turned to writing the Articles of Confederation, which would set up a new government for the newly independent country with weak central power so as not to challenge the power of the privileged families in the states.

After the Declaration was issued, the war was on in earnest. Up to this point, it was largely the Massachusetts militia managing the course and tone of the war. With the people's militia leading the war effort, this was starting to look like a war of, for and by the people. The throngs of crowds cheering on the delegates sent from Massachusetts to discuss the war emphasized the support the people showed the militia forces. It was clear that something had to be done to regain control over the situation. One of the first orders of business was to replace the military leadership since the militia leadership in Massachusetts was mostly from the "rabble" of ordinary colonists. Some of the officers were even willing to share their salaries with their soldiers. George Washington was chosen to take charge of the whole military effort. Coming from a long-established aristocratic family with strong royalist roots, he was considered a fair representative of those in power to execute the war effort. Additional officers were taken from select families across the colonies to keep things fair and balanced. Recruiting based on family instead of talent meant less-qualified military leadership who consistently put their own welfare above that of the troops, but this was how it was done in the time before Napoleon Bonaparte showed the virtues of professional officers.

The leaders debated whether the war fit in with their personal needs and eventually determined that it would help free them from the overwhelming personal debt they owed to the British nobility. Once they established firm control over the leadership, tone, and direction of the war, they finally felt secure enough to order up pamphlets to encourage people outside of Massachusetts to also sacrifice for the cause. The radicals in the independence movement asked Thomas Paine to put together a pamphlet consistent with their way of thinking. The result was the hugely popular *Common Sense,* in which Paine highlighted how impractical the idea of monarchy was and proposed a government that would be much closer and engaged of, with, and for the people. He took inspiration from the government in the United Netherlands. He proposed such popular ideas as a government committed to "Securing freedom and property to all men, and above all things the free exercise of religion." The pamphlet proved critical to building support for war effort. But it also called for a response, something to keep the ambitions of the people in check. So John Adams wrote his own pamphlet, *Thoughts on Government,* to make clear that the government should be dominated by a small minority at the top. He argued that, although far from ideal, the new government should be based on established and tested ideas. He suggested basing the new government on how the British government operated, stating: "At present, it will be safest to proceed in all established modes, to which the people have been familiarised by habit."

The response to the call to arms from the colonists was generally muted. Antipathy was most strongly felt among the lower classes in the south—Delaware, Maryland, North Carolina, South Carolina, and Georgia. They had had far more trouble with their local leaders than anything the British were doing to them, so they couldn't understand why they should fight for the local government against the British government. Neither of the governments was intended to serve and protect their interests. Meanwhile those familiar with the events leading up to the war saw the whole thing as cooked up for the benefit of the merchants and smugglers in Boston. To most people it just seemed better to keep out of the whole mess and let the elite fight it out amongst themselves and just see how well they could manage without citizen soldiers.

With the lack of enthusiasm for the war, the small number of recruits came mostly from populations of freed slaves, criminals, and recent immigrants trying to feed themselves in a society that was stacked against them. Such a limited supply of troops meant the military tactics had to shift away from using soldiers as expendable fodder—as was and would remain common practice in Europe—to acting more strategically with the limited human resources available. They favored more ambushes in wooded terrain and targeted enemy leaders with sharpshooters. Many of these tactics they learned from observing the continent's original inhabitants, in whose tribes the foot soldiers were typically much more highly valued than they had become in European militaries. But this approach was a serious violation of European wartime etiquette, showing just how desperate things had become.

The profound lack of commitment and shared sacrifice extended outside of the military as well. The concept that people "should" and would commit themselves to a nation was not firmly established until the French Revolution, and, without that blind, unconditional nationalist fervor, it wasn't long before the colonists had lost what little patience for the war economy they may have started with. The costs of goods, when available at all, were going up to maintain the income of a select few, but people were still expected to give up their produce to the army at prices dictated to them. Many farmers refused to sell, hiding their produce to sell to the British, who at least offered more secure currency. Others actually cut back production, figuring it wasn't worth the effort for the price they could get.

The attitude of the people, however, was nothing compared to the lack of commitment from the wealthy classes. In Virginia interest from slave owners spiked only when the British offered freedom to any slaves who took up arms against the colonists. But, for the most part, those who didn't take the opportunity to advance their position by serving as officers could and typically did pay to send replacements for themselves in the drafts for the state militias. They continued to live their lives of increasing luxury—adding to the strain on limited goods—without giving any thought to the serious deprivations of the army. To make matters worse, they often took advantage of their positions to extort high prices for products sold to both colonial and British armies and to their poor neighbors. General Washington, in fact, considered this sort of war-profiteering to be an even bigger threat to the war effort than the British military forces.[1]

Like the signers of the Declaration of Independence, most of the members of the first Congresses were from the wealthy classes. This meant that, like the military leadership, Congress, too, suffered from a lack of talent. With the rather extreme exception of John Adams, who was not only well-known for putting in long hours but was also the only "Founding Father" who didn't own a slave, they were not accustomed to work. Most of them returned quickly to the comfort of their estates after the first years of the war to escape from the difficulties of the independence struggle. Thomas Jefferson, too, retreated to his Virginia home, taking a two-year stint as Governor of Virginia, ending disastrously with the defeat of Virginia by the British after Jefferson could not convince the people to fight for the cause. Those who did stay in public service preferred state politics, where they refused the support needed to organize a national war effort since providing such would have meant personal sacrifice on their part. And with meaningful work so difficult on the national stage, many in the national Congress simply used their position to increase their own wealth. Always desperate to get ahead and keep up, the upper classes typically found ways to turn a bad situation into an advantage for themselves.

With the lack of support from the people and local leaders, the new country struggled to raise funds and organize materials for the army. Fortunately the French were willing to provide support. It was part of the continuing effort of their aristocracy and nobility to gain and maintain their position in European society against the encroachments of the British nobles. By 1777, in fact, 90% of small arms carried by colonial soldiers and all artillery, tents, and uniforms came from France.[2] It was a difficult alliance for some to accept, however. As British citizens, many considered France to be their mortal enemy, although few perhaps could say why. As such it hadn't been too long ago that some in the colonies had been fighting against the French. It was the ages-old animosity between the French and British that made the alliance possible, so old habits and hatreds simply had to be overcome. Those at the top tended to be much more flexible in their alliances anyway than the people who felt more sincerely the hatred for the enemy the leaders had previously (when it better suited their needs) convinced them was a threat to their livelihoods.

Eventually, after throwing themselves completely into the war effort with their own military forces, the French saw an opportunity to deal a decisive blow to the British forces in the South. Fortunately for the future of the new country, General Washington caught on to the plan and positioned his troops to participate in what turned out to be the decisive sequence that ended the war. By being involved in the final battle, the United States improved its leverage in the peace negotiations. They improved them again by ignoring their treaty obligations to France and negotiating a separate peace with Britain. There is very little honor among competing nations.

It looked for a while, however, that, after agreeing to terms with Britain, the leadership in Congress would let the peace slip through their hands. The dysfunctional Congress struggled to get the required number of people together to ratify the final peace treaty. For starters, the Congress was on the run from the people. They were being threatened by unpaid soldiers fed up with their lack of concern for ordinary people. They had to relocate first from Philadelphia to Princeton and then to Annapolis. Furthermore, the representatives were not inclined to leave their states. It was in the states where most people anticipated power would reside. Being absent from the states during the critical consolidation of power could have significant implications for their families' position within the new social, political, and economic hierarchies. It, therefore, wasn't until just before it was set to expire that the treaty was finally ratified and the peace was secured.

Selling an unpopular Constitution

The war did not resolve the challenge faced by the rising upper classes in North America. With a new nation they were indeed able to achieve a higher degree of separation and independence from Britain. They would still have to prove themselves worthy in those circles, but at least they no longer had to compete with them within the same national institutions. They would have power to create their own laws that would favor them instead of having to exert effort to avoid laws designed to favor the privileged back in Britain. But there was now a new problem: the people were starting to get utopian ideas. Most people just wanted to be left alone; they saw government as an institution for the privileged minority to manage their affairs and wished to be touched only minimally by it. But Thomas Paine's pamphlet had riled some people up, making them feel that the war was for them, not just by them. They wanted to form government in line with their own ideals and values.

In the early days after the war, there was an opportunity for the people to make some progress for their cause. The war disrupted some of the control enjoyed in the states. And the leaders from the states also struggled to work together, each jealous of the other's power and wealth. In addition, many from the most prestigious families were temporarily excluded from power. They had been implicated as British loyalists in opposition to the cause of independence. The people were therefore able to make headway in many of the states. The top priority was securing basic rights for everyone. Simply getting the rights they had enjoyed as British citizens secured officially in the states required effort. These basic rights included freedom of press and legal guarantees for fair trials.

Freedom of Religion was another battleground where the people had more success in some states than others. Rhode Island and New York, which were already well-known for religious tolerance, naturally went the furthest. In states like Massachusetts and much of the South, where religion was tied up with how the state's people were controlled, the road was much more difficult to travel, and little progress was made. In these states business and politics were conducted through the churches, their spiritual significance being secondary. People were still required to attend services at and contribute financially to specific churches. Among the most progressive and noble protections introduced by a state during this period has to be included North Carolina's protection of Native hunting grounds stipulated within their Bill of Rights.

The era of progress by and for the people was short-lived, however. Soon those at the top realized the threat, and decided to put aside their competitions and take care of business. Damage had been done already with significant protections hard-coded into many of the states. There were concepts from the states that many later insisted be carried over onto the national level. But before new systems could be envisioned that would give the people real power to set the direction for the states and the nation, the privileged minority had mastered the situation. The people were, after all, at a real disadvantage against the power of wealth and connections. They would much rather focus on rebuilding their farms and families damaged by the war—demonstrating their strong work ethic, unable to and uninterested in exploiting the labor of others for these efforts—than get wrapped up in states' governments.

After restoring their control in the states, the country's leaders found themselves no better suited to running the country in peacetime than they were in coordinating resources, the economy, and the troops during wartime. And the challenges were only slightly less dire. Debt racked up during the war was one of the most pressing problems. It was a public problem, however, beyond the capabilities of a government designed to facilitate the personal ambitions of those at the very top only. It was a problem that could be resolved only when its solution could be aligned with the personal interests of someone with power.

Instead of dealing with the debt problem, which seemed irreconcilable at the state level, they were much more concerned about protecting their base of power in the states and limiting any competing power at the federal level. The catch was that many had ambitions that were out of reach of state power. The southern landowners wanted to expand westward, seeing additional land occupied only by the Natives that could provide additional sources of wealth if brought under their control. But they needed shipping rights through New Orleans to make the new lands viable. Meanwhile the northern merchants wanted access to more foreign ports to build up their shipping empires and to participate more fully in the profits of global trade.

The states did not have enough international standing to negotiate with foreign powers to make either of these ambitions possible. Even if a state government could get an audience with a foreign nation, many of the states had given up trying to repay the debt owed to these nations and so had little hope of convincing these nations to make friendly concessions to them. The bottom line was that both North and South needed a federal government to negotiate with other nations to get what they wanted. The problem was that the goals of the two regions were often mutually exclusive. The country could expand westward and gain access through New Orleans by giving up ambitions for new trading routes or vice versa. The federal government would have to choose between the ambitions of one elite over the other. People who feel a sense of entitlement to privilege do not like to take risks, and a battle over control over a federal government was a big one. Federal consolidation meant dramatically more power for significantly fewer families. In fact, competing interests between the states got so bad that the North even talked of secession to set up two separate nations to avoid having to compromise.

In addition to these pressing concerns was the fact that the people were still way out of hand. In Massachusetts war veterans and farmers rebelled in protest of pro-banker policies and an ironic Stamp Act introduced by the state's leaders. There were no federal troops to bring in to put down the rebellion, and the state couldn't wait for federal troops to be called into service by the weak federal government of the time. Massachusetts would have to handle the problem with limited state resources. It was a wake-up call. They did not want the states to be the only line of defense between the leaders and the people. These events provided a much-needed sense of urgency that allowed the states to overcome their resistance and accept a central government to address their pressing concerns: solving the conflicts between the states, expanding the country's borders and trade, reducing debt, and keeping the political ambitions of the people in check.

A national convention was called to discuss a new federal Constitution. Each state recruited representatives from the very highest echelons, which inevitably meant that about one third of the total had actually voted against independence from Britain. While there was much animosity between North and South, nearly everyone could agree on one thing: people should be limited and controlled as much as possible short of pushing them to revolt. There was even persistent talk of a monarchy to keep people in line. Some even suggested the country should ask someone from a royal family in Europe to take charge. There was also general consensus that the states would be maintained as a useful tool to satisfy the interests and needs of local elite.

The convention had its troublemakers, however. For example, some of the representatives tried to suggest that the right to vote was a natural right—one of those inalienable rights people were starting to talk about that should apply to all humans equally—instead of a right that the state's leaders granted to those they felt were worthy. There was much riding on this point. If the right to vote were a natural right, then some would insist that it should apply equally to slaves and women, since they were equally as human as wealthy white men. If it were not a natural right, then the humanity of the individual would not be a determining factor in deciding whether they deserved the right to vote; their reliability in voting the "right" way could be weighed instead.

James Madison, one of the leading figures in the early fight for a federal government, argued forcefully for restricting the right to vote. He understood that, while the availability of land in the early days of the country gave a broad range of people more opportunity than they might have in other countries, this well would eventually run dry. At the convention to construct the Constitution, he suggested that "in future times a great majority of the people will not only be without land but any other sort of property." He continued to reason that, with a growing gap between the rich and the poor, a right to vote offered without regard to property ownership would mean that either "the rights of property and the public liberty" would be threatened or people would come under the sway of some unscrupulous wealthy oligarchy that could use their money to sway the vote in their favor.[3] Despite making such a profound and accurate prediction about the future, instead of arguing for a defense of people from such eventualities, Madison used the anticipated abuse to justify simply consolidating power in the hands of a few in the first place.

The philosophers at the convention suggesting that voting was a human right were eventually put in their place. Pointing to British precedents, the advocates for a restricted right to vote argued that property and wealth should be requirements for voting because people with more property would have more at stake. They also argued that those who were compelled to work for someone else would be dependent on them and, therefore, could not be counted upon to vote for their own interests. It was not only thinking that fit in better with the conventional wisdom of the time but also an argument that fit in with the will of the delegates, worth more than any logic one could apply to a question.

It was a clear indication that the independence the country had just fought for was intended for a slim few only. There would eventually come a day when the government representatives so openly admitting that the political and economic system denied such a large majority of its citizens a voice (and many even basic freedom and independence) would cause quite a scandal. This was long before that time. This was still a time when the country's rulers could openly discuss "freedom" and "equality" and have it refer simply to themselves without having to offer a vigorous defense or justification.

At the core of the new Constitution were James Madison's ideas on how to protect the social and economic privileges of the landowners.[4] Madison was disturbed that some of the ideas about equality and power being vested in the hands of the people, inspired by Thomas Paine's *Common Sense* and the preamble to the Declaration of Independence, were being discussed in the states. But these discussions were typically localized to a very small area—a few energetic champions of the people gathered together in a state capital, perhaps. To keep such local passions from spreading to the national level, Madison insisted that change in the new government should be difficult and slow.

The government would be split up into three branches not only to prevent anyone from easily usurping power but also to frustrate the hopes of any popular sentiments from affecting the course of government. The Judicial branch would be selected by the Executive and approved by the Legislative in order to prevent this potential defender of the rights of people, created to make sure the other branches behave constitutionally, from getting out of hand. Meanwhile the Senators would be selected by the state legislatures instead of by voters in the states like they would be for the House of Representatives. Since the state legislatures were typically fully controlled by those with the most wealth and/or land, the Senate would be a strong defender of the existing privileges, much like the House of Lords in England.

The elections, too, would be staggered for the different branches. For a campaign by the people to get all the right representatives elected to all these different branches of government would require years of dedication and financing before any serious change could be considered. Since most people had to work for a living and would have difficulty finding candidates who could afford to serve in positions with no direct pay, it would be very difficult to sustain the effort required to introduce real change in the proposed government, particularly against likely resistance from well-funded and powerful interests.

With these ideas as the foundation, a new Constitution took form. Like the Declaration of Independence, the Constitution was dressed up with a preamble designed to inspire confidence and trust. While it had no force of law and few people paid it much attention at the time, it would later become another source for the country's nationalist mythology. Ironically, perhaps the most inspiring language in the preamble was only a last-minute addition. The original text started out with a list of the states as the source of the legitimacy and power of the federal government: "We the People of the States of New Hampshire, Massachusetts, Rhode Island and Providence Plantations, Connecticut, New York, New Jersey, Pennsylvania, Delaware, Maryland, Virginia, North Carolina, South Carolina, and Georgia, do ordain, declare and establish the following Constitution for the Government of Ourselves and our Posterity." But this list was a bit unwieldy and would become outdated as soon as the first new state was admitted. So the original opener was replaced with the simpler "We the People of the United States." This language would later be leveraged in court cases to argue that the power of the government was intended to be vested in the people.

Most of the people outside of power were not fooled by the new Constitution, and support for it was difficult to come by. The fact that the political leaders thought it such a perfect instrument for the formation of the government was likely all the proof many needed. It was a sentiment one would expect to be strongly felt in South Carolina, where the plantation owners clung more viciously to their entitlements, oppressing not only the slaves but also the white independent farmers by monopolizing all the best land and restricting opportunities. Many in other states more affected by the war and the euphoria of hope after the war were disappointed to find in the Constitution an instrument designed to serve a single class. They saw it as a betrayal of what they saw as the ideals of the war they had been asked to sacrifice for.

Leading the charge for the Constitution were James Madison and Alexander Hamilton. Together they penned a large collection of essays to explain and rationalize the Constitution. They compiled all their thoughts together into a volume called *The Federalist Papers*. The "Federalist" in the title, which they also took as their party name, was a bit of misdirection since "Federalism" was generally understood to indicate a weak central government and strong local government, nothing like what was being proposed in the Constitution. To answer Madison and Hamilton's essays, others took up and gave voice to what the people were saying privately, eventually calling themselves the Anti-Federalists. Although most of these men used pseudonyms, their ranks are presumed to include notably George Clinton—Governor of New York and later Vice President under Presidents Thomas Jefferson and James Madison—and possibly even Richard Henry Lee—US Senator from Virginia, who had also served as President of Congress shortly after the war. A number of these writings from a variety of different sources were eventually compiled in *The Anti-Federalist Papers*. One such essay, signed "Brutus Junior," highlighted the unscrupulous background of the Constitution's framers:

> It is at the same time, well known to every man, who is but moderately acquainted with the characters of the members, that many of them are possessed of high aristocratic ideas, and the most sovereign contempt of the common people; that not a few were strongly disposed in favor of monarchy; that there were some of no small talents and of great

influence, of consummate cunning and masters of intrigue, whom the war found poor or in embarrassed circumstances, and left with princely fortunes acquired in public employment... *(Anti-Federalist No. 38)*

Another essay signed "THE YEOMANRY OF MASSACHUSETTS" suggested that the Constitution, and the war against Britain itself, may be nothing more than a ploy to secure power for a select few:

> it was not the love of their country they had so much at heart, as their own, private, interest; that a thirst after dominion and power, and not to protect the oppressed from the oppressor, was the great operative principle that induced these men to oppose Britain so strenuously. *(Anti-Federalist No. 40)*

This essay went on to assert that their right to pass their own judgment on the Constitution would not be forfeited, even though the likes of Benjamin Franklin and George Washington had endorsed it, insisting that "We do not conceive we are to be overborne by the weight of any names, however revered." To make the case the essayist pointed out that Washington was "living upon the labors of several hundreds of miserable Africans, as free born as himself" and therefore not the ideal spokesperson for freedom, despite his service as General.

The essayists argued that the framers did not share the ideals commonly held by the people. They made it clear that they could not support a Constitution that promoted rule by and for a privileged minority. An essay entitled "The Use of Coercion by the New Government," signed "A Farmer and Planter," explained with surprising clarity the undeniable connection between wealth and power, lamenting the lack of mitigation in the proposed Constitution:

> Aristocracy, or government in the hands of a very few nobles, or RICH MEN, is therein concealed in the most artful wrote plan that ever was formed to entrap a free people.... Does not riches beget power, and power, oppression and tyranny? *(Anti-Federalist No. 26)*

In an essay that could have just as easily been written in the second half of the 20th century, the essayist known as the "Centinel" pointed to the poor distribution of wealth and opportunities in the country as a serious concern that must be addressed if the country wished to have a free government:

> A republican, or free government, can only exist where the body of the people are virtuous, and where property is pretty equally divided. In such a government the people are the sovereign and their sense or opinion is the criterion of every public measure. For when this ceases to be the case, the nature of the government is changed, and an aristocracy, monarchy or despotism will rise on its ruin. *(Anti-Federalist No. 47)*

Alexander Hamilton, arguably the most prominent Federalist, openly acknowledged that the consolidation of power into the hands of the elite would be inevitable:

> From the natural operation of the different interests and views of the various classes of the community, whether the representation of the people be more or less numerous, it will consist almost entirely of proprietors of land, of merchants, and of members of the learned professions, who will truly represent all those different interests and views. *(Federalist Papers No. 36)*

But he insisted that they could be trusted not to abuse that position, and represent the interests of others with the same vigor as he would fight for his own interests:

> But where is the danger that the interests and feelings of the different classes of citizens will not be understood or attended to by these three descriptions of men? *(Federalist Papers No. 35)*

Hamilton went on to reassure that, if the elite did unexpectedly rule against the will of the people, they could simply rise up against the government (and its army) to punish the offenders and restore balanced government:

> Let it, however, be admitted, for argument sake, that the expedient suggested might be successful; and let it at the same time be equally

> taken for granted that all the scruples which a
> sense of duty or an apprehension of the danger
> of the experiment might inspire, were overcome
> in the breasts of the national rulers, still I
> imagine it will hardly be pretended that they
> could ever hope to carry such an enterprise into
> execution without the aid of a military force
> sufficient to subdue the resistance of the great
> body of the people. *(Federalist Papers No. 60)*

He was suggesting that an armed people would act as a check on elite power, a sentiment that would later come to be written into the second amendment to the Constitution, giving people the right to bear arms. This is clearly a very weak check on the abuse of power. The country's leaders could get away with a lot of abuse before people finally felt compelled to resort to this extreme and desperate act that would be unlikely to produce a happy ending for the people or the country, even if "successful" at overturning the government. This, however, was what Hamilton was proposing to keep power in check.

The elite were in an uphill battle getting public support for the Constitution against mounting popular disapproval. They didn't just want to ram this thing through, though. They surely could have, since the rules for choosing delegates for the states' ratification conventions were set by each state, with control firmly maintained by a few families. Instead, given the pockets of unrest and dissatisfaction already witnessed, they wanted the legitimacy afforded by debate. They would, however, need to control that debate. With the money available to them, they overwhelmed people with pro-Constitution pamphlets and articles. But the other side was still getting their message through. And their ideas were resonating with some of the delegates and the people they were talking to. In an effort to simplify the matter for people, the Federalists took steps to silence the other side of the argument. They used their considerable power and influence to deny critics of the Constitution a voice in official publications and their control over coveted postmaster positions to block their outgoing mail. When all else failed, they simply bribed ratification delegates. Too much was at stake for them to play by their own rules. The *appearance* of debate was all they really needed, anyway.

Confronted with such powerful opponents and being unable to mount the effort required to develop any compelling alternative, the critics of the Constitution started to give in. They turned their attention from trying to prevent a government for and by the elite to trying to limit how much harm it could do. The Constitution had given the federal government its powers but was restrained only by the power held in the states. What was needed was something like the Bill of Rights that many of the states had introduced to protect people from abuse of government.

Adding a Bill of Rights was a compromise some at the top were willing to make to push their Constitution into law with broader support. They refused the demand by many to include the Bill of Rights in the original document, but reckoned that, by promising to implement a Bill of Rights after ratification of the Constitution, they could win over the last measure of support they needed. Few people actually believed the Federalists would fulfill their promise after gaining power, but, combined with buying off key decision makers in swing states, it was enough to get the Constitution ratified. Only North Carolina and

Rhode Island remained as holdouts. The Constitution went into effect, and the formation of the new country proceeded without the holdout states. These two states waited to see if the Federalists would keep their promise before committing to the new federal government. It is possible that, without their stand, the Bill of Rights protecting the rights of the people and minorities of all sorts would not have been included as part of the foundational law of the country.

Even with the Bill of Rights in place, not many people of the time were under any illusion that the people's vision of the country had been brought to light. For starters, the protections afforded by the Bill of Rights required the cooperation of the Supreme Court to ensure that the government respected people's rights. But since the Supreme Court Justices were appointed by the President and approved by Congress, it was soon co-opted by the Federalists, allowing them to ignore many of the protections promised to people. The Bill of Rights applied only to actions of the federal government. For the time being and for more than a century to follow, the states could stomp on any rights that were not explicitly protected by their state constitutions.

Many at the top thought that the ratification of the Constitution would finally put the ideals awakened by the war to rest. They were genuinely surprised by the general public's interpretation of and continuing demands for "liberty." They would have been completely shocked to find "liberals" still continuing to fight for liberty more than two hundred years after the Declaration of Independence. For the leaders, the concept of liberty was tied to class, a different form of liberty depending on what class you were in. Applied to the top, it meant freedom to live as they wanted, to enjoy the privileges of their birth, which included exploiting the labor of others. Applied to the slaves, however, it obviously meant something dramatically less. Applied to white working men, it was somewhere in between these two extremes. For women, it often meant something closer to what the slaves got. It was the ability to convince enough people that they already had liberty—a talent that developed slowly over time—that allowed the whole system to last as long as it did.

CHAPTER 2

Competition at the top

Assertions that a government run by elite will rule in the interest of the people are proven illusory, as Alexander Hamilton expertly wields the government he created for a rising banking industry. After pushing his power grab too far, an opening develops for a new political class leveraging popular discontentment for their own benefit. The rise of these two competing elites cause the southern slaveowners to become nervous and are eventually forced to deal with their decline in power and status.

Enter the bankers

Most of the discussion during the framing of the Constitution was on protecting the privileges of the southern landowners. But it was a rising banking elite that emerged after it took force as the primary beneficiary of the powers the Constitution granted. The resulting competition at the top led to a loss of public voice, freedom, opportunity, security, and even life for many of the country's people.

National and international bankers did not have to wait long to learn that they were the victors in the "revolution" that had just been won. Their opening was provided by General George Washington. He had accepted the post of the country's first president after ratification of the Constitution only reluctantly. Chosen for his reputation earned in the war, in office Washington served much more as a symbol for the nation than as a political leader. He focused on the difficult questions of how a "President" was supposed to behave and represent the new country in ceremonies. This focus left a power void that Alexander Hamilton stepped into. An illegitimate child who relied on financial support from neighbors to get through college, Hamilton could not count on raising himself up to the status he believed he deserved through typical channels. Instead he would have to raise his position like many after him would, by fighting for the cause of people who were already wealthy and powerful. As head of the Federalists Party and with a network of loyal followers in and out of government, Hamilton was well positioned to direct the government in the interest of a newly developing and rising banking establishment. By doing so he dramatically raised his own stock and financial security.

Hamilton didn't create the wealthy power brokers he would end up aiding by handing out privileges to his friends. There was already a substantial consolidation of wealth, both in Europe and the United States. For example, by 1770 the top 1% of Bostonians owned 44% of the wealth in Boston. In New York state 30 people (in a population of around 20,000) owned ¾ of the land, renting it out to settlers for an additional source of income.[5] By virtue of their wealth and family connections, they had much greater opportunities available to them than most people, allowing them to increase their wealth without having to work at it.

In Europe, the monarchies and aristocracies were fighting against the incursion of the rising wealthy elite into government power circles and high society. But in the United States, Hamilton was in a position to welcome them in and provide them with first-class treatment, hoping to enrich and empower himself in the process. The debt crisis arising from the war was made to order for that effort. While the nation's debt was a problem for the war veterans who were paid in debt certificates for their service and sacrifice to the new country, it presented a golden opportunity for those who already had enough to live on. Desperate to build or rebuild farms, the soldiers had to sell off their debt certificates and land grants at deep discounts to the wealthy, who were eager to exploit their suffering. As a result, by 1790 the vast majority of the US-held debt was in the hands of a tiny minority of wealthy speculators, mostly in the North.[6]

A desperate country spelled opportunity not only for massive profits but also an epic power grab. Hamilton worked swiftly to exploit the conditions to establish the wealthy firmly in power, creating an interdependent relationship between the government and the bankers. Neither could be successful unless both succeeded, so each would have a vested interest in the well-being of the other. It gave bankers incredible leverage over the government and made sure keeping them satisfied was always the government's top priority.

The people, however, were going to be a problem. Their suspicions about the government serving a small set of core constituents were being confirmed. Something had to be done to redirect their attention away from the obvious abuses. Building out the mythology and symbolism of the nation, an early form of nationalism, was Hamilton's most powerful tactic and George Washington his greatest tool. It was easy to make Washington into a national icon. Wars were always good for making legends. To add to it, Hamilton increasingly portrayed Washington as a man of the people. Ironically, however, there could hardly be found a more potent example of the old landed aristocracy. Back in England, the Washington family had been strong supporters of the monarchy. They left England for North America only when Oliver Cromwell's forces disposed of the King and things looked bleak for the monarchy. In the colonies the Washington family had only grown wealthier, making Washington the country's wealthiest president ever.

Washington was also extremely pliable. In a letter to one of his colleagues in Virginia (Edmund Pendleton) in September 1793, Washington confessed: "I give my signature to many Bills with which my Judgment is at variance." He willingly gave his good name and reputation to draw attention away from government policies that were increasingly opposed to the "general welfare." He was, therefore, an extremely valuable asset that Hamilton wanted to leverage as long as he could. So despite the President's failing health and faculties and his vigorous protests, Hamilton convinced Washington to serve a second term as figurehead for the Hamilton government. The additional term from Washington bought Hamilton more time to take freedom and opportunities from the people in his service to the bankers. But he still had to move quickly if he wanted to secure his gains.

The Bank of the United States was arguably Hamilton's greatest achievement for the banking interests. The Bank had broad influence over national policies and was the benefactor of many government advantages. Not only was an elite increasing its control over the government and country, it was predominantly a foreign elite. The Bank was 70% owned by foreign investors, who had far more influence on the direction of the country than any citizen did. While Hamilton expected the citizens of the United States to demonstrate blind patriotism, he facilitated the development of an international banking class that would operate independent of national loyalties and boundaries.

Hypocritically, while actively putting up his own patriotic front, Hamilton warned future generations to "Guard against the impostures of pretended patriotism" in the President's farewell address. It seems he understood the indiscriminate power of nationalism and didn't want it used against his bankers as readily as he used it himself for them. Elite rule always came with a high degree of anxiety about maintaining ill-gotten power and wealth. The anxiety motivated the elite to take more extreme action to suppress and oppress the people.

The French Revolution complicated matters for Hamilton because it increased the risk that the people would reawaken and make new demands on the government. Hamilton had been successful up to that point because many people accepted that government was always for the elite. It didn't matter much to most people if the government served the landed aristocracy or the banking establishment. But the French Revolution was a popular movement, with heavy involvement, support, and enthusiasm from the people. It advanced the ideas of government for and of the people, proclaiming Liberty, Equality and Fraternity for everyone. Such ideas were dangerous. As such the French Revolution had a profound impact on

Hamilton. It motivated him to advance a more hard-lined government to protect against the advances of the people, much as Communism and the Russian Revolution would do for leaders generations later.

Thomas Jefferson, chosen as Washington's first Secretary of State, was among those hoping the French Revolution would inspire people in the United States. Being a member of the landed aristocracy in the United States meant he was on the outside now looking in as the bankers' power increased. Combating an established power base heightened Jefferson's rhetoric about the rights of ordinary people. He saw in Europe a land where a tiny minority was in charge at the expense of the people. And he observed much of the same in the United States, and getting progressively worse. Living in France since the War for Independence, Jefferson had seen the beginning days of the revolution and got caught up in the optimism and enthusiasm of the people there. Although dismayed by the increasing violence as the revolution progressed, he hoped the ultimate success of the French Revolution would provide new energy, optimism, and ideas to lift the United States onto a different track.

In a note published with Thomas Paine's latest work, *Rights of Man*, Jefferson wrote "He has no doubt our citizens will rally a second time around the standard of Common sense" and referenced the "political heresies" of the Hamilton administration as motivation.[7] He was terrified at the rhetoric of John Adams and Hamilton at a dinner party at the White House, in which he recalled Adams and Hamilton praising the British system of government. Referring to the British government, Adams had said that he felt that "if some of its defects and abuses were corrected, it would be the most perfect constitution of government ever devised by man." Hamilton was more extreme, suggesting that "it was the most perfect model of government that could be formed; and that the correction of its vices would render it an impracticable government."[8] Hamilton was, in fact, often heard showing support for the idea of a monarchy, hoping that the current form of government in the United States would fail so he could bring in his own monarchy.

To help balance out the growing power of Hamilton's Federalist Party, Jefferson helped form the Republican Party and usher in the two-party system that would dominate US politics. The party was also called the Democratic Republican Party, from the popular "democratic republican" societies that Hamilton tried to suppress. The existence of two competing parties each apparently representing different elites—the landowners versus the banking establishment—shattered the myth of benevolent and unbiased elite politicians making compassionate decisions with the whole country in mind. People who had believed the myth about elite rule representing the will of the people were confused and angered at these developments. Even President Washington found the developments disturbing.

Power was too tightly controlled by the Federalists, however, to allow the Republicans to break them. It was only the Federalists' overreach that ended up destroying their reign. One of the federal government's powers that the Federalists took too far was the ability to levy taxes on goods. It provided Hamilton a way to pay down the debt owned by the bankers without having to take from the wealthy to do it. As long as the government didn't explicitly target ordinary people at the exclusion of the wealthy, most were willing to let the tactic slide. However, one particular tax, the tax on whiskey, was too obvious. Whiskey was by far the easiest and cheapest way for Western farmers to transport their excess grains to eastern markets, where it was consumed mostly by other ordinary consumers, since the wealthy preferred other alcoholic beverages. Those with the greatest wealth and influence not only were spared the tax, but they also typically served as tax collectors in the new regime as they had under the British, continuing to take their cut directly from the top before it got to the government. It seemed clear that it was a tax intended to funnel money from those with the least to the wealthy and influential.

When protests broke out, Hamilton's government tried to contain them by keeping news of them from reaching other parts of the country. When that didn't work, he had to take more drastic measures. To raise a force to put down the protests, he had George Washington introduce a draft. The draft was widely evaded and led to more protests and riots. But eventually a sufficient force was raised and prepared to take on the people. Hamilton gave the operation a patriotic appearance by having Washington himself lead the troops to hunt down the original protestors. It was the only time a sitting President led troops into the field, and it was against his own constituents. Such an overwhelming show of force by the government was enough to break the will of most of the protestors. Those who were captured were marched mercilessly to Philadelphia to stand trial for treason. The scene must have reminded many of how the British troops reacted to tax protestors before the war. Since voting rights were limited to people with property and wealth, many of the protestors had even resurrected the legal complaint "Taxation without representation." The government was clearly working in the interest of the elite and not bothered by oppressing and silencing citizens to achieve its goals.

After the fiasco of the so-called Whiskey Rebellion, Hamilton resigned from his official position in government. But he remained the effective leader of the Federalist Party, and, as such, he managed the presidential election of 1796 from his private law office. In the election, Jefferson's Republican Party enjoyed greater popular support, but the Federalists had the voting system rigged in their favor. For starters, most people could not vote because of the property requirements. In seven of the sixteen states, the presidential electors who would cast votes in the Electoral College were chosen by state legislatures, which the Federalists controlled. Even with everything lined up against them, the vote was close. The deciding factor proved to be Jefferson's class, which alienated enough of the electorate in the South and gave Federalist John Adams a three-electoral-vote margin of victory. Awkwardly, as runner-up, Thomas Jefferson became Vice President, according to the rules of the time. Once in office, Adams spent much of his time at home in Massachusetts, leaving the day-to-day business of governing to Hamilton's men once again. Leftovers from the Washington presidency, these were men of dubious talent but stern loyalty to Hamilton. Work to suppress any popular movement and entrench the banking elite continued at a feverish pace.

Support for the Federalists was fading fast when they were handed a gift from Europe. The Federalists had always been strong opponents of France and the French Revolution, fearful of the populist ideas coming out of it. They also wanted to curry favor with the British to maintain and expand access to trading ports. Attempts by the wealthy in France to manage the passions of the French people caused the Revolution to take a decidedly sinister turn that seemed to confirm everything the Federalists were saying: the people could not be trusted. People who had supported the Republicans because of their pro-France position were easily brought over to the gleeful Federalists, who peddled fear and hatred of France. Under this manufactured threat, Hamilton not only pushed through an increase in the size of the military, but he also managed to get himself put in charge of it. He could, therefore, deploy troops as needed to support his agenda. And if war broke out, he would be in a position to be the leader who emerged as savior, much like Napoleon Bonaparte would do in France.

Many people were deeply concerned over Hamilton's control over the military, but it was nothing compared to the negative reaction people had to the Alien and Sedition Acts. These acts included a collection of new laws designed to give the Federalists greater control and secure their position from the changing moods of the people. The Naturalization Act meant that immigrants, who tended to vote Republican, would have to wait longer before becoming citizens and gain the right to vote even if they had enough property to meet restrictive requirements. The Alien Friends Act allowed the President to deport "dangerous" aliens. The Alien Enemies Act, which was supported by both sides, allowed the deportation of immigrants from countries that the US was at war with. And the Sedition Act made it illegal to speak "maliciously" against the federal government, its officials, or laws. The Federalists tried to convince people that the restrictions on their freedom were necessary because of all the French spies infiltrating the country. Their true intent, however, was betrayed by the exception they made to the Sedition Act, allowing for people to speak out against Vice President Thomas Jefferson.

The Acts were set to expire only after the election of 1800, which would give the Federalists a chance to "steal" another election and then further advance policies designed to strengthen their hold on power. Among themselves, the Federalists talked about crushing the Republican Party and putting an end to thoughts of social and political equality. Republican editors were persecuted, some were convicted, and many others left the profession in fear. But the number of Republican newspapers actually increased under the greater restrictions. For many it was the provocation they needed to become more involved. Telling someone in the United States they could not do something almost always had that effect.

The Federalist Party suffered a significant blow when private letters from Hamilton discussing his potential uses for the army were presented to Adams. He included such uses as going to war with Spain, Britain, or maybe even Virginia, a Republican stronghold. It was the wake-up call Adams needed to finally realize the truth that Hamilton had been in charge all along. Finding his personal independence, Adams refused to play along with Hamilton's plans for the Alien and Sedition Acts, dramatically limiting the damage the acts could have done to the country and its people.

However, if Adams really wanted to stop Hamilton, he was going to have to take the French threat away from the Federalists. To do so meant going against the wishes and obstructions of his own party. He had the support of most of the country, however. People were weary of the extra taxes imposed to keep the country on a war footing. By the time of the 1800 election, enough progress had been made in warming relations with France that the fear advantage manufactured by the Federalists had been lost. While Adams still enjoyed his reputation as a non-elitist Federalist, obstructions by his own party denied him the political boost one typically gets from brokering a lasting peace. The peace didn't come in time to make a difference in the election.

The election of 1800 was the last gasp for the Federalist Party. Without fear, the days of the Federalist Party were numbered. They continued to exploit Washington even after his death at the end of 1799, but their nationalism toolbox was lighter and weaker. They had become toxic and were completely incapable of speaking to the needs of the population. Some Federalist candidates even refused to "lower themselves" to be in the company of ordinary voters. On top of little popular support, the Federalists also had to deal with the fact that they didn't like their own candidate. John Adams was simply too independent for the party. Despite being the party's best hope for popular support, Hamilton couldn't get behind him. He even wrote a 54-page pamphlet against him, doing significant damage to his party's chances.

The Republicans had everything going for them in the election, but they still found a way to blow it. Because of poor planning and an unusual rule, two Republicans ended up tied in the Electoral College votes. The tie meant the decision was pushed over to Congress, where the Federalists still had significant influence. After holding the country figuratively hostage for an extended period, the Federalists were able to demand pro-banking concessions from Jefferson as part of their terms for accepting his election as President. The features of the Constitution designed to prevent change had worked, to a degree.

The election of Jefferson brought a new hope to the country. Jefferson, in fact, called it the "Revolution of 1800." Being a member of a privileged class himself, however, it seemed unlikely Jefferson would implement any dramatic changes in who had access to freedom and opportunity even if he hadn't made the agreement with the Federalists. Jefferson kept most of the Federalist government appointees arguing that doing so would help the country heal from a traumatic election. And his commitment to a small federal government reduced the checks on Hamilton's bankers, who continued to leverage their debt holdings and influence over the economy to their maximum advantage. Although the Republican Party talked publicly and in the press about expanding the role of ordinary people in government, they did little in the states to change suffrage or otherwise improve the role people could play in government.

Jefferson did inspire hope and trust, however, leading to greater public turnout for elections. Instead of reciprocating that trust, the Republicans remained uneasy about their hold on power. They experimented with new ways to ensure that the elections turned out their way and continued to build out the nationalist mythology in order to keep public approval and acceptance high. Soon the Republican Party started looking around for some new way to rally the people in support of the government. British attempts to execute a blockade against a French Empire that had spread across Europe (violating US neutrality in the process) gave the pretext they were looking for. The young Speaker of the House, Henry Clay, tried to sell war to the people by arguing that the United States had to be about something more than just making money for bankers. He suggested war could be a tool to demonstrate broader interests. Eventually his arguments won the day, and after a brief period of preparations, the United States declared war, choosing a side in yet another of the countless battles between France and Britain. Instead of fighting for the people, the government had opted to fight the British.

The political elite

After the Federalist Party's overreach led to its demise, the Republican Party found itself essentially unopposed. It opened up a period of one-party rule, referred to as the "Era of Good Feelings." Most candidate and policy decisions were made inside the party hierarchy, with little feedback from the people. It was what made it possible for James Monroe to become President. He was yet another Virginia landowner who was not very popular. So firmly in charge were the Republican leaders that, instead of campaigning *before* the election, Monroe took a goodwill tour to New England *after* the election in order to smooth over ruffled feathers in the North.

By the 1824 elections, however, factions were starting to develop within the Republican Party. The bankers were still powerful even though their Federalist Party had fallen. They managed to infiltrate the Republican Party and were trying to change the party's direction from within. Their interference made it difficult for the party to decide on political candidates. The lack of unity in the Republican Party, in turn. made it possible for political outsider Andrew Jackson, the "hero" of the Battle of New Orleans, to surprise the political establishment and pull in more of the popular vote and more of the Electoral College delegates than any other candidate in the 1824 Presidential elections. Since no one won a majority, however, the decision was once again pushed over to Congress, where John Quincy Adams had a distinct advantage as a career politician and son of President John Adams. The Republicans chose one of their own, inciting calls of political favoritism from the opposition.

The loss was a difficult one for political operatives outside of the establishment, but even in defeat, the election provided a ray of hope: the popular vote was expanding and becoming more important. Trying to do right by soldiers in the War of 1812 was putting pressure on states to expand voting rights. So, too, was westward expansion. In order to lure settlers, the western states presented an alternative to the elite-controlled politics of the older states by offering voting rights to a larger segment of their populations. This, in turn, put pressure on the eastern states. To avoid losing too much of their labor force to western migration, they also increased voting rights. More states also opted to allow voters to choose electors for President instead of leaving the decision in the hands of the state legislatures. Holding onto power and keeping the people in check became much more complicated.

To exploit the changing political landscape, a new class of politician emerged. While the Republican Party was increasingly committed to establishing and protecting the privileges and power of the bankers who had infiltrated the party, the new politician was focused on obtaining and enjoying the prestige and privileges of power for himself and his friends. There was power and privilege to be gained from the people, ideal for those who couldn't get in through business connections. Forming the "Democratic Party" to emphasize their use of democracy, their aim was to create a new political elite.

Because they were not committed to a particular policy outcome, the new politicians could take advantage of the growing electorate left unsatisfied by the party committed to the wealthy. Immigrants, religious minorities, working class, and independent farmers were among those available to the new party. The pro-wealthy party (whose name changed from time to time, from Federalist, to Republican, to Whig, and then back to Republican) kept the bar so low that it took very little to appeal to these voters. The Democratic Party didn't actually have to do much to satisfy the needs of a particular constituency. Simply acknowledging their issues was usually enough. Implementing bold policies, in fact, would have been counter-productive. It would have run the risk of alienating a portion of their electorate and got in the way of enjoying the prestige associated with political power. Struggling with complex issues that involved serious compromises on all sides was not part of an elite lifestyle.

Control of information and spin were critical to the Democratic Party if they wanted voters to keep coming back and not lose hope. Voters needed to know why the reforms they were promised didn't happen and believe that a vote for the Democratic candidate would lead to relief in the future. Newspapers were a great tool to control information, and soon most people were getting most of their news and political insight from firmly controlled and strictly partisan newspapers. As the political parties grew more sophisticated, they learned how to tailor their messages to specific audiences. Sometimes promises for one group would contradict promises made to another, but this wasn't much of a problem for a party that had little intention of implementing any of the promised reforms.

Nationalism was hugely important to how democracy could be used by the new party to control the vote and achieve a mandate from the people. It provided a way to shift attention off issues that were important to people's daily lives and onto more abstract ideas. By encouraging people to connect a significant part of their personal identity with the nation, they could make a threat to the nation out to be a personal threat to one's identity that should take priority over all other issues. War heroes were, therefore, incredibly valuable pawns for the new party. The government invested heavily in nationalism in order to gain popular support for war sacrifices, and that investment shined brightly on war generals. There would be a handful of military generals who would rise to the office of the presidency off of the mythology created about them and the wars they led. Hamilton had picked up on the value of the George Washington "brand" to change the country with the power it afforded. In 1828 Andrew Jackson took advantage of his war mythology to become President, overcoming the Congressional decision at the end of the election of 1824. There were even times (most notably and unsuccessfully during the 1846 war with Mexico) that the government would actively sabotage, restrain, and smear their generals in hopes of keeping those who were not easy enough to control from becoming political competition.

Much of the Democratic Party playbook for manipulating the voters was developed during the administration of the party's founding president, Andrew Jackson. Once in power, he put the whole weight of his office and the federal government into building and defending his monopoly on power. He built out a political machine capable of intimidating voters to help ensure the electoral mandate. On a more political level, he secured not only the White House and Congress but also the Supreme Court. The Democrats had seen how much power control of the Supreme Court had afforded the Federalists, so Jackson (and future presidents of both political parties) was anxious to pack the bench with as many loyal party men as he could.

Maintaining power also required taking on any competing powers. For Jackson this meant curtailing the power the bankers enjoyed through the Bank of the United States. It also meant confronting the South Carolina slaveholders when they tried to nullify a particularly harsh tariff that the Democrats had engineered in order to win votes from the middle states. Jackson saw it as a challenge to his federal government and sent forces to the South Carolina border to keep them in their place.

Party discipline was critical to the control of the Democratic Party. Independent thinkers and people whose first loyalty was to the voters instead of the party leadership were run out of office. For years after leaving office, loyalty to Andrew Jackson remained one of the most important criteria used in choosing Democratic candidates. It got so bad that James Polk not only asked Jackson's advice on whom he should marry, he followed it loyally once he got it.

Other aspects of the Democratic Party are best understood looking at the administration of Martin Van Buren. He had served as Jackson's Secretary of State and succeeded him as President. It was his reward for helping to create the political behemoth that was the Democratic Party. After working so hard to arrive there, Van Buren was intent on relaxing and enjoying his status. But his plans were spoiled by a financial crisis spurred on by Jackson's reckless attacks on the banks without offering a viable alternative. Not wanting to aggravate the southern leaders who considered any growth in government power one step closer to a federal ban on slavery, Van Buren's options to respond to the crisis were limited. He responded to the crisis as the government would respond time and time again, by first protecting the interests of the bankers on whom the economy relied and then getting the government out of the way for a long and painful recovery for everyone else. It was a decision that prolonged the crisis and cost Van Buren his reelection.

The fallout from the Van Buren presidency also demonstrated a key characteristic of the Democratic Party. After 12 years of Democratic rule, people were absolutely fed up with the party's promises followed by policies and execution that only went to strengthen and enrich the party establishment. As a result the election of 1840 had one of the three highest turnouts in US history. 80% of the eligible voters came out, many to protest the power and arrogance of the Democratic Party. The Republican Party even changed its name to the Whig Party in 1833 to make the most out of Jackson's extreme power grab and Van Buren's lack of action and concern for the people. It was a reference to the British political party opposed to the monarchy. This was often how the party of the wealthy managed to return to power despite their reputation and focus solely on the needs of a tiny constituency. Eventually the Democratic Party would disappoint their voters sufficiently to send voters back into the waiting hands of the only other option. The biggest challenges for the wealthy party were waiting patiently for it to happen, avoiding the temptation to force it prematurely, and then getting as much done for their constituents while they could before the electorate remembered why they'd turned to the Democrats in the first place.

The Whig (and later Republican) Party didn't just sit back and wait for the vote to come to them, however. They were engaged in many of the same election tactics used by the Democrats. They, too, nominated war heroes when they thought they could be counted on to support their policy objectives. They, too, tailored their messages to their audience, although obviously not with the same flexibility the Democrats enjoyed. Whereas the Democrats could promise the northern Capitalists to maintain tariffs to protect their local markets from competing imports while promising the southerners and others to lower tariffs, the party of the wealthy was stuck with a pro-tariff platform. So instead they tried to appeal to the electorate with more nationalist parades, songs, slogans, barbeques, and attacks on the power hunger of the Democrats in hope that would be enough.

Since the Democrats soaked up the votes of people the wealthy refused to deal with, the party of the wealthy was constantly on the lookout for new ways and excuses to limit the right and access to vote for these groups. There was no population denied the vote that was predominantly wealthy, not in the United States. So every new segment of the population that got the right to vote would likely be a target for the Democratic political machine. To make matters worse, fighting against the right to vote would just make the devotion of new voters to the Democrats that much stronger and unwavering. It was a trap the party of the wealthy constantly struggled to work their way out of, often finding themselves fighting against the democracy the other party championed.

With both parties trying to manipulate voters and the electoral system, it's unsurprising that participation was rarely as enthusiastic as it had been in the election of 1840. The choices between candidates were typically very bleak. Either you could choose someone you knew was just in politics to help the rich and powerful become more so, or you could choose someone you knew just wanted the prestige and privileges of political office. Even the Democratic Party candidates were perfectly willing to cater to the wealthy when that was what was necessary to get there. Serving the people was rarely at the top of their actual agenda. Championing the causes of the people was being used as a tool to oppress them.

The decline of the landed aristocracy

Despite actual and imagined pressure from the growth of the power of wealthy and political elite, the southern landowners in the United States remained relevant and reasonably powerful well beyond their counterparts in most of Europe. Studying their desperate attempts to retain power gives us insight into how elite rule created anxiety and led to desperation and extreme behavior. In their desperation to retain their privileges without adapting to a changing world, they not only did damage to their own position but also imposed a massive cost on the country in terms of productivity, international reputation, and competitiveness. In the end, it was the people who paid the largest price in more losses to freedom, opportunity, and security.

The northern wealthy class never felt they needed to create a firm alliance with the southern landowners.

This left the southern landowners as easy pickings for the Democratic Party. But it also left them extremely defensive, always afraid the northerners would come after their privileges and rights. This fear persisted despite the fact that four of the first five presidents were from Virginia and of landowning families. It persisted despite having won significant concessions during the writing of the Constitution, including the right to both count ⅗ of their slaves as humans for representation purposes and to consider them property for most other purposes. Since the fear persisted, however, every inch that the wealthy establishment in the North advanced, the southern landowners imagined the government was an inch closer to taking away their precious privileges and entitlements. The elite often viewed the world in zero-sum-game terms. They believed that, in order to move forward, someone else must move backward, and, likewise, if someone else was moving forward, they must be moving backwards.

At the core of the southern landowners' privilege was, of course, slavery. It was how they were able to afford their life of leisure and extravagance. Ironically, despite having fought for the right during the Constitution debate, the "peculiar institution" of slavery very nearly faded away on its own after the war. Before the war, slaves were typically used in tobacco, rice, and indigo plantations. The war ended the competitiveness of the United States in most of these markets. South Carolina, the heart of the slave South, even acknowledged the lack of viability of slave ownership and banned the import of slaves in 1787. In 1792 they forbade even the import of slaves from other states. In 1794, however, new inventions made cotton an ideal wealth maker for plantation owners and eventually established slavery firmly in the southern economy. In 1804 South Carolina opened up slave imports again until the United States government shut down legal imports in 1808. With the reestablishment of wealth generation from slavery, by 1815 more people had arrived in the New World from Africa through the slave trade than had arrived from Europe. In a total population of 8.4 million, 1.4 million were slaves.[9] And even after the import ban, 250,000 new slaves arrived before 1850. This very blatant form of denying people freedom and opportunity in order to achieve status and security for a tiny minority gave significant cover to the other elite, who were doing the same, only more discreetly.

The southern slaveholders had several effective ways to keep the rest of the population in the South from challenging their position. The most common and arguably most successful was simply turning the free whites against the black slaves. The landowners made the poorer whites fear the black slaves as morally and culturally inferior. In order to get them to accept domination, they painted a picture of what freed slaves would do to the white population. This made the whites grateful to the southern slaveholders for keeping the black population under control. Hopelessness against an all-powerful elite also developed. With a long history of minority rule in the South, many of the whites just wanted to be left alone. Towns, cities, and government all served the landowners, so ordinary people wanted nothing to do with any of them. To escape the influence of biased government, they fled to the hills.

Even with people isolated in the hills, however, the paranoid slaveholders still saw them as a threat. They leveraged their control over state government to determine which churches would be allowed to operate freely in the states.

Any church that refused to preach the morality of slavery ran the risk of losing state support and tolerance. It was at this time, therefore, that many Christian denominations split into northern and southern churches. The spirituality and freedom of the people were being limited for the good of those with the most power.

Controlling information was again a tactic aggressively exercised. To keep the northern abolitionist messages from getting through and "corrupting" the southern people, the southern slaveholders worked with the post offices to filter out and censor mail from the North. While they encountered resistance to such censorship at first, it became more accepted over time. And under the Jackson presidency, they finally had a President willing to let this censorship go on without offering any federal resistance.

A very potent tool for controlling information was public-education policy. There was an unspoken agreement between the southern landowners and the rest of the white population about education. The landowners preferred to educate their children with private tutors or by sending them to Europe for social training and status enhancement and so had little incentive to build up public education. Meanwhile the rest of the white population were suspicious of anything provided by the state and assumed that public education would be indoctrination instead of opening up new opportunities. They preferred to live simple lives completely detached from the affairs of the landowners. While perhaps not as effective as indoctrination, an uneducated population was less likely to demand changes and easier to keep in line. As a result, by 1840 North Carolina had the lowest literacy rate in the country at just 72%, compared to a literacy rate around 98% in New England.[10]

Limited education opportunities and restricted religious freedoms were high costs for the country to pay in order to maintain slavery and the privileges of the southern landowners. Another big cost was the country's difficulty organizing national infrastructure projects that could have improved the country's standard of living and competitiveness in world trade. The South fought attempts to organize roads and canals at a national level because they feared that a federal government with powers to organize such projects would be powerful enough to end slavery. Without national coordination of projects, the country enjoyed none of the economies of scale a national project would have and experienced many of the difficulties associated with traveling across national boundaries even when just crossing state borders. Perhaps the best example of the cost of poor national coordination was the railroads. Because each state operated independently, the tracks were laid at a variety of widths. Changing cars at state borders was required to travel between different regions, making interstate travel more troublesome than it had to be.

State infrastructure projects, however, were different. The southern landowners had little to no ability to limit what was done in northern states. And state infrastructure projects could be a very effective way to transfer public funds to well-connected local Capitalists (New York State's Erie Canal project being a notable exception) and so often got enthusiastic support from people in power. These projects were designed to provide companies owned by well-connected individuals a handsome profit since there was little concern for the public costs. Smaller state projects compared to large federal projects meant less oversight over corruption but also a chance for more people to exploit government for their benefit.

Another cost associated with the maintenance of the privileges of the southern slaveholders was the deterioration of the country's international reputation. The divide between what the country believed about itself and what the rest of the world thought of it increased greatly. The United States may have wanted to think of itself as the Land of the Free, but the fact of the matter was that people were desperate to escape into Canada, known by many in the United States as the "Land of Liberty." Meanwhile the government kept being put into a position where they had to defend slavery in international courts. There were several cases involving runaway slaves in which the United States had to demand that other countries compensate US slaveholders for lost slaves. There is no way to look like let alone be a leader in freedom and opportunity while defending the institution of slavery.

Southern fears of a powerful federal government also prevented the country from developing stronger trade relations. For example, an opportunity for the United States to lead a Pan-American conference offered a chance for the country to improve commercial ties between North and South America and, therefore, make the US more competitive against Europe. But the insecurities of the southern landowners dealt a double blow. Looking for any way to embarrass President John Quincy Adams and the North, the South blocked Adams' attempt to have the United States lead or even to participate in the conference. The opportunity was lost. Adding insult to injury, in an attempt to conceal their true motivation, the southern landowners actively promoted the idea that South America should be feared and distrusted for their racial diversity. The character of the people who believed such propaganda was poisoned in order for the slaveholders to avoid the appearance of losing power.

Despite the fears of the southern landowners, for the most part, the leaders in the North were not resolutely opposed to them. As long as the southern landowners didn't get in their way, they weren't inclined to get in their way, either. In fact many of the northern Capitalists benefited greatly from the institution of slavery without having to take the personal moral stain of being directly involved with its maintenance. Many in the North profited from the availability of cheap cotton. They used the cotton in the manufacturing of cloth and clothing that was sold back to the slaves, the only customers who would accept it, since it wasn't high-enough quality for anyone else.

There were also times when the northern wealthy party courted the southern slaveholder vote with candidates intended to appeal to them. Zachary Taylor, for example, was not only a hero from the war against Mexico, but he also owned a plantation in Louisiana. Both of these facts helped him gain votes in the South. Sometimes the strategy backfired, however. John Tyler was added as the Vice President for William Henry Harrison's campaign in order to court the southern-landowner vote. When the president—the oldest up to that time—died after giving a long inaugural address on a cold Washington day, the party ended up having to disown their vice president, who didn't represent the party's policy focus.

The clear immorality of the southern slaveholders' exploitation of other people's labor also provided incredible cover for how the northern Capitalists achieved their wealth and position. As long as the South held people in actual bondage, the Capitalists didn't look so bad. At times the southern slaveholders would ruin the deception, however, by pointing out the similarities between the exploitation of labor in the North (sometimes called "wage slavery") and their own. It was something the Capitalists were particularly sensitive to. So when the abolitionists started attacking the southern landowners for their aristocratic privileges, it hit a little too close for the northern Capitalists. They turned their attacks against the abolitionists in defense of the southern slaveholders in order to prevent an anti-elitism campaign from gaining momentum.

Slavery was also a powerful bargaining chip for the northern Capitalists. When they could get something in exchange for their acceptance of slavery, they didn't hesitate. The debate over the route for a new transcontinental railroad provides a useful example. After the southern landowners finally conceded the need for national infrastructure, the northern Whigs exchanged opening Nebraska to becoming slave states in a compromise to get southern approval on a northern route for the railroad. The northern route would be more profitable for the northern Capitalists compared to a southern route being considered. This was how compromises happened in Congress—trades between elites where the people were the ones who suffered.

There was no issue that riled up the southern landowners more than tariffs. The reasoning behind tariffs was simple enough. Like much of Europe, the United States struggled to catch up with Britain in terms of industrialization. In order to compete with the quality and price of British goods, the industrialists asked the government to impose a tax on goods coming from abroad to make the US-made goods more attractive to domestic consumers.

Presumably once US techniques were up to international standards, the tariffs could be lowered.

The problem was that the tariffs could be seen as a tax on all consumers that provided the greatest benefit to a small minority, the owners of industry. It increased the profitability of the companies while making both domestically produced and imported goods more expensive. And since the southern landowners imported most of their goods from Britain and sold much of their cotton to Britain, they not only faced higher prices on goods but also had to deal with retaliation from Britain on the goods the South was exporting. The southern landowners couldn't get into manufacturing to take advantage of the tariffs themselves. They didn't have the expertise, they didn't have the local market, since the lower classes were so poor and produced most of what they needed themselves, and they didn't have the labor, since the slavery model was poorly suited to industrial work.

The issue of tariffs also served as a proxy for the fight the southern landowners felt they needed to put on in order to protect their (immorally gained) privilege and wealth. If the northern Capitalists could impose this tax on them without protest, then they thought it would be nothing for them to impose their moral standards on the South as well.

The main battleground for the southern slaveholders was representation in Congress. The South benefited from a higher natural population increase. They also got credit for ⅗ of the slaves they managed to bring into the states. This helped the southern states compete in the House of Representatives. What upset this advantage was the steadily growing immigration. Wars and other disruptions were pushing more people from Europe to North America.

Since opportunities were much more evident in the North than in the South, many more immigrants came to the North than the South. This meant not only larger populations and thus increasing representation in Congress for the northern states, but also more settlers from the North available to populate and vote for freedom against slavery in the new western states.

In order to get more seats in Congress, the southern landowners needed to expand slavery into new states, ideally faster than states that banned slavery joined. To make the case for more slave states, the southern slaveholders came up with some rather fantastic arguments to counter the obvious moral objections and inconsistencies with the slowly expanding mythology of the country. For example, they argued that by spreading out the slave population, the risk of a slave rebellion would be reduced. They even argued that it could serve as a potential steppingstone to eventually ending slavery, since a high population of slaves in one area would complicate integration. But much more likely, the slave population would grow to fill new territory with new slaves procured from slave breeders in Virginia, thus mitigating any benefit of greater dispersion.

They also argued that, without new land for cotton, there was a real threat that the United States would lose its global position as a cotton supplier. Since in their zeal for maximum short-term profits the southern landowners pushed the land hard, it was wearing out quickly. New land needed to be dedicated to cotton in order to keep the industry going. Jefferson Davis even argued that the South needed to expand because slave labor was "a wasteful labor, and it therefore requires a still more extended territory than would the same pursuits if they could be prosecuted by the more economical labor of white men."[11] Although difficult to tell from his argument, Davis was not pleading for some outside force to end slavery for the sake of efficiency and economy. Profit was a northern preoccupation that the South liked to denigrate. But despite that, the landowners were not timid about using an economic argument to suppress freedom and opportunities for others, a trick they learned from the Capitalists.

They even argued that the Constitution protected their rights to extend slavery wherever they liked, insisting that denying the right to slavery in new states and territories was discriminatory. Their right to travel with their "property" to new lands was being restricted just because they were from the South. It was another example of the elite arguing for freedom and opportunity for themselves only. They also suggested that, since the Founding Fathers didn't seem to see the blacks as being equal, there was no reason why the country should ever give them equal rights. They were actually suggesting the country limit its moral compass to what a small minority expressed in the 1700s. Such is the power of nationalism to cloud people's minds to reason.

To manage the declining representation in Congress, the southern landowners used their influence to push through a "gag rule" that essentially blocked the Congress from considering any petitions from citizens about slavery. It wasn't as if the Congress was going to resolve the issue, anyway. It was far too complicated an issue for Congress to deal with. But just talking about it was embarrassing to the southern slaveholders. John Quincy Adams, as Senator after his presidency, frequently tried to find a way around the rule to get petitions on to the floor. The commotion he created produced more coverage and awareness than had the anti-slavery petitions been allowed to be raised and dealt with normally. One of the more sensational petitions was from a grassroots group in New England petitioning Congress to be allowed to secede to avoid having any association with slavery. Adams didn't support the extreme measure called for but did support the sentiment behind it and more than anything thought the right to petition the government should be preserved.

When all else failed, some of the southern states simply threatened to secede in order to compel the North to agree to their terms. They threatened to secede if Missouri were not admitted as a free state and again when California and New Mexico were up for consideration as free states. In the latter case, another "compromise" was brokered. California was admitted, while New Mexico was delayed. In exchange for admitting California as a free state, the South also got the right to send bounty hunters into the North to claim escaped slaves. The South was then able to leverage this rule to terrorize the northern black population. Bounty hunters were not very particular about whether the person they found was actually a former slave or not, so no one was safe. There were checks on the border, but since the judges seeing the cases were paid more for returned slaves than for denying a claim, it wasn't too hard to get through with a false claim.

The amount of territory the United States was expanding into where slavery made sense was severely limited, making the battle for each new state that much more intense. In short the land had to be suitable for cotton for it to be well suited for slavery, and much of the western land simply wasn't. That's why the southern landowners were so anxious about Missouri, and later Kansas and Nebraska. It was also why they got so excited at the prospect of Texas and got behind the war with Mexico to "liberate" it. It was why they supported attempts to overthrow the Spanish in Cuba before Spain ended slavery there. And it was why they supported the takeover of Nicaragua (funded by Cornelius Vanderbilt, who wanted to build a canal there) after the leader of the invasion reversed a long-standing ban on slavery in the country.

Eventually the southern landowners' anti-federal government rhetoric, designed to manipulate both southern populations and northern Capitalists, developed a life of its own. Lincoln had come out clearly opposed to federal restrictions on slavery where it already existed. But despite posing little genuine threat, the southern Democrats made him and the northern "Yankees" out to be the enemy in an attempt to win the election of 1860. They insisted he was a threat to the freedoms and culture of all southern whites. They had painted themselves into a corner with their rhetoric and had no other choice but to secede—the logic of their words demanded it. War broke out in an attempt to preserve the union, Lincoln's top priority. It was a gruesome and horrific war that gave a sneak peak as to what war would look like after full industrialization.

Like the French peasantry who celebrated the early stages of the French Revolution thinking that it meant an end to the aristocracy, many in the South celebrated the end of the Civil War and the defeat of the southern slaveholders. It meant they could stop dying to protect the landowners' slaves and prestige. They assumed the landowners would be dealt with, finally freeing the southern whites almost as much as it would free the southern blacks.

The southern landowners might very well have expected the worst as well. But there were several reasons why they got off very lightly. It is true they sustained significant damage to their plantations during the war. And they lost slavery, the largest contributor to their wealth and privilege. But there was no sustained effort to punish them. As already mentioned, the northern Capitalists did not, generally speaking, have much of a problem with the southern landowners. Their existence and privilege didn't offend them as much as it did the rest of the population across the country. Additionally, going after the southern landowners might bring up questions about their own privileges and their exploitation of labor. It really was best to leave these issues alone.

The southern landowners were also still very well connected within the country's political circles and enjoyed the respect and admiration of people aspiring to be accepted within the highest echelons of the upper classes. President Andrew Johnson, who succeeded Abraham Lincoln into the White House, was just such a man. He was a pro-union Democrat from Tennessee, a slaveholder, and owner of a successful plantation. But the southern landowners did not consider him part of the aristocracy because he was not born into it; he had worked his way up instead. He resented them for not letting him into the club. So when the southern landowners had to come to him and apologize for seceding (or for the mistake they probably felt guiltier about: losing the war to defend their secession), Johnson felt as if the wrong done to him had been righted. He could finally be accepted into the aristocracy he had been jealous of his entire life. Johnson pardoned the southern landowners and worked to get their land returned to them, instead of distributing the land to the poor whites and/or blacks, as many expected would happen.

And finally, with all the effort the southern landowners had put into their manipulation of the white population, they were very useful for keeping people in line. Ruling a defeated people through their conquered leaders was a common technique used by conquering forces. It was better than trying to use occupying forces to bring order to an area.

Under the banner of supporting the "American Dream," a radical faction in Congress did actually get behind the efforts of the freed slaves to participate in the new South. The radicals suggested that the idea of a privileged class was contrary to the ideals of the United States. They insisted that the land previously owned by the slaveholders should be distributed to allow more people to enjoy freedom and independence. But their opponents argued that this would violate the sanctity of property and set a nasty precedent. There was a valid concern that if the southern common-ers were to be free and independent, then the northerners would be next. The Republican Party could never allow that. The northern and southern elite could easily agree on this point. The freed slaves would not get the "40 acres and a mule" promised by the Republicans at the end of the war. Instead the confiscated land was sold back to wealthy whites, often at prices below the value of the land.

Despite eventually being let down by the conquering North, after the war the southern blacks were anxious to prove themselves good citizens and to take advantage of the benefits of citizenship in a country that billed itself as a land of freedom and opportunity. They were surpris-ingly sophisticated in their political, social, and economic tactics, devising strategies to achieve their goals within the rules. But the obstacles that party politics put in the way of grassroots candidates limited the number of blacks willing to run for office. So they were never represented in politics anywhere near their representation as voters. Given the general ability of the blacks to understand the principles of government, those who were elected proved themselves to be honest, earnest, and very competent.

Since the Democratic Party continued to support the southern landowners and black candidates were rare, a large voting block was left open for the Republicans to exploit with very little effort. When the blacks were given the chance to vote, they threw their loyal support behind the Republicans, finding them more palatable than the landowner-supporting Democrats. And it paid big dividends for the Republican Party. Many Republicans actually came down from the North to take advantage of the black vote and the promise of an easy electoral victory. Many of them were sincerely committed to improving conditions for the blacks, but most of them realized they could buy themselves into office at a small price and then put themselves and their friends into positions of privilege and influence. Corruption was, as elsewhere, in the majority.

In addition to office seekers, northern Capitalists also migrated down to the South to "invest" in new business and infrastructure. The northern Capitalists brought much-needed capital to a war-torn region. But like foreign investment in an undeveloped country of a later era, the Capitalists then took much more of the capital back North in terms of profits after the projects were completed. When an economic downturn hit in 1873, the investments came to a halt, not to return for another five years. They were quick to abandon the South when the economic conditions were not perfect for exploitation. The poor South, like the northern working class, was an escape valve for the northern Capitalists to insulate them from economic downturns. As a result, little of the wealth that the low-wage laborers in the area had created was left in the South.

The loyal blacks gave the Republicans 40% of the voters, which still meant they needed some help from the whites to stay in control. While the Democrats may not have been able to turn around the black vote, they certainly knew how to shave off white voters from the Republicans. The Republican reputation as loyal advocates for the northern wealthy elite was all they needed. So by 1874 the Democrats had won control in most of the southern states. The people had to choose between the Republican Party that served the wealthy Capitalists or the Democratic Party that served the struggling southern landowners. They returned to the southern landowners as the lesser of two evils by virtue of their being less powerful. And once back in power, the Democrats were able to work on limiting the vote and influence of the black citizens.

CHAPTER 3

The Capitalist heyday

Capitalists had their own version of the American Dream, one of exploitation spurred on by a relentless competition. But their hold on power had to become more subtle to keep the people in check. It was well worth the effort, however. Control over government produced huge dividends for those with wealth and the right connections.

Two versions of the "American Dream"

Nothing conveyed the ideals of Freedom and Opportunity felt by the people in the United States better than the "American Dream." It inspired many to take dangerous journeys to get to the United States and to start over from scratch in a new country. Many of the earliest settlers came to North America to have a fair chance at making their own life without having to serve the privileged classes of Europe. They represented the more-common interpretation of the American Dream, that anyone who was willing to work hard and contribute to the country would have a real opportunity to be successful. But even in those early days, many others came to exploit the land

and its people, often with a mandate to create wealth for European funders. They sought an opportunity to create empires off the labor of others. This was a dramatically different version of the Dream.

These two versions were not compatible with each other. People who were willing to not only put themselves above everyone else but also to sacrifice the public good for their own benefit limited the opportunity for others, sometimes dramatically. The trade with the Native inhabitants in the early days of settlement provided a clear example of the impact unrestricted opportunity can have. Most of the traders treated the Natives with respect, realizing the long-term potential for trading relationships. A minority, however, had no respect for the Natives and preferred to take advantage of them to make a quick profit. They didn't worry about the consequences for other traders, settlers, or the colonies. By stirring up reprisals, their abusive treatment of the Natives cost the livelihoods and lives of countless honest settlers and traders.

Slavery offered another striking case. Most of the early colonists were looking for a place where they could own their own land and create a life for themselves with their own hands and freedom from responsibilities to an overbearing aristocracy. These were the people Thomas Jefferson eventually came to celebrate in his writings, referring to them as the "yeoman farmers." In contrast there were other colonists who came to the continent to establish their own empire, to live off the labor of others like the aristocracy of Europe did. Believing themselves to be of superior breeding, they felt entitled to a life of aristocratic leisure, not expecting to have to work for long before they could retire to it. They rationalized that others were better suited to hard work and they better suited to the advancement of "culture" and civilization. In reality, however, they were just looking for a shortcut to comfort and security completely foreign to the popular understanding of the "American Dream." Slavery on an ever-increasing scale was their solution.

The scale of the "peculiar institution"—as slavery was often called—expanded dramatically with the influx of economic refugees from Barbados. Slavery there had developed on a massive scale after sugar production became big business, pushing people off their land as plantations became larger and larger, thanks to the labor of increasing numbers of slaves. But the migrants didn't come to the mainland with idealistic plans to break free from that highly exploitative way of living. On the contrary, they came in search of their piece of that lifestyle. And for them there was no compromise on slavery. It was their birthright as members of a self-fashioned elite that could not be denied them by anyone or any government. As such, slavery demonstrated clearly the cost of the elite's view of the Dream to the country and its hard-working and honest people (including the slaves themselves), not only in lost productivity but equally to the spirit, vitality, integrity, and morality of its people.

Those who imagined themselves above everyone else masterfully exploited people's belief in the Dream to defend their rights to exploit, convincing people that any threat to their unlimited exploitation was an attack on the Dream for everyone. If the right to ply the Natives with alcohol to get a better trade deal was limited, it would surely lead to the government taking over all Native trading and operating it as a monopoly. If the right to encroach on land occupied by the

Natives was limited, it would surely lead to the government eventually letting the Natives re-occupy land occupied by settlers. If the Congress could take away a slaveholder's slaves, it would surely lead to the government confiscating other property, perhaps people's oxen next. Or, more obliquely, if the government had the power to take away slaves and deny a landowner the freedom to hold other people, they would also have the power to deny other freedoms. So firmly did people hold the belief in opportunity for all that this sort of reasoning actually worked surprisingly well to convince people to support policies that were not in their own interest or the interests of the country as a whole.

With the spread of industrialization in the United States, capitalism similarly developed with both honest, hard-working, sincere, and civic-minded individuals on the one hand and those looking for a shortcut to wealth and privilege on the other hand. The majority of Capitalists saw a need or an opportunity to improve people's lives and pursued that vision with a passion that was often celebrated as part of the character and psyche of the country. Then there were the schemers, people looking for ways to exploit labor, consumers, or public environments to advance their own position at the expense of others. They weren't motivated by the fire of innovation or a chance to improve the country but simply by the game of acquiring more and more wealth. These Capitalists believed that the only rule that applied was what they could get away with, including by writing their own rules. And like so many others, their pursuit of the second (exploiters') Dream inhibited others from pursuing the first (people's) Dream.

While some of the early industrial Capitalists came from wealthy family backgrounds trying to diversify and stay ahead of a changing world, most of them came from more-modest beginnings. Increasing productivity in farming allowed some people to accumulate enough money to venture into new businesses with dreams of improving the world. Hardworking farmers found they were able to produce more at less expense and, even despite the declining prices for their product, earn a higher profit. This was particularly true if they were near a large city where they could sell their extra produce. Meanwhile declining costs of food meant that people in the cities had a little extra left over to see where their imaginations could lead them.

These self-made Capitalists tended to start out believing in the popular version of the Dream, that through hard work they could achieve a high level of financial security while contributing something important to the country. Depending on the strength of their character and their experiences with wealth and competition after achieving success, many slipped into the second Dream before realizing what had happened. Capitalism provided large, enticing rewards for those who were most manipulative and often squeezed out any well-meaning community-oriented Capitalist who did not follow his competitors into manipulative practices.

Some of the wealthiest people in the country got their start with outlandish forms of manipulation and exploitation. For example, John Morgan made his first fortune during the Civil War buying worn-out weaponry and then selling it as new to the US government at a huge markup. He made another fortune by connecting the first telegraph wire to Wall Street so he could make stock decisions based on information no one else had yet. Similarly Daniel Drew (who would later become a "successful" steamship and railroad magnate) made his first fortune driving cattle. He would keep them thirsty until just before they arrived at the destination and then pump them full of water to make them look better than they actually were. This was apparently more profitable than just taking care of them properly. Unsurprisingly with this sort of ruthless beginning, once these men got started, they milked everything they could from people through the empires they built. Because of this ruthlessness, they were popularly referred to as "robber barons."

The landscape was a tough one for Capitalists in the United States going up against established global industrial leaders. But the United States enjoyed several competitive advantages in their industrial competition with Britain—the entrenched leader—and the rest of Europe. The first of these, capital, we've already mentioned. In capitalism, in order for the country and its people to develop industrial capacity, money had to be accumulated in the hands of individuals who were willing to make decisions for the country on how to use resources and people. Their reward for making those decisions and taking risks with the country's resources was a large cut off the top of any benefits produced. US involvement in international shipping and improved efficiency in farming helped consolidate enough capital for the early stages of industrialization.

Another advantage was the large domestic market. Governments could and did regulate the flow of goods across national borders. In addition to regulating the trade of dangerous goods, it was very common for governments to impose tariffs on imports so that goods coming from outside of the country were more expensive than goods from within the country. This way, local industry could theoretically improve their efficiencies and quality without having to deal with the advantages already enjoyed by competitors in other countries. But since most countries engaged in this sort of protectionism, attempts to sell products from the United States into Europe would run up against the trade defenses imposed by the European governments. The large and growing population of the United States could be a valuable domestic market for industrialists to grow their capacities over time without having to worry about access to foreign markets.

The problem with the domestic market in the United States was that people did not have much disposable income for manufactured goods, and so most of what people needed they or their neighbors built themselves. The railroads dramatically changed this situation, improving the potential of the domestic market for Capitalists. First the railroads made it possible for farmers to sell excess produce to a larger market. This combined with improved farming to increase profits and gave farmers cash to buy goods. Secondly, the railroads reduced the costs of transporting products into the West, making manufactured goods a compelling alternative to homemade goods. While this frustrated local artisans, it meant people had both means and opportunity to buy manufactured goods. Capitalists could then count the domestic market as a competitive advantage.

Britain's head start was too great for the United States to overcome through ordinary market forces, however. New technological innovations were required to upset the current competitive advantages enjoyed by Britain. The country's early commitment to education with an emphasis on new thinking as opposed to rote memorization of old thinking was key to unlocking that innovation. This spark to challenge how things had always been done was applied on top of the strong technical know-how of the country's artisans. These artisans brought the fruit of innovation, hard work, and training of generations to bear on the new challenges and opportunities.

Lastly, there was access to labor, people willing to apply themselves to create wealth. There was never any shortage of people willing to work hard in the United States. The challenge was to find people willing to concede most of the value created by their work to someone else. The United States was, after all, competing with Europe, where there was an ages-old tradition of people working for the benefit of a tiny minority at the top. To compete, industrialists in the United States had to find a way to push people to work harder for less.

In the capitalist free market, lower labor costs were achieved by managing the supply of labor. The more people there were looking for the same sort of work, the lower the cost of labor. In order to keep the supply of labor in eastern cities high, many of the early industrialists tried to limit the exodus of people from eastern cities looking for more freedom in the new states. It was this pressure that helped compel many of the eastern states to expand their voting rights to more of the population, to keep up with the competition offered by new states and limit migration.

Eventually just as more efficient farming produced excess profits for some, it produced unemployment for others, most notably farm laborers. Greater efficiency meant fewer people were needed to do the work, pushing many people into the cities in search of an income. The first of these economic migrants were women, who were in the majority in early factories. But soon the floodgates opened up, letting in waves of new labor desperate to find work. It was a great relief for the industrialists in the cities. With a new supply of labor, the industrialists could be more open to westward migration as a way to get rid of people inclined to protest the industrialists' treatment of the new and growing working class.

The biggest labor advantage for industrialists in the United States, however, came from immigrants. Many of the early immigrants had passed through the cities on their way to set up their own farms and communities in the West. It was the vast availability of land as the United States expanded at the expense of the Natives that fueled the reputation of the country as a Land of Opportunity. As time went on, land became more difficult to come by, and more Europeans came to North America fleeing wars and famine and, therefore, could not afford to go further than the cities. Their situation was desperate, and so they were perfect for the industrialists. With the steady inflow of new labor, the poor were competing with each other to push wages lower and lower until families needed to send women and children—as young as four years old, but six was much more common—out to work to be able to afford to live. The more desperate life got for the working class, the lower labor costs dropped.

The Capitalists actively promoted the United States as a destination for immigrants, hyping it as a Land of Opportunity and selling the "American Dream." The companies offering the transportation across the Atlantic were in on the propaganda, too. It quickly occurred to them that if the transport companies got together and agreed on price and quality standards, they could make a fortune taking advantage of people's desperation for a new life. With collaboration, prices went up, and safety went down. And since their businesses were at sea, there was little governments could do to regulate them and bring relief to people. The "American Dream" was a gold mine for those willing to exploit it.

After their desperate crossing, the immigrants' expectations were immediately dashed upon arriving in their new country. They went into a vast pool of unskilled labor, competing against each other for the worst-paying and most-dangerous jobs. Many came with advanced skills only to find no market for them. Using technology to replace skilled jobs with unskilled jobs was another way the industrialists kept labor costs low. Any skilled task required someone with unique talents that could demand a higher price. Automating the task eliminated the extra cost and added more competitors to the unskilled labor pool, applying additional downward pressure on salaries. In this way, innovation provided benefits predominantly to the wealthy while seriously damaging the livelihood and self-esteem of ordinary people.

Low self-esteem was a valuable tool for driving and keeping salaries low. It helped that the economic migrants were already extremely vulnerable because of all the changes in their lives. The lives of recent immigrants were completely changed, of course, but life was changing for people within the country, too. People were losing control over their lives at an alarming rate, with fewer and fewer people working for themselves. Between 1800 and 1860, the percentage of the non-slave workforce that was self-employed (mostly in family farms) dropped from 83% down to 48%.[12] And by 1850, 59% of white males in the country owned no landed property.[13] This represented a significant loss to people's access to the American Dream.

Many of the new factory workers had moved from roles as artisans that demanded a unique skill and, therefore, provided a source of respect, to unskilled positions in factories. The move involved a dramatic drop in income, which provided a direct challenge to one's perceptions of self-worth. For farm owners and farm labor forced into the cities by the increasing productivity in agriculture, the lifestyle and living conditions changed dramatically. In a capitalist society, productivity increases have victims, people whose lives and livelihoods are destroyed. Capitalists preyed on these victims.

The loss of control in one's life was that much harder to bear when contrasted with the incredible rise in fortunes of a tiny minority. This was the timeframe when the term "millionaire" started being used. The top 23% wealthiest people owned 92% of the land by value.[14] By 1860 the top 10% owned more than 85% of the urban wealth. That was even worse than the South, despite its outrageous exploitation of slave labor, where the top 10% owned 60% of the agricultural wealth.[15]

Not ashamed to kick a man when he was down, the industrialists insisted that it was the poor's fault for not being able to find work, even though it was clear there was not enough work for everyone. An example of this from a later time was Henry Ford. In his early days he had championed world peace and the idea of affordable transportation for more people. But in 1931 Henry Ford suggested that the economic crisis the people were suffering was self-made, because "the average man won't really do a day's work unless he is caught and cannot get out of

it. There is plenty of work to do if people would do it."
The hollowness of his argument was laid bare, when a few
weeks later, he laid off 75,000 workers.[16]

The Capitalists tried to turn the "American Dream"
and strong work ethic against the people. They tried to
convince struggling families that if hard work was what
people valued, then making success that much harder to
achieve for some people would make the victory that much
more meaningful. They argued that the poor did not want
help establishing a level playing field—they didn't want any
help *at all*. The argument let the Capitalists off the hook
for fixing the inequities in the system or paying the social
costs of their wealth. It also kept the club of successful and
influential people limited to those who were willing to buy
into and be changed by the unique ethics and morals of a
manipulative and exploitative economic system. Changing
the system from within would be nearly impossible.

The wealthy were able to shield themselves from the
troubles and suffering of the working class by living in
their own neighborhoods in the cities, vacationing in the
country, and avoiding routes and neighborhoods that would
expose them to the harsh realities under which the poor
lived. And the middle class was happy to act as a buffer
between the rich and the poor. In exchange for a little extra
financial security, the middle class could also be counted
on to help drive the economy with their purchases. They
had become voracious consumers, producing enormous
amounts of garbage while building up the US economy.

Human life lost practically all value. With labor so
easily replaced, the industrialists saw little incentive to
invest in safety or healthy work environments. The living
conditions for the poor were also abysmal and added to

the sense of hopelessness and dread. Deteriorating work-ing and living conditions meant people were dropping like flies—with nearly as little remorse expressed as if they were just flies. And with the loss of self-esteem came greater social problems ranging from increased crime to alcohol and sexual abuses.

During times of economic prosperity, life was tolerable for most of the working class. But the economic system that produced such fabulous wealth for people at the top also resulted in regular economic crises that struck down the working and middle classes, like a war being waged in their neighborhoods would. The most serious of these crises included 1837, 1857, 1873, 1893, 1907, 1919 and 1929. In fact many people refer to the period of 1873 to 1896 as the "Long Depression" (or before the collapse in 1929 as the "Great Depression"), since it was an extended period of economic woes and the period in which the robber barons reigned. At times the suffering seemed to defy basic economic principles. Farmers couldn't afford to sell crops while people in the cities couldn't afford to buy food. People suffered both supply and demand problems. It was failure on an epic scale, and yet anyone questioning Capitalism was dealt with quickly and firmly.

The wealthy limited their pain from downturns in the economy by using the working class as their release valve. Unlike the southern landowners' slaves, when the economy turned, they could simply shed their labor to cut costs and respond to a diminishing market. Since they had already established that the poor were poor because they were lazy, they didn't even have to worry about taking responsibility for the human suffering that resulted from this self-serving tactic. The crises were great for the wealthiest, in fact:

labor was cheap, unions struggled to hold together, and companies could be acquired cheaply, thus thinning out the ranks at the top.

Clearly the wealthy didn't have much incentive to solve the crises, and so, unsurprisingly, no one seemed to know how to prevent the economic meltdowns or to have any ideas on how to end them once they started. It was always a big mystery, beyond the ability of human control, a fact of life, apparently. But as mysterious as the government, bankers, and economists tried to make the downturns out to be, their cause was almost always traceable back to the greed of bankers and Capitalists.

Much of what the banking industry dealt in was unreal wealth. They stored the money of depositors and lent that money out to other people while still claiming the original money was available for withdrawal at any time. For every dollar they brought in they could create a dollar of unreal wealth. There's nothing inherently wrong with this—it was part of the rules of the game of Capitalism. The problems arose when bankers and Capitalists took too many risks with unreal wealth. Once someone tried to convert a large quantity of unreal wealth into real wealth, the system collapsed, and the country's working class suffered. But any talk of regulating the banking industry and preventing abuses ran up against protests that the government was limiting the opportunities of bankers and that the opportunities of hard-working citizens would surely be next.

The government acted confused by these basics of economics, failing to understand that the elements that helped the economy prosper in the first place (capital, markets, labor, and innovation) would be the key to recovery. They took care of the bankers and the Capitalists, of course. After

Alexander Hamilton made bankers indispensable to the country and its government, the politicians felt they had little choice but to give them a free pass, despite having caused the crisis. They insisted this was needed to keep the crisis from getting worse. To help industrialists, the next step was often to increase tariffs. It was essentially a tax on the poor to keep the Capitalists going with higher prices on goods. Later this was replaced by tax cuts for the wealthy, leaving everyone else to shoulder the increased social costs of a suffering labor force.

After taking care of the first element of an economy (capital), the government was content to let the economy slowly and painfully recover on its own. Before the Civil War, the South had fought to keep the government from assuming powers to help suffering people, but even after the war, there was little inclination to help. Instead the politicians would attack the poor and middle class. They argued that people were suffering as a consequence of their poor decisions. They had bought too much and let their standard of living improve too quickly. Never mind that they had done these things on the assurances from retailers and banks through misleading and manipulative advertising and in-store sales tactics that accepting the loans and credit offered them was not only safe but wise. The message was that people should know better than to trust other people. It was a mistake that people paid for dearly with extreme loss of financial stability and severe economic hardship.

Control by Capitalists adapts

Since the country's inception, government had been domi-nated by the elite—people with either the right connections or a great deal of wealth before entering office. This elite rule was considered a virtue by some, viewing people of lower social status as incapable of independent thought and decision-making. The argument persisted that people without much wealth or who worked for someone else were not sufficiently independent to cast a vote.

There were, therefore, numerous schemes to limit the vote of the lower classes, typically put forward by the party of the wealthy since the Democrats benefited from the expanded vote. In the early days of the country, before the mythology of a government of the people was built out, there were property requirements people had to meet before they could vote. But the property requirements were slowly dropped as people were asked increasingly to sacrifice for the good of the country, during wartime in particular. Some states implemented laws denying the right to vote to people who accepted unemployment benefits from the government. They argued that people who needed help from the government could not vote objectively. Intelligence tests and poll taxes were also quite common, to keep out a certain type of voter. The Republicans insisted these measures were necessary to reduce voter fraud. It was an ironic suggestion since it was they themselves who used fraud to suppress working-class votes. Just looking at the voting results, it was evident the working class was not rigging elections in their favor. In fact, the poll tax increased the incidence of voter fraud since all the Democrats had to do to "earn" the vote of the poor was pay their poll tax for them. They were some of the cheapest votes they bought.

One of the most successful political defenses against the interference of the people in politics was to split the electorate with manufactured hatred and suspicion.

The southern slaveholders created and inflamed animosity and fear between free whites and the black slaves. Likewise representatives of Capitalists turned the descendants of previous immigrations against new arrivals. Before the Civil War, immigrants were coming from northern and western Europe—Britain, Ireland, Germany, Scandinavia, Switzerland, Denmark. After the war, the bulk were coming from southern and eastern Europe—Italy, Greece, Austria-Hungary, Russia, Romania, Turkey. The leaders leveraged the nationalism running rampant in Europe to turn the working class against itself and prevent them from uniting against the wealthy.

While never hesitating to hire an immigrant whenever a "native" worker was unwilling to work for less, the Capitalists still managed to convince the workers that the country (speaking to the earlier immigrants) had to unite to confront this immigration threat. Soon secret organizations started to appear to organize "native" workers to intimidate and oppress the immigrant population. Whenever someone asked one of the members of these secret organizations what they were doing, they would always insist that they knew nothing. So the movement came to be called the Know Nothing Movement, and their party, officially the American Party, was known popularly as the Know Nothing Party. It operated like so many other nationalist parties, trying to get laws passed that protected the "rights" of the early immigrants and limit the rights of the new immigrants. So instead of the country setting an example for how people of different cultures could get along while retaining their original character, they intentionally imported the hatred and distrust from the old countries into the new environment to serve the purposes of those with the most power.

And fostering hatred did significant harm to the country, turning diversity from a real and significant asset to an engineered and harmful liability.

As one would expect, the party of the wealthy (in turn the Federalists, Whigs, and Republicans) enjoyed significant campaign-finance advantages over the Democrats, which they leveraged to strengthen their position. It was not unusual for the Republicans to spend more than ten times what the Democrats did. With that sort of spending disparity, they could drown out any conflicting ideas through repetition and confusion. Since little additional information could get through, they could also say whatever they wanted to about their opponents. For example, the Republicans asserted that criminals supported the Democrats, so no one else should. They advised people on all the reasons they should fear farmers and labor. They even went so far as to suggest that supporting the demands of farmers would be bad for Christianity.

Over time the industrialists were able to simply kill off the will to vote. By controlling who could and wanted to run for election in the major parties, they managed to keep the options bleak for the working class. And since the government rarely did anything for the people anyway, it came down to voting for the candidate who would do the least harm. That's hardly inspiring to get out and vote, a commitment that often required a day off work to register and then a day off to vote, losing income most working-class people could hardly do without.

If all else failed, the industrialists could use their economic power to try to impose political power. In the early days, ballots were open to public scrutiny so employers could simply forbid their employees from voting a certain way under threat of being fired. After the secret ballot came into use, the factory owners used the threat of closing down the factory and firing all the employees if the election did not go their way. As time went on, these threats became more sophisticated, making people feel that a vote against the industrialists was a vote against jobs.

People who were allowed to and bothered to exercise their voice through the ballot box found it filtered through several levels of government and representatives before appearing (often unrecognizable) on the other side. It was taking representative government to its extreme abstraction. Senators, for example, were elected by state legislatures, not by the people. The extra layer allowed the industrialists to manipulate the selection and turn the Senate into an upper house of Congress, similar to the House of Lords in England. State legislatures were so easy to manipulate that, in the second half of the 1800s, most of the senators were clearly representing industries or companies instead of the states they came from. Likewise, the Electoral College system removed the election of the president from the people so far that it was not uncommon for the person with the most votes to lose the election.

Even with all these advantages, the Democrats still managed to leverage the power of the people to their benefit. But that was the worst-case scenario for the industrialists, because third parties could make little headway. Since the Democrats could take the working-class vote for granted and they desperately wanted cooperation and funding from the Capitalists, they were often nearly as aggressive in pushing pro-business interests as the Republicans were. For example, the first Democratic president elected after the Civil War (President Cleveland in 1884) went out of his way to prove his willingness to make concessions while ignoring the pleas of the people. When farmers in Texas asked for $100,000 to recover seed stocks after a weather disaster had wiped them out, Cleveland denied them support. He claimed that if the government helped out, they would become dependent. But he didn't hesitate to approve $45 million to perk up the federal bond holders. He didn't care if they became dependent on the government—that ship had long since sailed.

Whoever was elected was easily bought off anyway, since economic power controlled political power. If an industrialist wanted support for a new venture that required government sponsorship, he simply had to deal a politician or two into the profits, and suddenly he had a dedicated and enthusiastic advocate for the cause. Since members of Congress traded favors among themselves, a small number of committed supporters were often all that was necessary to push through a project.

Beyond politics there developed a separate nexus of decision-making for the country, one without a sense of community, rules, or a long-term vision. It was a growing power that would race the country back to the sort of large-scale exploitation of the majority by a minority that had taken place in European aristocracies. It developed not as part of a premeditated plan of world domination but simply followed the logic and thinking of the day. The new philosophy of Capitalism encouraged people to focus on maximizing one's own personal income. They believed that only with each person fighting for his or her own interest would the greatest overall good be produced. Personal—or worse still—government concern for the poor could do irreparable damage to the system, they argued.

For those at or near the top, it became a game to see how much money they could accumulate and how little they could get away with giving back, to see who could exploit consumers, labor, and natural resources the most. It was a game in which the team that started out with the most money and those that were willing to push the rules and disregard for others to the limit enjoyed a significant advantage.

When it came to exploiting consumers, control over information was important, just as it was in politics. The free-market concept assumed perfect flow of information. But in the real world, no one had access to all the facts or knowledge of all the options or all the risks. It took too much effort for a person to be an expert on everything, so people had to trust each other. That was a trust many Capitalists were perfectly willing to exploit. Capitalists controlled what information the consumers got and often gave downright false information to mislead them.

Exploiting labor, however, was the real strength of the professional Capitalist, constantly finding new ways to leverage their economic-power advantage to get more profit from employees. And once one Capitalist found a new way to exploit, they all had to follow; such was the nature of competition. There were a number of new innovations for exploiting labor that took hold in the second half of the 1800s. One of them was the company town. Companies set up whole villages for their employees, paying salaries in village currency and controlling prices on items sold at the company store to get back a large portion of the salaries. Another innovation was to switch to payment based on output instead of by hours worked and charging the employees for materials (such as dynamite) used. On the surface, this looked like a decent scheme to reward hard-working employees, but in practice it offered new ways for Capitalists to manipulate labor into lower wages. They adjusted the prices of dynamite to manipulate take-home pay, and they slowly increased the batch size people were paid for. The best example of the latter was from the mining industry, where some miners were paid by the cartload. As time went by, the carts the company used got bigger and bigger, while the pay per cart was stagnant.

When the pressure from labor for fair wages got too strong, companies gave in on wages but simply increased the prices they charged their customers in order to maintain their high profits. It was a strategy that meant a never-ending cycle of ever-increasing prices that drove up the cost of living faster than salaries could keep pace. It made employees feel like their lives were on the right track, only to have more and more difficulty making ends meet. It added to the despair of labor and caused chaos in the economy. When people first got a wage increase, they often went out and spent more, which boosted the economy and encouraged industrial expansion. When the increased prices kicked in, people were punished for trying to improve their standard of living, finding their extra dollars going less far and then punished again when industry had to quickly reverse direction and lay people off. By that time, those at the top had already made another fortune off the confusion.

Inflation wasn't the only way Capitalists sent the always-fragile economy into turmoil. There was a regular flow of get-rich schemes that bankers dreamed up that would become popular for a while and fail dramatically, taking the economy with it. It was not uncommon for companies to spend much more time and energy artificially inflating their stock value than actually improving efficiency and sales volume. They did this in order to prevent unwanted buyers from taking over the company and to increase their own theoretical value, which they could leverage for loans in order to invest in increasingly risky business ventures. It took just one big player to get nervous at all the unreal wealth, however, and convert it to real wealth for the whole economy to crash.

One of the more remarkable ways the wealthy controlled the nation was through their philanthropy. Because of their enormous wealth, those at the top had an opportunity to impact the look and feel of communities in ways unavailable to anyone else. They used it, like everything else, as a tool for their own purposes. When they donated money for buildings (such as libraries), they made sure the architecture communicated the greatness and ideally the benevolence of the Capitalist. It was their way to achieve an extra measure of immortality, lasting monuments to their wealth, and to silence any complaints about their abuses.

Philanthropy also extended to national monuments, to stoke the mythology. While the Capitalists expanded their business to exploit people and resources in other countries (Standard Oil had 70% of its business coming from abroad by 1885[17]), they needed the people to remain loyal to the nation to prevent revolt. They invested in new monuments and art to express the mythological past of the country. For example, in the second half of the 1800s, with the Civil War fading from people's memories, they built up the mythology about Lincoln and his role as the emancipator beyond what the facts could sustain by themselves. It was a narrative that helped convince people that they lived in a country that offered more freedom and opportunity than it actually did.

With time on their hands and an itch to make a difference for their class, sometimes the elite of the Capitalists would even enter into "public service" directly. In his day JP Morgan not only offered to lend the government money to pay US military officers to lead an attack on strikers, but he also actively contributed to the bailing out of the banks on several occasions, making sure he got his cut, of course. In 1921 Andrew Mellon (the second-wealthiest person at the time) was chosen as Secretary of the Treasury, where he pushed through a tax cut for the wealthy ahead of the Great Depression in 1929.

Within the United States, corporations and the wealthy had usurped much of the public policy decision-making and strategic allocation of limited resources. They chose which industries and technologies should be invested in. They chose how natural resources should be exploited. They chose how people should spend their lives, how their energies and talents would be deployed. And they made these decisions not with concerns for the public good or with any sort of public consensus, but in their own interests, to maximize their own short-term profits. Political power may have been the obvious power structure in the country, but it was nothing compared to what economic power could do.

Taking advantage

To be clear, the takeover of the government by a wealthy minority was not part of an evil master plan to enslave a population. Instead it evolved naturally from the starting assumption that there was an upper class of people who deserved special privilege and were better suited to rule. It was the same line of thinking that was used to support hereditary monarchy. From that starting point, desperate people simply followed the rules, stacked in their favor. Privileges then built on top of privileges because power and wealth produce more power and wealth. Not only did the rules make it easier for people with wealth to accumulate more, but also the social hierarchy made people anxious to please the wealthy and win their favor. This is how the party serving the Capitalists came to be so extreme. It wasn't so much that the Capitalists coveted or felt they needed additional privileges, wealth, or power, but more that those in the party were anxious to please and so went to increasingly greater extremes to prove their commitment and get noticed. The result was active support and advancement of pro-wealthy policies and the withdrawal of government from interfering with the blatant and open exploitation of labor and consumers.

The wealthy elite and their surrogates never had an easier time of running the country to their benefit than after the Civil War. Because of their support of the slave-holders, the Democrats had to rebuild their image after the Civil War. As a result, the power of the Republican Party was so overwhelming that they were able to turn the whole interface between politics and economics around. Politicians didn't need to be rewarded for service to the wealthy. Instead political appointments were made by the Capitalists to give their members extra advantages. Positions were given as gifts to help offspring of wealthy families become independent and generate their own revenue streams. Once in these positions, people would enrich themselves from the position; that was the nature of the reward. Corruption was everywhere. The presidency itself became an honorary position whose main responsibility was to appoint people to government positions as dictated by the party. So confident in their position, the Republicans openly nominated to the highest positions people who had been implicated in corruption scandals. There was no check on the blatant abuse of power because all branches of government were covered and controlled.

Knowing and being able to count on the right people in government and politics was key, typically more important than skill or hard work, in determining success. Connections opened up unique opportunities not available to people without the proper acquaintances. Strong government contacts were critical to getting in early on commercial steamboating and railroading, for example. In both cases technological innovation had created an enormous gap between what people were used to receiving and paying for transportation and what was newly possible. It was a gap that meant huge profit potential for people who got in early because they could charge much more than it cost to operate and didn't have to offer much in the way of safety or services to bring in customers. The government connections gave one access to technology, land, and often even exclusive monopolies.

Government funds flowed out for different railroad projects without much oversight on how the money was spent. People used their connections (and bribery) to secure railroad grants, skimmed up to 50% off the top immediately and then enjoyed both free land offered by the government as part of the deal and profits from running the railroad, if they even bothered building a railroad capable of producing profits. It was a great racket and a fabulous way to secure a new generation's position in the highest social ranks by milking the people *and* the government.

The customers weren't complaining—they were desperate for the faster travel offered by steamboats and railroads. They were typically unaware of the risks they were taking until it was too late. Accidents happened regularly, though, often leading to death. To shield themselves from financial accountability for these accidents and deaths, the railroads managed their stock ownership carefully so that they could siphon off all profits, leaving nothing for the families of the deceased to go after. The rules of the game allowed this, and those who wanted to succeed against competitors willing to do it had to also do it. Eventually the public outcry was too much for the government, however, and they finally stepped in to regulate basic safety standards where lack of information or realistic alternatives made market self-regulation practically impossible.

One of the more compelling and disturbing examples of the industrialists' control was the government response to labor's campaign for fair wages, reasonable hours, and safe working conditions. Instead of taking a balanced, unbiased approach, the government threw everything it had in support of the owners. Local police, state National Guard, and even the federal military stood and acted on the side of the employers in most cases, actively oppressing labor strikes and protests. The federal military became necessary because too many of the National Guardsmen came from the working class and therefore could not be counted on. While recruiting for the National Guard shifted to the middle class, the military was called in around 700 times to suppress labor collaboration over a period of some 25 years.[18]

The loyalty and discipline of the local police and army soldiers were often taken for granted. It was expected they would do their job without complaint and without realizing or acting on the fact that the commands were contrary to their own interests. In some cases the police themselves were being so poorly paid for the work they were doing that the strikers, desperate for a living wage, were actually getting paid more than the police. But when the police in Boston tried to strike for better wages, Governor Coolidge told them they were too important to be allowed to strike (but not important enough to pay decently).

Here, too, control of information was critical. If the strikers could be made to look violent and therefore in need of control, then public opinion might support the government action. The problem was that the strikers tended to be disciplined in their peacefulness. So to win the public-relations battle, many employers planted evidence of violent plots and even hired instigators to try to drum up violence among the strikers. In one case a railroad company went out of their way to attach US Mail cars to a train held up because of a strike. Holding up the mail, a federal offense, was all the excuse the Democratic president needed to justify dedicating federal forces to move against the strikers. Passing on just the "right" information to the government was what made the difference.

The Supreme Court continued to be a useful tool for those at the top as well. Years of rule by and for Capitalists meant that the Court was pretty well disposed toward the rights of corporations and capital instead of the rights of individuals. They fought relentlessly to limit the ability of labor to strike, boycott, or even organize themselves into unions. They took laws intended to restrict abuses by corporations, found ways to avoid applying them to corporations, and at the same time used them to obstruct labor's efforts to negotiate more balanced terms for employees.

In addition to labor negotiating powers, another issue on which the Supreme Court worked for the rich was the income tax. The government relied on revenue from tariffs and taxes on specific goods. It was an income strategy that meant most of the government revenue was coming from ordinary people, while most of the benefit went to the rich. The goods targeted were often ones favored by ordinary consumers and in all cases represented a much higher percentage of the working class's income than for the rich. A graduated income tax would put more of the burden of the government *for* the rich *on* the rich. It was an idea that made it through Congress thanks to the efforts of western Congressmen, who tended to be more independent than their more easily controlled eastern counterparts. But by a single-vote margin, the Supreme Court shot it down as unconstitutional, claiming that taxes had to come from the states proportional to population instead of proportional to wealth. The states were once again the refuge for the elite. It would take a Constitutional amendment before the income tax could be brought to light.

As we've seen, because of their influence in the country, the industrialists could always count on the government to support them in times of economic crises. To insulate them from the effects of the economy, the government implemented a small cocktail of relief that included some combination of: bailing out the banks, raising tariffs, which increased the cost of goods for everyone, and offering businesses government resources to find ways to cut costs (helping corporations lay off people). To pay for this welfare for the wealthy, the government cut spending at a time when no one else could or was willing to spend money to keep the economy going. Most of the actions the government took actually hurt the economy, delayed recovery, and often increased the likelihood of future economic collapses.

While the government seemed oblivious (or worse, uncaring) to what needed to get done for the economy to recover, the people understood that someone simply needed to spend money again. They realized that getting people working and earning who weren't already was the best use of government resources. To try to explain this to the government, people often rallied in favor of government-led infrastructure projects. But instead of listening, the government responded with police to disperse the crowds of concerned citizens. It is a tribute to the strength of the mythology of the country that it could withstand such blatant evidence against the nationalist beliefs and still survive.

Instead of trying to end the crisis itself, the government asked churches and private charities to step up and provide relief for the poor. A Capitalist society that insisted that people were greedy and selfish and that the best thing anyone could do for the economy was to think of oneself needed charity in order to keep from falling into complete anarchy. Predictably the charities found themselves unable to cope with the need. Donations simply were not keeping up. In the larger cities, it was organized crime that stepped up to help people suffering. It was a great way for them to improve their relations with people in the city and help make it look like the laws (particularly prohibition of alcohol) and the police enforcing them were what were unreasonable.

Foreign policy was also executed to serve the wealthy. In the early days, this meant negotiating trade deals for the merchant elite or clearing away foreign powers from land coveted by the southern landowners. Before industrialization, war was bad for business and so something that the country typically tried to avoid. After the Capitalists found there was money to be made in wars, they switched sides and became rabid advocates for war. They also found they had to support wars as their hate-filled rhetoric of fear and mistrust of others got out of hand and left little option other than military action.

The industrialists soon began to realize the potential for exploitation of foreign labor and markets as a way to respond to changes in the United States. Capitalism required constant expansion, always looking for new labor and markets to exploit. But by 1890 the frontier in the United States was declared officially closed by the Bureau of Census. Most of the land taken from Natives had been claimed. While the population would continue to grow, the sort of opportunities the Capitalists had gotten used to would be harder to find. Labor in the United States was also becoming more difficult to exploit, meaning the demands of labor were more difficult to suppress. Rampant inflation was the result of the conflict between labor demands and the need to report increasing profits to shareholders. Foreign countries offered new opportunities, new markets, and new labor to exploit. Since the people being exploited could neither vote nor cause social unrest in the United States, they would in fact be easier to oppress in order to push labor costs lower. The only cost would be to the country's reputation and the security of its citizens abroad, of little concern to the Capitalists who could protect themselves and cared little about nations.

As the United States surveyed the international landscape, they had to decide who they would compete against and who they would collaborate with to achieve the maximum gains for the wealthy. Spain, on the decline, was one they decided they could confront. After someone pointed out to the president where the Philippines was, the United States attacked the Spanish military presence there in response to Spanish provocations in Cuba. While the war with Spain was quick and the US Capitalists got huge concessions in the Americas, the acquisition of the Philippines was much more complicated. The Filipinos were hoping the Spanish defeat by the United States would mean independence for them. Instead the United States insisted that the Filipinos were incapable of ruling themselves and spent seven long years fighting—resulting in the annihilation of towns as large as 17,000 inhabitants and the loss of 4,200 US lives—before the United States had "convinced" them the West was more "civilized."

Mexico, too, was an easy target. US Capitalists had invested heavily in the exploitation of Mexican natural resources (silver, lead, copper, coal, and oil), and the Mexican people were starting to resent it. To keep companies from European countries and, increasingly, Japan from trying to break in on what the United States government had secured for its Capitalists, they expanded the Monroe Doctrine to warn any foreign companies against investing heavily in the Americas. When a new government came to power in Mexico, threatening the US position, the United States declared war to ensure the rights of the Capitalists operating in the country. The country's reputation as a bully was developing quickly.

Japan presented a surprising challenge for the global ambitions of US Capitalists. In 1905 they were dealing Russia a surprisingly severe military defeat, which would open up a number of different opportunities for them in global power politics. To direct them away from competing with the United States in the Pacific, President Theodore Roosevelt arranged to host a peace conference. By taking the lead this way, the Japanese could be directed back toward Asia instead of out into the Pacific. To make the point clear, the president painted the country's naval assets white and sent them on a "goodwill tour" through the Pacific in a barely masked attempt to intimidate potential adversaries. The ploy resulted in a naval arms race that heightened tensions for generations.

Meanwhile it was calculated that Britain and Germany were not to be toyed with. As a result, compromise was the preferred solution for competing interests in the Samoan Islands. Each had built up their own local power bases, which competed against the others as a sort of proxy contest between the three countries. It was not sustainable, and eventually it was decided that US and Germany would split the Samoan Islands and that Britain would be granted the Solomon Islands. It was a win-win-win situation—only the Native residents of these islands lost out.

The same sort of "compromise" was brokered by the United States to divide the spoils in China. Up to that point, the nations of Europe had been competing with each other to exploit China, viewing it as a great market for the country's manufacturing goods despite the country's general lack of interest in western products. Eventually the United States helped bring about a cooperation among the exploiting countries that allowed them to establish a firm upper hand against the resistance of the Chinese people.

If the US Capitalists were the top priority of the US government, the global Capitalists were a close second. There was a whole world of people to exploit open to them. The story of the Panama Canal presented a compelling example. A canal connecting the Atlantic and Pacific Oceans had long been a dream of the Capitalists in the United States. A French company owned the canal rights through what was at the time northern Colombia. They wanted out, so they lobbied Congress in the United States to buy the rights from them despite the fact that the US already had an option negotiated to build in Nicaragua. The United States agreed to pay the French company, but Colombia refused the transfer of rights. The agreement was about to expire, so Colombia wanted to negotiate new rights with the United States. Dissatisfied with the delay, the United States encouraged a rebellion in the region, sent its navy down to block Colombian forces from responding, and broke Panama away from Colombia. To avoid losing face with the French company, the United States paid them for the Colombia rights. Non-binding deals with foreign Capitalists were a matter of honor, completely different from treaties with foreign nations or Native peoples, which the United States considered less binding.

While direct and active support from the government was less common but always welcome, the consolidation of wealth in a small minority was facilitated most by a government that was willing to stand by and let abuses of labor and markets to continue unregulated. So the Capitalists were often keenly promoting the notion of a small government, one that would not interfere with their control of the economy. The government was typically the only defense the people had against the wealthy, and, without that protector, the people's freedoms and opportunities shrank dramatically.

A compliant government also meant the Capitalists were in a position to experiment with their own form of utopia, in which the ideals and ideas of Capitalism were taken to their natural extremes, bringing enormous wealth and privilege to those fortunate to be at the top of the Capitalist pyramid. Of course, what this meant for people outside of the tiny minority at the top was something much closer to dystopia than utopia.

With government out of the way or acting in their favor and labor sufficiently brought to heel, one of the greatest remaining obstacles to more efficient exploitation and greater profits was the competition between the different Capitalists. The answer, of course, was collaboration. It was in the railroad industry that the idea of collaboration took off and expanded to utopian levels. The railroads in the East had been laid more densely than in the West, which meant that consumers and labor had more options and, therefore, more leverage to combat abuses. If the railroad tycoons could eliminate the competition, they would be in a stronger position to dictate terms. Cornelius Vanderbilt led the way. Instead of investing in a broad network across the country, he concentrated on buying up all the significant railroads in New York State. Next he turned to buying out or killing off the Pennsylvania railroads to eliminate any sort of competition. Less competition meant higher prices, poorer service, lower safety, and fewer options. The idea caught on in other industries as well. John Rockefeller brought the concept to the oil industry, becoming so powerful that he even managed to dictate terms to the railroad companies. He not only got discounted rates from the railroads, but he also took a cut whenever they shipped his competitors' oil, driving up their costs and prices for everyone.

When people started to complain about the increasing costs and decreasing value provided by the railroads, some of the states tried to regulate them. But the business-friendly Supreme Court blocked them. In 1886 the Supreme Court voided around 230 state laws attempting to restrain corporate exploitation.[19] They argued that corporations as legal entities deserved the same protection of their property that an individual would expect from the 14th amendment, which stated that "No State shall make or enforce any law which shall abridge the privileges or immunities of citizens of the United States; nor shall any State deprive any person of life, liberty, or property, without due process of law; nor deny to any person within its jurisdiction the equal protection of the laws." Trying to regulate the railroads was restricting the rights of corporations, they argued. It was a convoluted argument by any measure but made particularly tragic when the same court was ruling that the 14th amendment did not protect the rights of freed slaves in the South, for whom it was written. The Court's decision that corporations were people with rights equal to or greater than human citizens would have profound implications for the country and was a clear indication of where the federal government stood in the fight between corporations and people.

Hostile takeovers weren't an option for everyone, however. Few industrialists had enough money or nego-tiating talent to buy out enough of an industry to make a difference. Instead many industries developed what were called "trusts," a more collaborative path to consolidation of market power. They were often facilitated by a banker, who took a large cut of the profits for their efforts. US Steel was the biggest trust, but they also formed in other industries, including cottonseed oil, linseed oil, lead, whiskey, and sugar. Once control over the market had been successfully achieved, the Capitalists behind the trust could pass the organization over to talented administrators, continue to siphon off the wealth created by the organizations' employees, and dream up their next money-making scheme. This continued the trend of separating decision-makers from mandate makers. The managers of the companies were driven to increase profits even when doing so went against their human instincts, leading to greater exploitation of labor, markets, and the environment.

Once a trust was created, they moved immediately to take everything they could from the market. They had to, in order to satisfy the profit demands of the masterminds behind the trust. They also had to make sure no competitor came in to disrupt their advantage. In several cases, they even bought up patents and buried the technology to prevent a new company from coming in and beating them on price or service with new technology. It's what happened when individual minority interests served as the overwhelming driving force of an economic system. In order for a minority to stay on top, they were holding up progress—not at all how you'd want a free market to work.

The Supreme Court actually looked at ways to regulate these trusts. It turned out that even the Supreme Court had limits on how far they were prepared to let the Capitalists abuse consumers. But this time the states came to the rescue of corporations. In an attempt to lure companies and their meager-paying jobs, they invented new ways to allow corporations to get around the Supreme Court rulings. Not only were countries competing to get the Capitalists to exploit their land and people, but states, too, were competing with each other, desperate for what little scraps the industrialists could leave for their citizens. The multiple layers and "checks and balances" of government were serving perfectly as designed to prevent the people from achieving gains against the elite.

While the industrialists embraced collaboration on a utopian scale among themselves to maximize the exploitation of markets and labor, they insisted that any other form of collaboration was dangerous to the capitalist economy. So when labor tried to coordinate their efforts to balance out some of the enormous power enjoyed by corporations, the industrialists protested loudly. Not only did such coordination challenge the negotiating supremacy of corporations, but also there was no telling what a coordinated labor movement could do to the position and privileges of the Capitalists. Hoping no one would notice the irony, they insisted that consolidation of labor demands was not consistent with a free market and, therefore, should be forbidden, for the good of the country.

This was, of course, after Abraham Lincoln's Gettysburg address, in which he put forward the notion that the United States was a country with a "government of the people, by the people, for the people." The wealthy were testing just how blatantly far off that mark they could continue to operate without resistance. They would eventually learn that, in order for government of, for, and by the elite to persist, it would have be more subtle in its tactics.

CHAPTER 4

The people struggle

The people wrestle with different ways to gain control over their lives and country but end up being defeated in the effort by two world wars. After the wars, fear of Communism is stoked to achieve firm control over the people. After the absurdities of the Communist witch hunt are made clear, the people take another stand in an era of rebellion.

Government for the people tries to emerge
Since the days of the early colonists, there had always been a persistent thread of anti-elitism in the United States. People who didn't aspire to achieving a position in society where they could exploit others freely were outraged by the landed aristocracy of Europe. It was why many left Europe. They resented people who enjoyed special sources of wealth and an extra voice in governing. In the United States, this anti-elitism manifested itself early in such forms as the anti-Masonic Party, having seen many in the upper classes organize in Masonic lodges. It showed up within the abolitionist movement upset about

the southern aristocracy and their inhumane privileges. And many realized that the Capitalists were no different. Instead of special revenue sources and power by virtue of land ownership, they got their privileges from their control of wealth. The more wealth one had, the more power and the more potential to generate more wealth one had. And the Capitalists were leveraging that power to make life difficult for ordinary people.

To escape the influence of the eastern elite, people headed West, into the frontier. Many were lured there by the exaggerated claims made by the railroads, only to find land that was difficult to work in most places and weather much less predictable and less stable than what farmers east of the Mississippi had to deal with. To make matters worse, the settlers of the western frontiers didn't actually succeed in escaping the reach of the elite. They were dependent on bankers for mortgages and loans to cover seed costs until harvesting. They were gouged by railroads and other monopolized services. These forces combined to dramatically increase the risk for farmers. But despite the importance of the agriculture of the new frontier to the economy, security, and well-being of the country, Capitalism failed to compensate them for that risk. It showed how poorly the free market actually worked and how important wealth and connections truly were.

It did, however, take some time before the industrialists and their political parties could gain solid control over the electorate in the West. This offered the farmers a measure of political freedom much greater than what their eastern counterparts had. It gave them room to establish third parties that competed successfully against the Republicans and Democrats. Eventually most of that third-party interest consolidated into the Populist Party, which fought for a better chance at the "American Dream" for the farmers.

In an attempt to expand its base, the Populist Party also tried to add some of the labor demands (for example, the 8-hour workday) to their platform. But labor had largely given up on politics as a means to advance their interests. Since they lived among the political control of the major parties, there was no hope of getting anywhere through political channels. Instead they focused most of their energies through unions, their only hope to stand up against the power and influence of the Capitalists. When labor did turn out for a political party, it was for the Socialist Party, which experienced some success during the first decades of the 1900s. Unlike in Europe, there was very little interest in the Marxist-inspired Socialist Labor Party or the later Communist Party in the United States. The idea of a violent revolution existed much more profoundly in the propaganda of the Capitalists to encourage the middle class to fear the working class than in the hearts and minds of the workers, despite the desperate situation the workers were subjected to.

The middle class tended to buy into what the Capitalists were selling, both figuratively and literally. They bought into the fear: fear of farmers because of the example of the French Revolution, and fear of labor after the example of the Russian Revolution. They also bought the manufactured goods that the Capitalists were selling, in many cases buying them on credit. They racked up debt to drive the economy forward, enriching both Capitalists and bankers.

There were times, however, when the middle class broke out of their consumption-induced coma and realized what the Capitalists were doing to the working class and to the ideals of the country. It was newspapers and artists that were largely responsible for awakening the middle class to the abuses of the robber barons in the late 1800s. But the newspaper industry had to go through a rather significant change in order to serve the role. Up to that point, newspapers had been competing largely on sensationalism. They were willing to make up and exaggerate facts in order to draw in more readers. They had contributed greatly to the demand for war against Spain in 1898, creating sensationalism and furor to sell newspapers. A handful of newspapers started to compete on investigative journalism, shining a bright light on the abuses of business and government while exposing the plight of the working class. They discovered that having high journalistic standards not only felt good because they were making a real difference but also sold newspapers. Writers and artists, too, had to break away from their comfort zone and the direction of the art trusts in order to raise awareness of the suffering of the working class. But when they did, they portrayed vividly the daily lives and living and working conditions of the working class to a middle-class population that was finally prepared to see what was really going on.

As in Russia before the Russian Revolution derailed the momentum, intellectuals began to imagine alternative forms of government, economy, and society. Writers imagined a future where people's contributions were respected and sought after, with a wave of more than 100 different utopian novels sparked by the 1888 publishing of *Looking Backwards* by Edward Bellamy. Many novels also forecast a bleak dystopian future if conditions did not change.

With people increasingly united against the abuses of the Capitalists, the government started to back down from their unrelenting and undisguised support of the wealthy. It happened, however, only very slowly and extended only as far as was absolutely necessary to prevent a total collapse of the government.

Knowing that there was growing public discontent at the beginning of the 1900s, the Republicans panicked when the assassination of President McKinley promoted Theodore Roosevelt to Commander-in-Chief. Roosevelt had attracted the attention of the public when he weakened the political machines in New York (of which the Democrats made much better use). He was both popular and unpredictable. Being difficult to control, he was a risk for the Capitalists as Governor of New York State, and many imagined the Vice Presidency a safe place to sideline him.

Fortunately for the Republicans, however, he proved easily moderated in office after he became president. He pursued a conservative approach he called "stand pat," waiting to see if change was really necessary. He did go after a few of the more egregious trusts but let most of them continue with business as usual. He had, after all, accepted campaign donations from many of them. His hands-off conservative approach allowed for a massive increase in the number of trusts during his administration. He also continued to stand firmly behind business owners against labor. In one example, he supported the owners of a coal mine against labor even after the owners were found guilty of dirty and insincere dealings with labor and the government. One of the few concessions he made to the rising anti-elitism was the symbolic change of the name of the Executive Mansion to the White House, hoping to make the office seems less ostentatious and the government less elitist.

It was only at the end of Roosevelt's terms as president that he got firmly bitten by the Progressive bug. What awakened him was an encounter with some banks that tried to leverage an economic downturn to reverse the offensive against trusts. They claimed that the economic problems were not caused by greedy Capitalists trying to corner the copper market but instead by the regulations on greedy Capitalists. Roosevelt exploded and fed off the anti-Capitalist sentiment that was gripping the country, adding his own strong, fighting personality to the effort. It came too late for Roosevelt, however, as his second term was already coming to a close.

After four years of Roosevelt's conservative successor, the election of 1912 was the peak of the Progressive Movement. There was a single conservative candidate, the incumbent President Taft, up against three progressives: the Socialist candidate, perhaps the most progressive of the lot; Theodore Roosevelt, running under the new Nationalist Progressive Party that combined progressive economic issues with hateful nationalist and ethnocentric rhetoric; and the Democrat candidate, as always promising everything to everybody. The three progressive candidates combined to receive 77% of the votes, an impressive statement of protest from the people. The least progressive candidate, the Democrat Woodrow Wilson, convinced the most voters that he could do the most for them. As a former president of Princeton, it was hoped he would provide enough wisdom and avoid the traps of politics as usual to make a difference.

In office Wilson worked on the most serious abuses of the banks and other businesses. For starters, the government introduced new restrictions on the formation of trusts while trying unsuccessfully to close loopholes that allowed corporations to use these laws to suppress labor negotiations. Wilson put a great deal of personal effort into reforming tariffs in order to shift the costs of government off the backs of the poor. Breaking with the tradition set by Thomas Jefferson, Wilson gave his State of the Union address in person, lecturing the Congress on the need for tariff reform. Congress relented and accepted dramatic changes to the sources of government revenue, but it cost Wilson heavily in the Congress, where his new "enemies" were determined to limit his future successes regardless of the cost to the country.

Also significantly, Wilson appointed a couple of new Supreme Court justices who were committed to individuals' rights as opposed to focused on the rights of corporations or the rich. Louis Brandeis, in particular, was known for his incorruptibility by big-business money and as a champion for the people's causes.

By most measures, however, Wilson's most ambitious project was his attempts to secure world peace, his so-called "great adventure." It developed from thinking that had been percolating both in Europe and in the United States for years after many compassionate people were shaken by World War I. The war had taken barbarity and senseless violence to a level higher than even the Civil War had done. Wilson was set on finding a way to avoid future conflicts on such a horrific scale.

Wilson negotiated extensively and vigorously with the European nations to make sure that the peace terms for the Great War would include the establishment of a League of Nations, to give countries a place to discuss disagreements without having to resort to war. Ironically, in order to get the League of Nations included, Wilson had to accept other peace terms that would eventually make another war inevitable. And then, after all that negotiation and compromise, the United States Congress refused to ratify the treaty. Congress complained that they didn't want to be drawn into European conflicts. Wilson responded by explaining that the League provided a moral, not a legal, mandate to help out when troubles arose. They complained that the League might interfere with the country's dominance over the Americas. Wilson responded with confidence that he could get an exception carved out for the Monroe Doctrine. Ultimately, however, perhaps the biggest factor preventing Congress's approval of the treaty was retaliation for Wilson's win on the tariffs. After the president had embarrassed them, they were not interested in handing him another victory. Politics demonstrated itself again and again incapable of acting in the best interests of the country, let alone the world.

As horrific as it was for Europe, the soldiers, and even the people left on the home front, the Great War was good for the Capitalists. It produced a massive burst in government spending in industry. It also helped weaken the Progressive Movement. The jolt of nationalism required to convince people to sacrifice for the war also stopped many people from questioning the government's pro-Capitalist commitments. After all, to challenge the government was to weaken the war effort. At the end of the Progressive Movement, it could be said that some real gains had been achieved, but the wealthy were still clearly in charge of the government and the economy. If anything, the experience made the Capitalist control over the economy and government more sustainable against growing popular discontentment.

It didn't take long for the wealthy to regain ground lost in the Progressive Era. The Republicans returned to power with a platform calling for a return to "normalcy." With the 1919 passing of the 18th amendment, making the sale, manufacture, and transportation of alcohol illegal in the United States, the 1920s saw a combination of extreme government interference in people's personal lives, with a return of a minimalist approach to regulating the actions of corporations. People responded to the restrictions to their freedoms with open defiance, while corporations responded with a return to unfettered exploitation of labor and consumers.

With the return of Republican administrations, the wealthy were again well taken care of. By 1926 the top 1% wealthiest people owned 60% of the wealth.[20] More and more capital was being consolidated in the hands of people who could theoretically use that money to expand the economy. The problem was there was not enough market demand to encourage industrial expansion. Stagnant wages meant there simply wasn't enough cash in the hands of people to buy the basics, let alone anything new. Without a strong domestic market, there was no reason for the wealthy to create new jobs and keep the economy and the country healthy, regardless of how much money they were handed.

Since Capitalism offered no incentives for individual Capitalists to improve the spending power of a country's people, banks and Capitalists put much more effort into juicing up the stock-market prices than actually improving industry or wages. One of the major innovations of the time was to lure ordinary people and their money into the investment world. They were attracted by the lifestyle of the Capitalists: fabulous wealth and power and a life of luxury and leisure. As always, the banks were eager to loan people money in order to invest in corporations, driven by the guaranteed interest profits from the loans.

A new sport developed around duping the investing public. In one scheme, Capitalists would pool their money and buy a large quantity of stock in a particular company, driving the stock price up. People thought the company must be heading somewhere and so joined the bandwagon, at which point the original investors started selling at the inflated price. When the true value of the company caused the price of the stock to plummet, the original investors were gone with the money, leaving the small investors bankrupt. Like casinos, it was a great way for the rich to siphon off additional wealth from the poor. It also gave people hope that they may some day be part of the Capitalist elite, and, so in anticipation of that day, it was insisted that they should not challenge the special privileges enjoyed by the super-wealthy. It was, they were told to think, an opportunity open to anyone willing to take on the risk and do the "hard" work.

The artificial wealth created was no more sustainable than previous schemes, however. Before long the economy was destroyed again, once savvy investors started to realize broad prosperity without work was not possible. Since the government had fallen completely for the notion of prosperity through ever-increasing stock prices, they were committed to giving business and Capitalism free reign and, therefore, could offer no resistance to the complete collapse of the economy. Human suffering grew to unprecedented levels while Hoover, who had run in 1928 on the promise to eradicate poverty—and was so wealthy himself that he could donate his salary to charity for his entire career in public service—spent much of his time fishing.

Ahead of the 1932 presidential election, Hoover finally broke down and accepted that the government must do something. In an effort to demonstrate to voters that the Republicans did care about people, he funneled some government money to infrastructure projects in an attempt to boost the economy. But the economic impact did not come quickly enough to have much of an impact on the election.

True to the philosophy of government of the age, in the election neither the Democrats nor the Republicans emphasized the economic problems much. The economy remained something they considered largely outside of the concern of government. A change in the government's regulation of people's personal choices was, however, evident as both candidates came out clearly in favor of repealing Prohibition. The country was suffering, and alcohol seemed the most obvious way to treat the symptoms. A restored liquor industry would also produce jobs, and taxes on liquor would increase revenue for the government. With support from both parties, a Constitutional amendment (the 21st) was proposed by Congress shortly after the election and rushed through the states.

Once in office, however, the new president, Democrat Franklin Roosevelt (from a wealthy family himself), broke with all expectations and traditions and committed the government to provide relief to people. It was needed to prevent an open and widespread revolt, as desperation had grown to unprecedented levels. One of the first things he did was to shore up and clean up the banking industry. He closed down all the banks and allowed only those that could prove themselves trustworthy (around 75% of them) to reopen. When they did reopen, they enjoyed the full support and backing of the federal government. The move gave people who still had money confidence to keep their money in them.

Then the president fell for the same, old, tired thinking that had extended so many economic crises before: he cut government spending. Specifically he cut government salaries and soldier pensions. He failed to realize that when the government was the only entity spending in an economy, a reduction in government spending has a negative impact on the economy.

To make up for the government cuts, Roosevelt continued and expanded on Hoover's infrastructure idea. He started small, focusing in on national forests and parks in addition to helping fund some state and local projects. Seeing the success of these programs, the president decided to expand the scope dramatically. Such projects not only got people back to work and spending money in the economy, but they also allowed the country to build much-needed (particularly rural) infrastructure at a lower rate than would be possible at full employment, when the government would have to compete for labor with private companies.

The government paid extra attention to keeping corruption and waste down in these projects, to serve as a model for future government infrastructure projects. In some cases conditions made it necessary for the government to take over or start up new utility companies. This gave them a chance to demonstrate to private enterprise and their customers how business could be done and how customers could be treated respectfully.

The administration also helped organize industries in order to ensure fair salaries, safe working conditions, and fair profits. These were measures that some of the wealthy resented. They argued that "life isn't fair" and that it was not the place of government to try to make it more so. Before long, the Supreme Court, still reliably in the control of the rich, stepped up to protect the rights of corporations, ending the federal government's attempts to curb exploitation.

Meanwhile conditions just kept getting worse for farmers, particularly in the central states. These were not lazy people, contrary to what the wealthy back East might argue. Despite some very difficult years, most of them had stuck to it. As prices dropped in the 1920s, few gave up; instead, they resolved to work harder. The problem was that, the harder they worked, the more they produced, the lower the prices went, and the more damage they did to the soil. To make matters worse, the demand for food was also depressed, despite massive starvation. Eventually there were few farmers that could meet their financial obligations. And then the weather turned on them. Crop failures due to excessive drought left nothing to hold the soil to the ground. Windstorms drove the soil up into the sky, producing thick clouds of dust that made breathing—let alone walking and working—very difficult.

Things got so bad for the farmers that the federal government finally stepped in to help out. They encouraged and educated farmers toward soil conservation, ideas that they could have learned just as readily from the continent's Native populations if only they had bothered to ask. In the maniacal logic of Capitalism, the federal government also paid the farmers to destroy crops and kill off livestock in order to drive up prices while people were starving. But it was too little and too late for many farmers, who simply could not afford to keep going. Plus it did nothing for farm laborers who didn't own the land. Reducing output meant they were out of a job. It was also unconstitutional, according to the Supreme Court. After the program was allowed to operate for three years, it was ruled that the federal government was not empowered to help people in such active ways.

With all his efforts and breaking with traditions of not helping the people, there was a definite reversal on the employment decline after Roosevelt took office. After peaking at 23.6% and 24.9% unemployment in 1932 and 1933, it was down to 21.7% and 20.1% in 1934 and 1935.[21] But there were limits to how many people the government could employ while waiting for private enterprise to regain the confidence they needed to engage again. Roosevelt realized that if some relief were not provided, the ranks of the unemployed could easily become militant, taking their aggression out on the government or the wealthy. To forestall that outcome and keep Capitalism viable, Roosevelt pushed through unemployment compensation to help people get through the crisis without resorting to desperate or violent measures. He also introduced a new social security plan to take care of people who were too old to continue to work but who had never earned enough to save for retirement.

To help pay for these programs, Roosevelt increased taxes on the wealthy, a radical move. But if they weren't interested in contributing to the recovery of the country in their role as Capitalists by expanding production or research—or even by just paying employees enough to afford goods—then they could help pay for the government efforts to prop up the country until they were ready to step up again. It was argued that with extra power and privilege should come extra responsibility, particularly in such dire times.

After his reelection, Roosevelt responded to concerns from the rich about the growing federal deficit by making massive cuts in spending on infrastructure programs. The move increased unemployment again and slowed down economic recovery. By 1937, the unemployment rate had finally come back down to a still painful 14.3% (from, as we'll remember, a peak of 24.9%), but the cut in public projects shot it back up to 19.0% in 1938. It was clear that, in order to sustain the recovery, the government was going to have to continue its spending. There was no one else around to push the economy back into shape. Roosevelt introduced new projects, and the unemployment rate started to decline again.

After suffering a number of reversals at the hands of a Supreme Court still operating in the interests of the wealthy, Roosevelt threatened to expand the Court in order to get more justices that he could count on. The threat alone proved enough to encourage the Court to be more reasonable in its judgments, although clearly much damage had already been done. The tactic didn't sit well with voters, however. Instead of trying to reform the core problem with the Supreme Court, Roosevelt had simply tried to bend them to his will. The voters responded to this and the increasing unemployment caused by Roosevelt rollback of public projects by providing the Republicans a small comeback in the mid-term elections of 1938. The Democrats could not hide from their past manipulations of government for their own purposes, even when they were trying to operate in the best interests of the people, for a change.

By 1940, the renewed public infrastructure projects had reduced the tide of unemployment once again, going from 17.2% in 1939 to 14.6% in 1940, on its way to 9.9% in 1941. Although few imagined the recovery was over, it was generally regarded well and truly on its way. Additional government spending in supporting the British war effort and then joining it after the attack on Pearl Harbor in 1941 helped push down unemployment further, to 4.7% in 1942.

But once again, the nationalism of the war, tied with compromises the government needed to make to Capitalists to get them to participate in (and profit from) the war, was enough to bring to an end another brief period of government for the people and launch the country into another era of government exclusively for the elite.

Communism for the Capitalists

The idea of a people's economy, where the value created by labor would be enjoyed by labor, became mainstream with the theories of Karl Marx in the middle of the 1800s. Even before World War I and the Russian Revolution, there was significant agitation for humane treatment of workers throughout Europe, especially in Germany. Therefore Capitalists were already actively creating fear about the unknowns of change when the formation of the Soviet Union, with its autocratic rule and awkward lack of a people's economy or government, gave shape to fears of a society without Capitalists. It was part of the cocktail that allowed Hitler to be elected in Germany.

When Lenin took over Russia, he claimed that he was doing it for the workers. But instead of introducing a genuine workers' government, the Revolution simply replaced the Capitalists and landed aristocracy with bureaucratic or party elite who enjoyed special privileges by virtue of their connections and willingness to bend to the will of the party leaders. Its window dressings were all that was different from the elite rule of Europe and the United States. The perpetuation of the mythology of a workers' government, even after oppressing labor and consolidating supreme economic and political power in a totalitarian regime, played directly into the hands of the Capitalists. They could then suggest that giving in to the workers' demands would lead to the form of government and society exhibited by the Soviet Union. However, the opposite is more accurate: by not satisfying the simple demands of labor (for dignity and fair wages), a dictatorial regime was able to usurp both political and economic power using the labor demands as ideological cover.

Soviet Communism seemed custom-made for the Capitalists in the United States, since it helped substantiate a fear they were already trying to use to gain middle-class support for the oppression of labor. Throughout history fear had proved itself an incredible tool for governments to expand their power and overcome objections. People have often been willing to give up substantial freedoms in exchange for security from a (typically manufactured) threat. John Adams, writing before the Declaration of Independence, imagined that the people of North America had a higher resolve against such tactics. He wrote in his *Thoughts on Government:* "Fear is the foundation of most governments; but it is so sordid and brutal a passion, and renders men in whose breasts it predominates so stupid and miserable, that Americans will not be likely to approve of any political institution which is founded on it." In his first inaugural address, President Franklin Roosevelt had tried to strengthen people's defenses against fear tactics: "Let me assert my firm belief that the only thing we have to fear is fear itself—nameless, unreasoning, unjustified terror which paralyzes needed efforts to convert retreat into advance." And yet, in the United States, people had no unique resistance to fear tactics. Contrary to Adams' predictions, the people did not challenge the government's use of it to manipulate them.

The manufactured threat of Communism and labor was much greater than anything that existed in actual fact. As was happening in Europe, the threat was used to consolidate power and eliminate challenges. It happened early in the United States. At the beginning of 1920, the US Justice Department went on a hunting expedition for anyone who they might be able to tag as "Communist" to crack down on the growing workers movement. They made 5000 arrests across 33 cities in 23 states.[22] States, too, started to expel elected Socialists from their state legislature. In Milwaukee, the people responded by simply reelecting their Socialist representative, requiring him to be expelled a second time. The state ended up having to keep the seat empty in order to defeat the will of the people.

Laws began to appear across the country banning red flags and putting restrictions on speech, with an emphasis on limiting "disloyal" speech. By 1948, the government was requiring anyone involved in government to take loyalty oaths and Communists across the country to register themselves as such.

Teachers and professors were hard hit by the attack, as were the books they wrote. Books and art were being banned in the country, requiring creative interpretation of the Constitution. Hollywood executives were prosecuted for making Communism look good (or not making it look evil). Hollywood was even attacked for shining a light on the early abuses and real threats of Hitler, who had risen to power under the mythology that he and his National Socialist Party were fighting against the advance of Communism.

In 1938, the House of Representatives created the House Un-American Activities Committee (HUAC), designed to spot and handle extreme behavior both from the right and from the left. It was soon taken over to exclusively attack the left after the Fascist threat in Europe was defeated. The government investigated all public employees and offered no right of trial or defense before dismissing people who had ideas they didn't approve of. Private companies also performed their own internal searches for left-leaning individuals, taking advantage of the atmosphere to clear out anyone who might challenge the owners' exploitation of labor.

It wasn't until after 1954, when one of the more ambitious Communist "witch trials" was televised, that the ridiculousness of the domestic threat and its abuses became clear to people. The Capitalists would no longer be able to be quite as extreme in their tactics to suppress and control the workers.

Despite all the attacks on Communism, the retractors steered clear from an attack that would have resonated. One of the more compelling criticisms of theoretical Communism—a flaw that was shared with many utopian experiments over time—was its apparent assumption that people should and would all want to live their lives similarly. The thinking of the time suggested that a managed economy would require an incredibly high degree of conformity. It seemed like a weakness ready-made for the propaganda machines of the Capitalists in a United States that cherished freedom and individuality. However, the Capitalists wanted to impose a high degree of conformity on people as well. They aimed for a sort of "Capitalist commonism" in which all consumers, laborers, and voters would look and behave similarly, follow clearly defined rules of behavior, and think the way the government expected them to think. It was all designed to reduce labor costs, simplify product selling, and produce a compliant citizenry that would be easier to govern. Diversity was an obstacle for the wealthy and political leaders to be reduced and eliminated as much as possible.

The middle class was once again content to fall right into line with the desires of the Capitalists. They were desperate for security and predictability after the Second World War and the growing arsenal of weapons of mass destruction controlled by both the United States and, later, the Soviet Union. With a continuous stream of manufactured goods and automobiles to buy, typically on credit to deal the banks into the profits to be had, being like everyone else became acceptable and in fact what many people aspired to.

Television sets became ubiquitous, particularly in the suburbs. They were an incredible tool to homogenize the country, giving everyone the same "cultural" foundations. Since television programming was funded by advertisements, corporations had incredible influence over the content. They used that influence to encourage conformity and acceptance of the social hierarchy. Sitcoms portrayed a model for a "typical" family that no one could live up to in reality but were kept striving for. Quiz shows reinforced the idea that anyone who worked hard and followed the rules could win big money. To ensure this message, several quiz shows actually rigged the contests to show good and honest hardworking people winning while undesirable-looking people lost. A serious problem occurred when some of the people chosen to represent losers blew the whistle on the practice. Suddenly people didn't know what to trust on television. The response to the scandals had a cascade effect and encouraged even news programs to improve their standards for a while.

Organized religion stepped up to build communities in the new suburbs. Church attendance was part of the appearance of conformity, and religious affiliation became one of the questions used to evaluate whether someone was Communist or not. Church services were also a good opportunity to develop and foster social and business connections. With people increasingly belonging to a church in order to fit into a community, some preachers must have lamented the loss of sincerity in religious observance.

The Congress passed a series of laws to advance the conformity agenda and to prove their own conformity. Members didn't want to be accused of being Communists any more than anyone else did. In 1954 they added "one nation under God" to the pledge of allegiance, required recitation at many venues in that day and for decades to follow. In 1956 they replaced the national motto "E pluribus unum" (Out of many, one), which emphasized the country's strength from diversity, and replaced it with a motto designed to emphasize the new conformity: "In God We Trust." The message of cultural conformity was made clear and present when the new motto was required on all government currency in 1957.

Soon, to the fear of labor was added fear of standing out and fear of associating with people who stood out. In order to keep their position in society, the middle class had to enthusiastically follow the rules set by the rich and avoid getting noticed for independent thinking. Innovation naturally took a serious hit.

Not living up to the norm—particularly given the consequences of failing to conform—created a great deal of anxiety. What was portrayed as "normal" on television, in magazines, and in the churches was an artificial construction, outside of human nature, designed to encourage compliance and obedience. Few people actually lived up to these expectations. Few people's families got along as harmoniously as they were portrayed on television or how other families appeared to be. They didn't believe in what they were being told everyone should believe and what others pretended to believe. Many people felt that there must be something wrong with them for not being "normal." But no one could talk about it for fear of being reported. As a result, the number of professional psychiatrists doubled during the course of the 1950s. With doctor-patient confidentiality, the doctor's office was a place where people felt more comfortable admitting their true human nature.

Particularly in the middle class, feelings of inadequacy were often channeled—when not channeled through infidelity, alcohol, or drugs—through a drive to acquire more stuff. It was a way to demonstrate to the neighbors that they were happy. But soon it became a competition, with neighbors trying to one-up each other acquiring the latest consumer goods and automobiles. The stores accommodated this by offering to sell items on credit, finding interest on loans a valuable source of revenue. But keeping up proved difficult for most families, creating more anxiety and a greater sense of inadequacy.

A new and powerful fear

Another big payoff for Capitalists from the Communist scare was a new set of excuses to avoid having to cover the social costs of a labor force. Since Communism was evil—as was Socialism by association—anything that they didn't want to do could be labeled as Communist or Socialist to imply that it would be the first step to giving in to the Soviets. So when a scheme was developed to both help small farmers and lower the cost of food to consumers, the southern landowners, who were bothered by the reduction in cotton subsidies in the plan, tainted it by declaring it "Socialist." A plan to eradicate polio (which afflicted and profoundly impacted President Franklin Roosevelt) through public vaccinations was shelved as "Socialist." A national healthcare plan, which seemed to many as one of the basic and fundamental requirements of a modern civilized country, was killed off by the insurance companies by calling it "Socialist."

While the domestic threats of hidden Communists were no longer easily exploited by the Capitalists, there remained the foreign threat, particularly after the Soviet Union announced it had developed the atomic bomb. The international race for global domination over Communism took priority over any domestic issue. In order to "save the world for democracy," the people in the United States should be willing to make certain sacrifices to their welfare, financial security, and freedoms.

The United States and the Soviet Union found themselves locked in a battle for underdeveloped, non-aligned countries. These countries were viewed as vital for security, to keep the other side confined geographically, and as valuable targets for economic exploitation. In reality, however, they were most valuable to each side's elites as populations to exploit for power and wealth. To these countries, the United States and the Soviet Union offered two distinct paths to economic development. Each path promised higher standards of living for the country's citizens. The Soviet Union pointed to its own success with Communism. Before the Russian Revolution, Russia had fallen behind in industrial development. Since the Revolution, they had been able to dramatically increase their industrial and agricultural output. For underdeveloped countries, they offered their leadership on state-run economies, suggesting that their mistakes that had led to massive human suffering could be avoided. With a few years of sacrifice, a country could compete on the world market and raise its living standards.

In contrast, the United States offered investment from international Capitalists to build up the country's industrial infrastructure. The international Capitalists would frequently partner with locals willing to participate in the exploitation of the country's people and resources in exchange for a small share of the wealth generated. While typically providing greater freedom of expression and action, the United States model also created a much greater gap between a country's wealthy and its poor, mirroring what one saw in the United States.

The US model also required a great deal of the developing country's resulting wealth to be exported out of the country, into the hands of the international Capitalists. They had put up their investment with the expectation of higher returns than they could expect in their home country. Between 1950 and 1965, $8.1 billion was invested in Latin America, with $5.5 billion being taken right back out of the country in the form of profit. In Africa, it was even worse: a $5.2 billion investment was resulting in the loss to the continent of $14.3 billion in profit taken by Capitalists.[23] As people started to realize how much wealth was being taken from a country, unrest developed, and the reputation of the United States suffered. The US was clearly no ambassador for the ideals of freedom and opportunity for all.

In exchange for the loss of wealth, the US model could offer only a long and uncertain path to economic improvement for the workers. When a country first started to improve its industrial capacity, its main competitive advantage was the fact that its workers would work for less than workers elsewhere. If their standard of living improved, their competitive advantage would disappear as well, often resulting in a reversal of progress. If a country did manage to successfully transition to a more-skilled labor force, with higher wages, they would become a threat to other countries and be challenged accordingly. Sustaining their gains would be extremely difficult and require a weakening of relations with other countries.

Since the people of a developing country were typically resistant to giving so much of themselves and their country to foreign Capitalists, a strong hand in a country was required to gain access to resources, industries. and malleable labor. Anxious to secure power in as many countries and as quickly as possible in a race against the Soviet Union, the United States allied with and funded tyrants across the globe. These were people who actively and openly oppressed their people in order to get them to generate the wealth demanded by the Capitalists. Selling arms to these tyrants, to control their own people and to fight in proxy wars for the United States and Soviet Union, was another way the United States could siphon off more profits. By 1975 the United States was exporting $9.5 billion in arms[24] around the world, true merchants of death. The people in these countries might not have agreed, therefore, with the designation of the conflict between the Soviet Union and the United States as a "Cold War."

Both of the options presented to developing countries were pretty awful. In one model, the people paid a heavy price in liberties, individuality, and freedom, and, in the other, progress was slower for most people, and almost all of the wealth generated went abroad. It's no surprise that many countries tried to deflect the pressures from both the United States and the Soviet Union, insisting on their own sovereignty.

As a result of the pressure, people around the world were increasingly resentful of the United States. They realized the US actively and aggressively facilitated the theft of a country's wealth and resources while supporting oppressive regimes and encouraging conflict. The net result was a greater consolidation of wealth in the hands of a tiny minority. Because it was generally believed that the people in the United States chose their government, the people themselves became natural targets for anyone around the world desperate enough to lash out in anger against the exploitation and hopelessness they experienced. As a result, in addition to bringing or extending misery to developing countries, the Cold War increased the threat of terrorism, making it much less safe for people from the United States to travel abroad.

Despite the apparent animosities between the two countries, the Soviet Union and the United States soon developed a strong symbiotic relationship. The existence of the one was used skillfully by the other to conceal weaknesses and to gain control over its citizenry. As long as Capitalism continued to be practiced, Communists could claim that sacrifice was required to prevent the evils of Capitalism from taking hold. They could argue that, without a strong central government that suppressed human liberty, there would be income disparity similar to what one saw in the United States (or how the Soviet government portrayed it). Likewise, as long as Communism continued to be practiced, Capitalists and Capitalist governments could claim that the disparity of incomes and the high cost of the maintenance of a Capitalist elite were necessary to prevent Communism from taking hold, with its oppression and denial of human liberty. As long as the other ideology existed and could maintain the appearance of strength, they each had a perfectly suited enemy to rally their people against. They were each able to suppress calls for improvements or innovation in their economies or governments because of the threat posed by the other.

With the ever-present Communist threat, the United States flung itself without restraint into Capitalism, putting the rich firmly back in charge of government. In 1946, the Democratic president threatened to draft strikers into the military if they did not give up some of their demands for fair treatment. President Eisenhower recruited so heavily from big business for his cabinet that his Secretary of the Interior openly admitted, "We're in the saddle as an administration representing business and industry."[25] This was how far the people had fallen, thanks to Communism.

The threat of Communism proved real, but it was not labor that proved the source of the trouble but the Capitalists, who used Communism to extend their oppression of the working classes.

While the return of government for and by the elite meant the return of exploitation and policies favoring the wealthy, the attempts to roll back the social programs gained in previous administrations proved difficult. Every time the president tried to scale back a social program, the economy and tax revenues would sink. Yet the Capitalists still refused to accept that a more-balanced distribution of wealth was better for the economy than the wide disparities that Capitalism otherwise led to. It was, ironically, a clear sign that the wealthy were not acting as a coordinated cabal trying to maximize their own wealth. If they had, they would have realized that if all companies agreed to pay a little more in salaries, it would boost the economy, with the wealthy continuing to take in most of the increase. Wealth would expand upward. But the system allowed only for coordinated exploitation, not coordinated sacrifice, for increasing wealth.

Meanwhile, underneath all the fear and forced conformity, there remained the heart and soul of the United States, a people who appreciated freedom, individuality, opportunity, and anti-elitism. These were ideals that proved impossible to suppress for long. They started to break through in the 1950s, perhaps most clearly in the new Rock and Roll, which had evolved from the music of black communities. Once given the slightest release from the oppressive weight of fear, that suppressed energy exploded out in an era of hope and transformation.

It was the 1960 election that really woke people up. The Democratic candidate, John Kennedy, was up against incredible odds in the election. Not only had the Republican Party established a strong hold on the country's power through its use of fear, but Kennedy also had to contend with his Catholicism at a time when people still worried that a Catholic president would be more loyal to the Pope than to the country. What he had in his corner were the driving force and wealth of his father and the playbook of the Democratic Party. With fear wrapped up by the Republicans, they had to resort to hope—the strongest tactic against fear—and promises of more-responsive government. Because of the Kennedys' independent wealth, garnered from the investment industry, the campaign could operate free of party control and therefore go beyond what the party felt comfortable with. In a close race, hope defeated fear.

By running on hope instead of fear, Kennedy enjoyed certain advantages once in office. Whereas fear motivated people to recoil into a shell and hide, hope inspired people to become more active in the larger community in order to capture the potential expressed by the hope. Kennedy's inaugural speech, in which he implored people to "ask not what your country can do for you—ask what you can do for your country," allowed him to "cash in" on the investment made in nationalism and leverage it into a new civic mindedness. The impact was clear. During this era, seven out of ten new jobs were created in the non-profit sector.[26] And the Peace Corps was founded, an organization that did much to reverse the damage the Capitalists and the government were doing to the reputation of the United States within the global community.

Kennedy's administration was actually fairly moderate in their policies, at least compared to the hope they inspired. But they did have some notable achievements. In an attempt to protect consumers, they placed limits on dishonest advertising and regulated unsafe products. The pharmaceutical industry, in particular, was in need of regulation after numerous deaths shed light on the fact that it was often cheaper for a pharmaceutical company to pay off wrongful-death claims than to take reasonable safety and quality precautions. By introducing the Clean Air Act, the administration took protecting consumers to a whole new level by attempting to reduce environmental damage and transfer more of the associated public costs to the source of the problem. They also pressured the television industry to develop content to satisfy the viewing public instead of as part of the advertiser's campaign to standardize the country's purchasing. This opened up an era of innovation in television content, testing and expanding the socially acceptable bounds. The administration also made some concessions to the working class: adjusting the minimum wage, investing in community projects, and introducing a program for low-cost housing. These programs not only helped the poor but also boosted the economy.

The Kennedy administration even tried to tackle the problem of inflation. They went toe to toe with US Steel, demanding they find a way to end their inflationary practices. The problem was that labor's demands were in truth very reasonable and as such could not be ignored forever. But the investors also had certain profit expectations that were difficult to meet without maximum labor exploitation. The investors were not expecting to encounter any real risk in their investment and naturally carried more weight. Ultimately the administration convinced US Steel to become more responsible by threatening that, if they didn't, there would be anti-trust and other investigations of the company. Kennedy quickly regretted being so aggressive with big business, however. He dedicated much of the rest of his term to winning back the support of big business, offering tax breaks and other advantages to the wealthy while incurring increasing budget deficits that would soon have a disproportionate impact on the poor.

Many companies simply moved their operations off US soil, looking for a place where the workers were willing to be exploited and where the government was willing to accept the environmental damage done by their operations. It was another case of nationalism and patriotism used to keep the people in check, while Capitalists enjoyed the full benefits of a global perspective. The working class was supposed to sacrifice and put up with poor human rights in the name of the national good, but it was nothing for the Capitalists to deny any allegiance to the nation their political lackeys kept praising. Globalization meant that US Capitalists need not be limited to enticing immigrants to come to the United States in order to keep US labor costs low. In many cases there was no reason to move the people. Technology had advanced enough that the jobs could be brought to the cheap labor at the whim of the Capitalist. And so began a global competition between countries for the investment of Capitalists, each country trying to outdo the other in allowing Capitalists to exploit their people and resources.

While countless people were left stranded and helpless after old industries abandoned the country in search of cheaper labor—people the Republican Party called "lazy" for not being willing to work—new industries rose up. With these new industries, the Capitalists were prepared from the beginning to block any attempts to unionize. They wanted to maximize their power advantage over labor, and unions were the greatest obstacle.

The exception to this trend of shrinking unions was in the public sector, government employees. As the government increasingly looked to balance its budget by cutting salaries, benefits, and headcount, more and more public-sector employees joined unions in order to defend themselves from an obviously powerful force on the other side of the negotiating table. The two union trends operating in opposite directions presented the Capitalists a wonderful opportunity to exploit. They were able to turn private-sector working-class employees who typically didn't enjoy union protections against the public-sector employees, who increasingly did. They successfully transferred blame for "high" taxes and budget shortfalls to "greedy" teachers, firefighters, police, and other government employees and away from corruption and favoritism in government spending.

With the rise of new fears—Communism, labor, nuclear war, etc.—the old fears introduced to keep the powerful in power were starting to break down. Most notably, the country was slowly beginning to challenge the way blacks and other minorities were treated. At the heart of the matter was that such discrimination was in direct conflict with the fundamental ideals of the country, the Land of Opportunity. Race conflicts were also an embarrassment in foreign policy when the United States was trying to present itself as the superior form of government and society.

Racial discrimination was even limiting the country's ability to invest in education, since any attempt at the federal level to fund education ran squarely into questions of segregation in southern schools. The country's inability to invest in education was particularly awkward when the Soviet Union started advancing out into space. It was a move that took the competition between the two nations beyond military competition to challenge the United States to also compete in terms of its people and education infrastructure. Time and time again, the Soviet Union embarrassed the United States by reaching space milestones first, until finally Kennedy committed the country to the bold and aggressive goal of landing on the moon. It was a move that would require more government commitment to education and science.

Ultimately it was not the national embarrassment at slipping education, highlighted by the successes of the Soviet Union, that motivated the greatest change but action from the people themselves. Awakened by President Kennedy to do something for their nation, people started to question the hatred they had been taught to feel toward their fellow citizens and the oppression many minorities lived under. Non-violent civil rights protests by regular citizens were met with televised displays of violence by police, including attack dogs, electric shocks, and high-pressure water cannons. After people saw clearly how the government responded to peaceful protests, public pressure mounted, and the government was finally shamed into acting on civil rights issues.

Hatred and fear lingered, however, in many parts of the country. Once fostered, these were difficult to extinguish. In the South in particular, where white fear of and feelings of superiority over the blacks were most strongly encouraged by the country's slaveholders more than a hundred years earlier, there lingered still a strong belief in a segregated culture. So when the Kennedy administration came out in favor of civil-rights reform, his approval rating in the South dropped from 70% to 30%. Even though the value to the elite had long since passed, the damage done by an elite desperate to retain power continued to be felt by the people and in the very soul of the country. The costs of elite rule were manifold and extreme.

After President Kennedy was assassinated while in Dallas trying to persuade Southern Democrats to stop supporting Republican pro-wealthy causes in exchange for their support in blocking civil rights legislation, the torch passed to his Vice President, Lyndon Johnson. While largely marginalized by Kennedy's staff, Johnson had completely fallen for both the inspiring hope of Kennedy and, unfortunately, the crippling fear of "World Communism" peddled by the Republicans. He brought both a rare sincerity and a talent in legislative strategy to both extremes.

Johnson also benefited from a desire to make sure Kennedy's death meant something. It helped the president push through dramatic civil-rights reform, an effort to correct some of the more glaring injustices perpetrated against blacks and other minorities. He also pushed through significant voter-rights legislation, including an eventual end to the poll tax, making the United States one of the last countries to eliminate this blatant expression of elite dominance.

Johnson also continued the trend of presidents nominating Supreme Court justices who favored people over corporations. It helped usher in a period in United States history during which the courts could be counted on to advance and protect the rights of citizens. In addition to working to protect the rights of a variety of different minorities, the Court also attempted to restrain some of the more outlandish attempts by the Capitalists to control the outcomes of elections.

In Johnson's 1964 election campaign, he presented the idea of the United States as a "Great Society," holding out the idealistic notion that the country could and should try to live up to something closer to its mythology. A major part of this effort would be a so-called "War on Poverty" to capture people who had fallen through the cracks. The war would include early-education opportunities, young-adult training for careers, support for schools and colleges, a US-oriented version of Peace Corps, health insurance for elderly (Medicare) and poor (Medicaid), and medical research to reduce the costs of healthcare. The idea was that if wars were good for the economy, as the country had learned from World War I and World War II, then surely a national, concentrated peaceful effort should have a similar effect.

If the country had been able to truly and sincerely focus on the effort, it may have proven hugely successful. Unfortunately, alongside Johnson's concern for people was the Republicans' fear of global Communism that drove Johnson to escalate an actual war in Vietnam beyond all reason. Predictably the war got the lion's share of the funding. For example, in 1965 the budget for the War on Poverty was $1.7 billion, compared to a military budget of $50 billion.[27] It is easy to imagine that if these figures were reversed, the US economy would have been in a dramatically different condition 20 years later than it was.

The growing dissatisfaction with the war and the methods used to escalate the war, combined with having to reduce the scope of the Great Society, destroyed Johnson's reputation, making him unelectable in the 1968 election. When Robert Kennedy (John Kennedy's brother) was assassinated, the Democratic Party was left in shambles, leaving the door wide open for the return of the Republicans and Capitalist rule.

CHAPTER 5

Pushed too far

*In a bid to regain control, the Republicans propose a new
enemy to fear and fight against: the people themselves.
But creating enemies of one's own citizens makes the
president paranoid, opening the field for a caring president
to slip in. Turns out, though, that the government is no
place for compassion and wisdom, fear wins out, and
the government presses its heel on the people again.*

War on Poverty

In the 1968 Presidential campaign, Republican Richard
Nixon appealed to the country by promising once again
a return to "normalcy." After a decade of reflection and
experimentation, accompanied by violent government
oppression, it was a message that appealed to many, particularly the large population that had committed themselves
to conformity in the 1950s. In an effort to fit in and be
accepted, they had invested much of themselves into being
"normal." To go against normalcy now would mean challenging the decisions and compromises they had made in
their own lives, difficult for anyone to do. So instead, they

did like most of us would and barreled ahead, following the path they had already chosen, without thinking about the full implications.

To be able to sustain their control, however, the Republican Party needed a new enemy, a group of people who threatened the security and identity of the United States. They needed an enemy whom promising to fight could excite and expand their voting base. Racist, ethnic, and religious hatred had largely played themselves out except for on the fringes of society. The threat of secret Communist agents running around the country had been taken too far and therefore had lost its potential. The external threat from the Soviet Union was still paying huge dividends but had limited potential in confronting dissent within the country.

The Republicans eventually stumbled upon a compelling solution. By refusing to cover the basic social costs of labor (calling such plans "socialist"), the government and Capitalists were able to push a growing segment of the population into desperate poverty. When one's ability to provide for one's family is threatened, desperation leads to extreme and often illegal actions. Those desperate acts (crime) could be highlighted as a threat to the security and identity of the country. Catching criminals would reflect well on the government's ability to respond to the demands of people, while not being able to keep up with increasing crime would simply confirm the threat and the need for more government powers. It would give the government the authority to get rid of the least contented in the society, scoring points with voters while doing it.

The first part of the plan worked like a charm. The poor responded, as anyone would, when the ability to control their own lives or even provide for their families was threatened. The murder rate doubled between 1963 and 1970. New laws, like the Crime Control and Safe Streets Act, did little to reduce the crime rate but did give the government more powers to fight it. There were widespread riots in each of the summers between (and including) 1965 and 1967. In the summer of 1967 alone, federal troops were called in on eight separate occasions. The increase in crime was just the evidence the Republican Party needed to paint the poor in the country as a threat. It wasn't the rich who were stealing money from people to live a life of leisure—it was the poor.

The country's conformists were easily trained to object to any sign of weakness in dealing with criminals. So when new Miranda rights designed to protect people against abusive police persecution that might result in a coerced false confession were suggested, there was significant back-lash. When a new right for even poor criminals to have the benefit of legal counsel was put forward, people complained that it was soft on crime. The poor were assumed guilty and therefore deserved no rights.

As part of the plan to return the country to "normal," the government went after the activists demanding change in the country. There were many of them left over from the turbulent decade of reform, with causes including the rights of farm workers, women, homosexuals, and Natives. For the conformists, they were all troublemakers, trying to upset the status quo. Suppressing the movements was something the Republicans could actually campaign on, and did as early as 1966, when Ronald Reagan was elected governor of California on the promise to control campuses and bring students back to conformity.

The Republican government didn't feel the need to conceal its active and aggressive war on the country's people. In fact, politicians stumbled over themselves to sound tough on citizens. For example, in November 1969 a massive anti-war campaign was scheduled in Washington, prompting Nixon to call up 9,000 federal troops to deal with them. Ahead of the event, Nixon's Deputy Attorney General was quoted as saying "We just can't wait to beat up those {expletive} kids." Likewise, after a student was killed by the police in one incident at The University of California at Berkeley—at the heart of the country's student movements—Governor Reagan said, "If it's a bloodbath they want, let it be now."[28] It's hard to imagine that the students had any interest in a bloodbath, but it certainly seemed to be part of the Republicans' agenda. The Republicans had people so completely entranced that when the Ohio National Guard fired on war protestors at Kent State, killing four students, only 12% in Ohio thought the government's reaction was unjustified.[29] People were convinced that the government was justified in killing its own protesting citizens.

Nixon's campaign against activists slowly wore down the activists' will to protest. The police were no longer permitting peaceful protests, and people were no longer ashamed by government oppression. The time had passed. Many people who were inclined to protest or demand change channeled that resentment into a counter-culture movement of "drugs, sex, and Rock and Roll" instead. The police followed them there and continued to try to pressure them into conformity. Tough on crime and on non-conformists had become the new domestic qualification for political positions. The number of prisons expanded as a result of the number of people being arrested increasing dramatically.

Having launched an all-out offensive against a large portion of the country's population, Nixon felt like he had enemies around every corner. He was extremely paranoid and untrusting. When a confidential report on the Vietnam War, one detailing how and why the country's involvement in the country had increased, was published, Nixon jumped immediately into action to defend the office of the president and the government, even though the report was mostly about the Johnson administration. He ordered the closing of the newspaper that had published the report, only to have his order reversed by the Supreme Court. The Court argued that the president did not have the right to silence newspapers. When Nixon found out that the person who had leaked the report was seeing a psychiatrist, he had a team break into the psychiatrist's office to try to find something to use against him. The caper was discovered. Next Nixon tried to influence the trial of the person who leaked the report, offering the judge the position of FBI Director if he ruled against him. Instead the judge cited the break-in as grounds to indicate improper prosecution and released the person responsible for the leak without any charges against him.

To protect himself from his enemies, Nixon started recording all meetings in the White House, imagining that he would someday need proof of an enemy trying to extort something from him. He didn't consider that recordings he was making to protect himself could be used against him, but that's just what happened. Even though the Democratic Party was still in disarray during the 1972 presidential election campaign, the Republican Party wanted to ensure their victory. The Party authorized a team to break into Democratic headquarters to find information and bug the offices. While Nixon wasn't directly involved in the planning, it was soon discovered that he had exploited his office to interfere with the investigation of it after the fact. He wanted to get the investigation delayed at least until after the election so had used the CIA to delay an FBI investigation. The evidence of his involvement was the president's own recordings. The man who had run on "law and order" against the activists argued that the law didn't and shouldn't apply to him, but the courts did not agree. When the investigation became public, it was over for the president. Facing nearly certain eviction from office by the Congress, the president resigned, the first president of the United States to do so.

Nixon's Vice President had resigned shortly after the reelection after being found guilty of accepting bribes and kickbacks. So it was Gerald Ford, who had been chosen from the House of Representatives to serve as replacement Vice President, who ascended to the White House. To try to get the country past the scandal before the mid-term elections in 1974 and to avoid investigations into other political wrongdoings, Ford quickly issued a pardon for Nixon, to avoid a trial. The country saw this as the president looking after one of his own, more hypocrisy from the "law and order" Republicans.

With the unpopular Vietnam War, decades of exploitation of consumers and workers by companies, and now the recent scandals in the Nixon administration, people were starting to question if the country was actually of, by, and for the people or just for a select few. People's confidence in the country's leading power centers slipped dramatically between 1966 and 1975. The military, for its part in the Vietnam War, slipped from a 62% confidence rating to 29%. Corporations went from 55% to 18% as they demonstrated their compassionless pursuit of profits at the expense of the country's people. And the president and Congress dropped from 42% to 13%.[30] It's hard to imagine their approval rating ever getting lower than that without the country falling into revolution.

It was in this context that the country celebrated the 200-year anniversary of the signing of the Declaration of Independence. It was a great time for the government to rally the country around nationalist sentiment, hoping to do so without raising additional attention to the fact that the country was still failing to live up to the ideals expressed in the preamble to that document.

Making the world safe for democracy

In the election of 1976, the Democrats chose a Washington outsider, former Governor of Georgia Jimmy Carter. Not being a typical politician was perhaps Carter's greatest selling point. He even campaigned on a promise not to lie to the public, a pretty radical concept at the time. He also ran against the Republicans' clear allegiance to the rich, saying in his nomination acceptance speech: "Too many have had to suffer at the hands of a political and economic elite who have shaped decisions and never had to account for mistakes, nor to suffer from injustice."[31]

After the turbulent 1960s, which saw the resurgence of people power, the Democratic Party felt the need to strengthen its democratic credentials. In 1972 Democrats introduced new rules to make their nominating-convention delegates more representative of the country, attempting to appeal to the new generation of freedom seekers. Reforms to campaign financing also intended to provide a balance against corporate and wealthy buying of elections. But the Republicans found a loophole wide enough to funnel ever-increasing quantities of cash to influence politics. Even foreign companies and countries were able to finance candidates, gaining more influence over the outcomes than any single US voter could have.

Given the distrust of Washington politicians, however, the money wasn't enough for the Republicans to steal the election, and Carter was elected. In office, Carter was hard-working, unpretentious, and committed to an open and transparent White House. He didn't have much patience with lobbyists and people trying to buy his favor or get him to act contrary to what was good for the country's people.

Continuing the efforts of the early 1970s, the Carter administration pushed to make voting easier, including making uniform rules for voter registration and even allowing for voting-day registration. As always, the Republicans fought the expansion of voting, realizing that anything they could do to make or keep voting difficult would keep the poor and working class away from voting for the Democrats.

Having to work with traditional politicians and political advisors, Carter quickly got caught up in the rhetoric, fears, and maddening logic of Washington, DC, however. Despite coming in with good intentions of helping people, many of the policies introduced during Carter's presidency were decidedly biased against the people. While claiming to place a high priority on social programs, Carter's first budget showed a $10 billion increase in military spending and a $25 million cut for milk for 1.4 million schoolchildren.[32] He weakened labor-safety and consumer-protection laws to help improve corporate profitability. So in practice, his priorities were first, military spending, and second, balancing the budget (made more difficult by the higher military spending). As a result, he was pushed into attempting to balance the budget on the backs of the poor. He failed to realize, as so many had before him, that it was the working class as consumers and wealth producers that drove the economy. Carter took a major hit in the polls for not living up to expectations. His approval ratings fell below even Nixon's approval ratings. He demonstrated what happens when good people try to do good in a system designed to favor the country's elite.

Where Carter really stood out was in foreign policy early in his term. He encouraged a human-rights-oriented foreign policy. On the one hand, he called the USSR and South Africa—among others—to task for their violations of human decency. Meanwhile to avoid hypocrisy, he challenged the United States to clean up its act and serve as a positive role model for the world. He attempted to reverse the awful reputation the United States had in the world through more enlightened and respectful treatment of other countries. For example, he signed a treaty to hand over the Panama Canal Zone back to Panama in the year 2000. Right-wing extremists like Ronald Reagan vehemently opposed the treaty, arguing that the Canal was simply too important of a national symbol to be lost. As we'll see, nationalism was very important to Reagan's political strategy.

To encourage US companies to transact business globally, according to the Capitalists' own professed principles of free and open markets, the Carter administration oversaw the development of the Foreign Corrupt Practices Act in

1977, which made it illegal for US companies or individuals to bribe foreign officials to win business. Getting the Capitalists to play by set rules (even if it was their own rules) was a significant accomplishment that raised the standard for international business.

Carter suggested that the Cold War could be fought not with aggression but by winning the ideological debate between democracy and totalitarianism. At a speech at Notre Dame in 1977, he argued that "Being confident in our own future, we are now free of that inordinate fear of Communism that once led us to embrace any dictator who joined us in that fear.... We can no longer separate the traditional issues of war and peace from the new global questions of justice, equity, and human rights."[33] He realized that fighting might with might required the United States to oppress its own democracy in order to prove its superiority to Russian oppression. He suggested that if the country believed in democracy and believed that Soviet Communism was not sustainable, then the country should put its faith in democracy. The country should encourage countries to move toward it instead of supporting regimes that deny it. That way, the Soviet Union would have to compete against genuine and complete freedom instead of easily refuted mythologies.

There were severe limits to how far the rich were willing to let this sort of thinking go, however. For them, the battle with the Soviet Union was not between democracy and Soviet totalitarianism but instead a contest between the Capitalist leadership of the United States versus the bureaucratic-elite concept of the Soviet Union. They had to demonstrate to the world that only the Capitalists could be trusted to run the world's governments and economies without giving up any of their power and influence. While the Republicans attacked Carter for not being sufficiently anti-Communist, Carter's vision also worried the Soviet Union. The USSR relied on the aggressive policies and the easily disproved mythologies of the United States for their domestic and international propaganda. They had to do something to provoke the United States back into their traditional role. Whether these concerns factored into the Soviet decision to invade Afghanistan or not is unclear at best, but it certainly did the job of scaring Carter into pursuing a more traditional foreign policy strategy. The government decided to support the Afghan rebels (the Taliban) in their fight against the Russians. The US offered both arms and financing to them, even though the Taliban demonstrated no interest in establishing a democratic and free system of government for Afghanistan.

Relations with Russia deteriorated quickly, putting an end to discussions for an arms-limitation treaty. The Carter administration increased its military budget, discarding any hope of achieving a balanced budget, and reintroduced registration for the draft, just in case. The draft registration was ignored by many to protest the absurdity of the new foreign policy direction. The cooler relations with the Soviet Union also dramatically increased the risk for accidental nuclear war. In November 1979 and June 1980, for example, early warning systems in the United States detected missile attacks incoming from the Soviet Union. They were false readings, but if relations had been much worse, it would have been more difficult for personnel to reach that conclusion and cancel automatic responses. To make it clear to the Soviet Union that the United States was once again fully committed to the Cold War, the Carter administration announced that the US would boycott the 1980 Summer Olympics in Moscow, a significant diplomatic insult and therefore excellent propaganda material for the Soviet Union. The symbiotic relationship between the ruling elite in Moscow and the Capitalists had been restored.

Government for the elite returns

The country's aggressive foreign policy came back to haunt the country at the end of the Carter administration, dramatically contributing to the president's defeat in the 1980 election. Events started to spiral out of control when the US-backed, Capitalist-friendly regime in Iran fell in 1979. A religious leader took charge of the country, setting up a theocracy similar to what a few loud-but-small-in-number fundamentalist Christian groups envisioned for the United States. The religion became the law, with morals strictly legislated and severe punishments for failure to comply. With so much Capitalist investment in Iran (particularly oil), these developments were, on their own, extremely troubling to some of the country's leadership. What made it a matter of national importance was the determination of the new Iranian regime to leverage the past misdeeds and exploitation of US Capitalists to make the United States and its people out to be the enemy around which to rally the support of their people.

The new Iranian government demanded the return of the country's former leader, who had fled for the United States for asylum and medical treatment so that he could stand trial. The United States refused. Taking advantage of this snub to their sovereignty, the Iranian government took US hostages, offering a prisoner exchange. It was a tricky situation for the Carter administration. Negotiating with kidnappers rarely involved clear-cut decisions. The Carter administration decided to execute a rescue attempt instead, but it failed miserably. The incident played perfectly into the hands of the Republicans, providing more fuel to the claims that Carter didn't have what it took to keep the United States safe. They argued that what the country needed to be safe was to get tough with the rest of the world. The country needed more enemies.

This was the context for the elections of 1980: deteriorating relations with the Soviet Union, diminishing concern for the working class, hostages in Iran, and a resulting oil crisis that pushed inflation and interest rates to new heights. To take on Carter, the Republicans nominated Ronald Reagan, to the surprise and dread of much of the country. Early in life Reagan had been a registered Democrat, a supporter of the New Deal and in favor of a fair tax plan for the working class. But after he was hired to host the General Electric Theater television program, his wealth increased dramatically, and he slowly lost touch with ordinary people. Eventually he was fired from the program when his views became too extreme. As governor of California, he spoke about violent suppression of student protestors. By this point, Reagan was viewed as not much better than a tyrant, like so many of the dictators the US had supported over the decades. It seemed certain that he would get the United States into a war of some sort with the Soviet Union or one of its proxies.

In the campaign, Carter continued to argue that the country could be great if it just believed in itself and became what it said it was. He wanted the reputation of the United States to be as good or better than that enjoyed by some of the European nations. In contrast, Reagan argued that the greatness of the United States would be proved by its military, that the country could impose its will on the world. He suggested that any country that disagreed with the greatness of the United States would face the US military, which could effectively end the debate.

Reagan also took a page from deep within the Democratic Party playbook: telling people what they wanted to hear with empty but energetic rhetoric that made few concrete promises. To a country struggling to make ends meet, he promised to lower taxes. To Capitalists he promised to dramatically increase the size of the military to feed the defense industry and to defend the interests of Capitalists abroad. To people concerned about the country's long-term future, he promised to balance the budget without addressing how he could do this with tax cuts and out-of-control military spending. To appeal to the religious right, looking for greater conformity and a return to the traditional values from before the 1960s, Reagan downplayed his record as California Governor when he supported abortion rights, homosexual rights, women's rights, and the environment.

Christianity had become big business, with considerable wealth and power to be garnered from it. Massive fortunes were on the line, and churches needed to keep people riled up about threats to their religious freedoms and their eternal souls; otherwise, there was a risk that church members would take their "business" elsewhere. Fear was once again a common tactic—and fear of democracy the phobia many encouraged. They told horror stories of the strong Christian population of the United States declining below a majority or a determined minority taking over the gears of the US-style democracy and forcing people to give up their faith despite thorough protections and guarantees of Freedom of Religion. To preempt a non-Christian majority from trying to impose its standards and values on Christians, they encouraged people to push for hard-wiring Christian morality into the country's institutions and laws and imposing its standards and values on non-believers.

Church leaders exploited their positions as authorities on the Christian religion and as spiritual leaders to encourage conflict instead of openness and flexibility. Their focus was not on helping people with real spiritual problems but instead on trying to gain political power and economic success by making the most of contentious issues. In short they were trying to form themselves into a new elite for the country, a religious elite. Since the Democrats were not in a position to speak to their issues, the Republicans were happy to accept these religious leaders and their followers into their fold for the extra votes they could provide. Besides, their message of fear and distrust fit well with the public themes of the Republican Party, so they were an easy voting block for the Republicans to appeal to.

After getting a large block of voters worked up about issues designed to raise their own political profiles, many of the televangelists and other similar large-church formats were hit by scandal when their leaders were found to be using church funds for themselves or failing to live up to the high moral standards they preached. They were engaging in elite behavior before even achieving real elite status.

With the two rather miserable options, most people stayed home on Election Day. Only 54% of the eligible voters cast a vote, which meant that Reagan's eventual win came with just 27% of the eligible voters.[34] Unsurprisingly, he did dramatically better with men (54%) than women

(46%), women tending to vote for human-rights causes that Reagan proposed taking a hard stand against.

With the election over, Iran released its US hostages. Having kept an eye on the election campaigns, they recognized that the outcome could not have gone better for them if they had arranged it themselves. It was hard to make the United States out to be the enemy of the Iranian people with someone like Carter as President. Reagan proved to be a much better tool for Iranian nationalism.

In his inauguration speech, Reagan clarified an important part of the Republican agenda while trying to direct people's attention away from the government's commitment to Capitalists. He said, "In this present crisis, government is not the solution to our problem; government is the problem. From time to time we've been tempted to believe that society has become too complex to be managed by self-rule, that government by an elite group is superior to government for, by, and of the people." He was trying to convince people that the part of the government that served the people and protected them from abuses of the Capitalist system was the problem and that only the government programs designed to support corporations should be retained.

Once in power, the administration removed government objection to massive mergers, allowing the power of consolidated wealth to be used more forcefully to push salaries down, consumer prices up and quality down, to funnel enormous profits to Capitalists. Reagan expanded deregulation of banks, leading to more risky investment decisions assured by the confidence that, if anything went wrong, the taxpayers could bail them out. In exchange for a $270,000 donation to redecorate the White House, the

Reagan administration removed controls on oil prices, allowing profits to increase by $2 billion. When a new pamphlet was educating workers on the dangers of cotton dust to textile workers, Reagan "solved" the problem by having the pamphlet destroyed. Reagan was showing quite clearly the sort of government he wanted to eliminate and the sort he aimed to maintain.

With the more permissive government, companies started introducing "planned obsolescence" into their products to take more from consumers. The idea was to build products so that they failed sooner, requiring consumers to buy new ones more often. The practice was very common in the US automobile industry, giving foreign car-makers (most notably in Japan) a golden opportunity to break into an industry that had, to that point, seemed closed to new competitors. The employees of the automobile companies paid the price for the short-term greed of their employers as the invasion of well-built cars from Japan eventually left the US auto industry in shambles.

To provide additional profits to the rich, Reagan once again transferred environmental costs of industry back to the public. There would be no incentive for corporate decision-making to factor in the impact of their decisions on the public, let alone long-term sustainability of the environment. It seemed to some that the administration had given up on the future, acknowledging that the world would soon succumb to environmental damage and therefore there was no reason not to exploit it while it lasted. It got so bad that Pope John Paul II warned: "Today, the dramatic threat of ecological breakdown is teaching us the extent to which greed and selfishness, both individual and collective, are contrary to the order of creation."[35] It wasn't too long before this that the Pope (Pius XII) was excommunicating anyone who was Communist; now it looked like the Capitalists were being called to answer for their sins.

Having run on fear and the dangers of the world, it was a simple matter for Reagan to funnel massive military spending to Capitalists involved in the defense industry. Because the threats the Republicans created were so terrible, no one could challenge the spending, particularly on such mundane and practical a basis as concerns over the budget. The US developed an awesome arsenal of new weapons that resulted in a whole new and terrifying arms race. For people outside of the reach of US propaganda, the leadership role the United States took in escalating this race made it difficult to believe that the Soviet Union was the evil one. In fact, just outside of the United States borders, a documentary film was released in Canada highlighting the dangers and truths about the nuclear arms race. It was so embarrassing for Reagan that he tried to suppress its release in the United States, but the federal court didn't allow the ban.

Within the United States, it was a completely different matter. Television and movie studios stepped up eagerly to support the anti-Communist rhetoric. They were happy to have a new and clear enemy to help advance plots. The constant threat and intrigue was also of interest to television news, particularly the new CNN, which started broadcasting news 24 hours a day in 1980. To keep viewers tuned in, they happily escalated any ordinary disagreement into a threat to the country.

With support from the public for a global confrontation with Communism, Reagan quickly returned to the practice of supporting any of the world's autocratic regimes willing to favor US Capitalists and oppose Communism. He sent advisors and intelligence agents to help rulers in El Salvador and Guatemala, and tried to reverse the electoral outcome in Nicaragua by supporting rebels intent on overthrowing the government. It was all a little too much for Congress, which denied the administration funds to continue to support the Nicaragua rebels, putting Reagan's operations there in jeopardy.

Without Reagan's aggressive rhetoric and military build-up against the Soviet "threat," it is very possible that the Soviet Union would have collapsed. They gambled heavily to try to provoke the United States—in Africa, against Israel, and then finally by invading Afghanistan—and this put a lot of pressure on their internal systems. With the United States acting like a serious threat again, the Soviet Union had what it needed to press its people further. In fact Reagan was so perfectly suited to the needs of the Soviet Union that some have since imagined he was working with them.

1983 was a particularly terrifying year. For starters, it was the year that the president announced his plans to militarize space, developing weapons to defend the country from orbit. In September of 1983, the USSR shot down a South Korean airliner that had accidentally flown into sensitive airspace, killing all the passengers. In addition to 268 other civilians, the plane was also carrying a US Congressman. Then, with relations extremely tense and trust at an all-time low, the Soviet Union registered a false positive on a US missile launch. It was their turn to realize, despite the Republicans' anti-Soviet rhetoric, that it wasn't a real attack and save the world.

October 1983 saw some significant military engagements that increased the tensions on both sides further. US forces operating in the Middle East trying to secure friendly governments were bombed by guerrilla forces, inflicting significant casualties and forcing them to retreat. That same month the US invaded Grenada, a tiny island in the Caribbean that was home to 118 offshore banks housing significant US Capitalist wealth away from US taxes. The invasion became "necessary" after a government that looked to be unfriendly to the United States gained power there.

With the escalation of US military activity, the Soviet Union put their nuclear-missile facilities on maximum readiness. And the Doomsday Clock—a symbolic indication of expert opinion on how close the world was to nuclear war—was advanced to 3 minutes before Armageddon, the furthest it had advanced. The clock had already been advanced to 4 minutes when Reagan won the election, such was his reputation as a madman. The organization in charge of setting the clock explained that, "There has been a virtual suspension of meaningful contacts and serious discussions. Every channel of communications has been constricted or shut down; every form of contact has been attenuated or cut off. And arms-control negotiations have been reduced to a species of propaganda."[36]

Meanwhile the administration pursued a muddleheaded strategy with Iran. On the one hand, they supported Iraq's autocratic ruler Saddam Hussein in his war against Iran. On the other hand, they sold arms to Iran in hopes that they would agree to use its influence in the region to convince guerrilla groups to release US hostages. Iran didn't help much, but they did appreciate the weapons. Since the operation was a secret, the Reagan administration was able to squirrel away the profits from the weapon sales to help support their war in Nicaragua. It wasn't until the official government in Nicaragua shot down a shipment of arms to the rebels that the country found out what the government was doing in its name.

As the Reagan administration became more aggressive against the world, it didn't take long for the world's peoples to respond. Finding no avenue open to protest US exploitations, some resorted to terrorism again. It was clear that the policies were not making the world safe for democracy. Dictators that the US was not supporting directly were getting legitimacy and recruits from the fear and hatred of the United States. Democracy was in full retreat.

To support the Capitalist elite back home, Reagan imposed an economic philosophy that mystified most of the country's economists so much so that many people called it "Voodoo Economics." The plan called for massive tax cuts for the wealthy accompanied with much more modest cuts for the rest of the country. Reagan tried to convince the country that money given to the wealthiest people would "trickle down" to the poor through increased spending and job creation. Without actually putting more real money in the hands of actual consumers, his plan called upon an age-old Capitalist trick, making sure people had access to easy credit. The economy could grow on the debt of the working class. Reagan, set on transferring as much wealth to the wealthy as possible, ignored a warning from his Department of Commerce showing that lowering corporate taxes would in fact result in a steep drop in capital investment.

Before long, Reagan's tax cuts and out-of-control military spending ballooned the budget deficit. To put this in perspective, during the last war (the Vietnam War), the United States ran an agonizing deficit of around $25 billion. Reagan's deficit during peacetime (not considering the Cold War as wartime) was around $200 billion.[37] The increased debt served Capitalists in two ways. First, the interest on the debt was another way for the government to transfer the wealth of the country to bankers and investors worldwide. Second, it put pressure on the social programs, which tended to be the first to be targeted in government cutbacks. Serious poverty remained good for creating both fear and a desperate labor force willing to accept almost anything for a poor-paying job.

It wasn't long, in fact, before Reagan did make cuts to Social Security and welfare. To reassure people that the country was not going backwards, they insisted once again that private charities and churches would take care of poverty. Back in the real world, however, it was clear that private charities weren't keeping up, as the number of people living below the poverty line in the United States increased by 25% from 1979 to 1983.[38] It was no surprise that Reagan chose to prove the greatness of the United States with its military instead of by the standard of living of its poorest citizens.

Public opinion on the welfare cuts revealed just how much control the Republican propaganda machine had, but also how shallow its messages actually were. They had demonized the programs of Johnson's War on Poverty by name in order to get support for cuts to "welfare," but people had not lost human compassion. While a *New York Times/ CBS News* poll showed that 44% of people thought too much was spent on welfare, only 13% said too much was spent for "assistance to the poor." 64% said too little was.[39]

People busy with their own lives had apparently accepted the talking points without thinking about the meaning.

The still-increasing isolation of the middle class in the suburbs served two valuable purposes for the Capitalists. On the one hand, it made it easier to restrict public services to the poor—often minorities—since they were isolated in the inner cities. This pushed more of the poor into crime, which was also typically isolated in the poor neighborhoods. On the other hand, living quietly in the suburbs, the middle class was once again able to disconnect from the actual suffering of the working class. It made it easier for them to believe that crime was committed by evil people, not people forced into the situation by difficult living conditions. Television programming helped enforce the image. In order to create interesting story lines and justify the increasing violence used to attract audiences, television, movies, and books had to establish criminals as clearly evil. It would not do for an audience to relate to the criminals who were being jailed and beaten by the police.

The country's inability to make strategic use of and cover even the basic social costs for its valuable human resource made many people desperate for some sort of relief. They were anxious to work and contribute to the country, but there were simply no jobs to be had. Many reluctantly turned to the assistance offered by the government, justifying it any way they could. No one wanted to have to get help, but they certainly didn't have the resources to start their own company or, in most cases, even to get skill training needed to enter most careers. Others felt forced into a life of crime, playing right into the hands of the wealthy trying to make them out to look lazy and immoral. There was little doubt that pro-business economic policies were having an effect. As early as 1965, even before Nixon had implemented his coordinated War on Poverty, there were 8 to 10 times more people murdered in the United States than in Europe, but between 1965 and 1980 that number doubled again.[40] There seemed to be no place safe for US citizens, neither inside nor outside the country.

For the Republicans, proving oneself worthy of office meant funding law enforcement and prisons. As a result, more and more of the country's citizens ended up in prison, particularly after the government started a broad attack on drug users. Whereas in 1974 the US inmate population was still less than 300,000, by 1980 that number was 540,000,[41] and by 1985 it was up to 743,000.[42] After 1976, when the Supreme Court ruled that states could return to executing criminals, Republicans competed with each other on who sent the most people to their deaths. Falling through the cracks in the United States economic system had dire consequences.

The Democrats could not afford to come out as aggressively against the poor, but neither could they tackle the economic conditions that led to crime, because doing so would put themselves up against potential campaign donors. Instead some Democrats attempted to appear tough on violent crime by going after the distribution of guns. It was a ploy that further divided a country committed to freedom, pushing legitimate gun owners (such as hunters) to the Republicans, who appreciated the extra support for their pro-business agenda.

The fortunes of CEOs and Capitalists increased fabulously under Reagan, and they showered him with praise. At the start of Reagan's term, a CEO was already making an outrageous forty times more than an average factory worker, but by the end of the decade the CEO was making 93 times more.[43] This was in stark contrast to the situation for farmers, who found rising interest rates difficult to cope with, and workers, who struggled and typically failed to keep up with inflation. The approach was essentially killing off the large market in the United States, since few people would be able to buy the products sold. The key to the long-term viability of this strategy would be to count on new, developing markets around the world. Theoretically a razor-thin middle class on a global basis tied with a free-spending upper class could create enough wealth and power for Capitalists to live well for a generation or two before having to deal with finding new ways to grow the economy.

With government support firmly behind corporations, union-busting was back in fashion. The government even engaged in some battles with its public-sector unions. The air traffic controllers, for example, were forced to go on strike to fight cuts in government spending. Reagan ordered anyone who struck to be fired, replacing those who were lost with military personnel until replacements could be found. Reagan's administration wasn't ashamed to use the incredible negotiating-power advantage the federal government had over labor to take more from the working class.

By the end of Reagan's first term, the country was fed up with his tactics. Whereas in May 1981, Reagan's approval rating was at 68%, by May 1982 it was down to 42% and had slipped to 37% by February 1983. By 1984 an IRS poll showed that 80% of the country believed that "The present tax system benefits the rich and is unfair to the ordinary working man and woman."[44] This wasn't "our taxes are too high"; this was "if the country needs a military to protect the interest of Capitalists, they should pay for it."

People were also slowly breaking free of the fear being sold to them by the Republicans. In 1980 the National Opinion Research Center at the University of Chicago reported that only 12% of those polled thought too much money was being spent on the military. As people realized that the military buildup was making the world less safe, out-of-control military spending started to lose favor. By 1982, 32% were saying that the government was spending too much on the military. In 1983 a *New York Times/CBS News* poll put that number at 48%.[45]

In April 1983 protestors gathered outside a conference put together as a publicity stunt to show concern for the unemployed. The protestors wanted a chance to present their situation during the conference, to present their frustration with the administration's pro-business policies and complete disregard for the plight of the unemployed. But they were denied. The conference concluded that unemployed steelworkers could be retrained to work in the growing computer industry, making available enough funds to train just a fraction of the unemployed. It was a clear demonstration of the disconnect between the Reagan administration and the challenges faced by the country.

Even the country's religious conservatives were fed up with Reagan, particularly after he had to confess that he was not even a regular church-goer. Once elected, the Republicans simply weren't desperate enough for the support of the religious conservative vote that they felt they needed to waste limited political capital on satisfying these voters. The changes they demanded would have been difficult to achieve under ideal conditions, let alone when combined with the other priorities of the Republican Party. For example, there were attempts in many states to get religion taught within public schools, but these attempts were shot down by the Supreme Court. To make any difference on this issue, the Republicans would have to change the Constitution. Banning abortions was another hot issue, but with 75% disapproval for an amendment making abortions illegal, that cause offered no easy win, either. Despite such obvious disappointments, the Republicans remained confident in their ability to maintain the religious conservative vote. At least the Republicans talked to the issues of people fearful of losing their religious freedoms; that's more than the Democrats were typically willing to do.

With growing disappointment with the direction the country was heading in, change was in the air. As David Nyhan of the *Boston Globe* wrote in an editorial: "There is something brewing in the land that bodes ill for those in Washington who ignore it. People have moved from the frightened state to the angry state and are acting out their frustrations in ways that will test the fabric of civil order."[46]

PART 2

ON A NEW PATH

The 1980s found the United States suffering through a crisis of trust. The Capitalist economy was built on the assumption that every person looked out for themselves, taking advantage of any available opportunity to improve one's own position. People were warned not to trust anyone and were frequently punished for putting too much faith in others, particularly those offering financial or product advice which could lead to personal and national economic ruin. Companies could be trusted to maximize profit, but that was hardly reassuring when deciding which products to buy. And then there was the government. There existed the mythology that the government operated "for the people," but it had seldom given much reason for the people to trust that it had their best interests in mind. Since Nixon's scandals and the continuing attack on the working class, the second half of the 20th century was a dark time. Even the country's religious leaders could not be trusted since they were proven to be willing to manipulate faith for their own purposes.

To their credit, the Republicans had found a way to encourage and leverage the mistrust in the country and use it to serve their own agenda. By blatantly serving wealthy interests, they proved how little the government could be trusted. They then argued that government should, as such, get out of the way. The intent appeared clear: to once again give corporations free reign to exploit markets, labor, and the environment. But it was a dangerous game. When people don't know who to trust—when even "experts" are found suspicious—then anyone could manipulate the people. It was similar crises of trust that allowed the French and Russian Revolutions to unfold as they did.

It seems some sort of change was inevitable. Eventually big business and the wealthy would consolidate enough power that the people would lose all hope in their innate ability to influence the government. If all trust was lost and all sense of control over one's life eroded away, the explosion of suppressed frustration would likely be destructive. It would be yet another revolution that brought on more of the same—or worse.

Fortunately there was a spark that led the country on a new path before this happened.

It was a quiet and subtle spark, much less than what anyone expected to change the course of history. But that was what made it work. Anything more dramatic would have enlivened passions and eventually come across as a personal attack on those in power, instead of a challenge to the systems in whose service they unwittingly operated. Since the conversation was focused on ideals and objectives (instead of idiots and objections), the path was much smoother than anything that had come before it, making it possible to stay the course.

CHAPTER 1

Who do you think you are?

*A compelling survey prompts people to
think about the country's promises and how short
it has fallen in meeting them. The political system
is run for and by those at the top. But that was
nothing compared to the opportunities to exploit
the people offered in Capitalism, especially
with government out of the way.*

The survey

In the spring of 1981, a college student performed a small-scale survey for her political science studies that presented respondents with a collection of simple statements about the country, many from historical sources. The respondents were asked to carefully underline the parts of the text they liked the most and cross out the parts they didn't like. The purpose of the exercise was to put together some picture of what people thought was important from the government, from society, and from an economic system.

For example, she presented them with the preamble to the Declaration of Independence:

> We hold these truths to be self-evident, that all men are created equal, that they are endowed by their Creator with certain unalienable Rights, that among these are Life, Liberty and the pursuit of Happiness. That to secure these rights, Governments are instituted among Men, deriving their just powers from the consent of the governed, That whenever any Form of Government becomes destructive of these ends, it is the Right of the People to alter or to abolish it, and to institute new Government, laying its foundation on such principles and organizing its powers in such form, as to them shall seem most likely to effect their Safety and Happiness.

"All men are created equal" was well-regarded, except the word "men" was sometimes excluded as a testimony to advancements in gender equality. "Unalienable Rights" scored positively while "their Creator" was considered positively by some and negatively by others. "Liberty and the pursuit of Happiness" had slightly more positives than the full phrase "Life, Liberty and the pursuit of Happiness" likely because protections for Life were uninspiring. Coming shortly after Reagan's inaugural speech, in which he said "government is not the solution to our problem; government is the problem," the phrase "Governments are instituted" scored a few negative votes. Even the line "it is the Right of the People to alter or to abolish it" received a near 40%

positive rating, giving an indication of the volatility of the country.

The survey also offered up a modified version of the Preamble to the Constitution:

> The purpose of government is to insure domestic tranquility, provide for the common defense, promote the general welfare, and secure the blessings of liberty to ourselves and our children.

The phrase "domestic tranquility" scored much better than "common defense," portraying a weariness of constant war, always with enemies of whom to be wary. And "welfare" continued to be a tricky word, with some negative responses while something more explicitly compassionate such as "support people in times of crisis" may have scored higher (although this clearly doesn't capture the full sense of the "general welfare" language).

The questions weren't restricted to political preferences and views. The survey also covered some questions about the economy, attempting to disentangle people's views on what I have previously referred to as the "Two Versions of the American Dream." Would people favor the Jeffersonian view that everyone should have an opportunity to succeed and make a useful contribution to the country? Or would people favor the Hamilton/Reagan view that no one's success should be fettered by the government or concerns for the general welfare? Would people view government attempts to regulate corporations and Capitalists as inconsistent with the Dream or as necessary in order to help ensure the viability of the Dream in a Capitalist free market?

The first statement intended to address these questions was: "In the United States, anyone willing to work hard should have an opportunity to be successful and contribute to the wealth of the country." It produced the strong positive results that one would expect. On a 5-point scale ranking how much people believed each statement (completely disagree, disagree slightly, neither agree nor disagree, agree slightly, or agree completely), 89% of the respondents said either agree slightly or completely. It seemed to indicate a tilt toward the Jeffersonian version of the Dream.

At first glance, the next survey statement wasn't all that controversial: "It is in the best interest of the country to make the best use of people's talents, skills, and strengths." 81% responded with positive agreement; 42% said they "agree completely." If a country believed itself superior to others, then they must also agree that their people are at the heart of its superiority and would want to make sure that advantage is used to its greatest potential. And yet there were only rare instances in US history where the country truly invested in its people. Since the early days of industrialization, the country's Capitalists had led more and more people into unskilled, thoughtless jobs that limited their potential value to the country—all in order to reduce labor costs to business owners. Even education had been sidetracked by the interest of those in power and corporations, seemingly with the goal of creating a more pliable and uniform citizenry that would be easier to rule over and to sell to. Despite a brief resurgence thanks to the Space Race, enthusiasm for education in the country's early days was difficult to find. As it was, there was much more interest in spending money on weapons than on teachers and textbooks. As some individuals increased their personal wealth dramatically, the country as a whole was deteriorating in global competitiveness.

There were statements designed to assess people's belief in the basic precepts of Capitalism, as well. For example, Capitalists put a great deal of faith in the "invisible hand" of the free markets. The statement "An open, competitive, and unregulated labor market is all that is needed to ensure a proper balance between labor and employers" was included to determine the depth of the belief in the Capitalist free labor market. It produced an interesting result, with a higher "completely agree" response (24%) than "slightly agree" (15%) suggesting almost a dogmatic commitment among some participants.

After the Republicans espoused the idea that the poor were to blame for not finding work, the statements "The unemployed typically cannot find work because they aren't looking hard enough" and "The unemployed typically cannot find work because they are lazy or unwilling to do what work is available" both received a fair amount of positive agreement—35% and 28% respectively. These numbers may have been higher if another statement—"The unemployed typically cannot find work because they lack the skills necessary to get hired"—had not given respondents another theory that was not as confrontational and fit better with people's personal experiences.

In contrast, "The government of the United States should be empowered to protect consumers and labor from exploitation by corporations even if doing so limits the upward mobility of some individuals" received only weak support at 53%. Only a few people (16%) said they "completely agree." Few people would suggest that the government was the ideal force to restrain the exploitation of labor and consumers by corporations, but with the absence of any other real viable options, it was seen as necessary.

People seemed to have more faith in the free consumer market than a free labor market. Most people realized large corporations had overwhelming power over individual (particularly unskilled) employees. 42% responded with positive agreement to "Consumer choice in a free and open market will protect consumers from abusive or deceptive corporations if the free market is left undisturbed by government." The United States was a very consumer-oriented society, with consumers imagining that they had more power and influence than they actually did. They simply took for granted all the regulations the government already had in place to protect consumers.

One area in which people were convinced that the government needed to be involved was the environment, where 72% agreed to "The government of the United States should be empowered to protect public resources such as the air, water, and places of natural wonder even if doing so limits the profits of corporations or individuals."

Unsurprisingly the statement "The country performs better when a small subset of the population is making decisions about research, product development, resource use, and urban development" received weak support. Only 7% of the respondents agreed with the statement, and 79% disagreed with it. It was a curious statement about the country's commitment to Capitalism. Although consumers have an impact on which products and uses of resources are successful, there is little democracy in how the country's resources—and people, for that matter—are "deployed" in Capitalism. People seemed to expect more say in decisions about the economy and allocation of limited human and natural resources.

More surprising was the response to the statement "A person's income should reflect the amount of work one chooses to contribute to society." It received a 79% positive agreement. Even among people who indicated an annual income greater than $250,000, the positive agreement was at 69%. It was intended to address people's sense of "fairness" of incomes obtained outside of labor, specifically income gained from the control of money (interest and profits). It is distinctly possible that many were thinking about recipients of welfare payments who were unable to find work instead of the Capitalists who got most of their income from sources other than work. The result eventually produced a great deal of conversation about how one's value was and should be calculated. Does it really make sense for the wealthy to enjoy both the power that is derived from controlling capital and the additional wealth from it? Is this any different from the feudal arrangement, where landlords enjoyed privilege and power by controlling land?

The student earned high marks for her research into and analysis of the country's political and economic beliefs. It was enough to help the student acquire funding from her university in order to expand the project on a larger scale (with some refinements). This caught the attention of an executive at General Electric. General Electric was at the time sitting upon a public-relations nightmare: a long and extensive history of environmental abuse. Sponsoring a survey to explore what was at the heart of the country and its people, what they valued, and what was important to them provided a wonderful preemptive public-relations opportunity. They took the effort national: they hired professional pollsters to work out the statement dynamics and took a cross-sampling of the country in order to reduce to a bare minimum any biases and ensure a fair representation of the country's population. In the end, the results were very similar to what the student had found. When General Electric published the findings, they pushed them heavily, and soon the whole country was involved in a national conversation about what the core values of the country really were.

At first people started to come together in small groups, meeting at universities, churches, restaurants, community centers, and public parks. They were discussing what made the country great and what the major shortcomings and challenges were. They discussed what the country was and what they wanted and expected from the government. They were also comparing what they were *told* they had (representative government, Land of Opportunity, etc.) with what they *actually* had. When provoked to think, people started to realize that there was a disconnect between what the country could be and what it had become, or perhaps what it had always been.

With reports of these meetings coming out in newspaper articles and news programs, the meetings grew larger. An organization (Supporting the Conversation) was formed to help people find their closest meeting and to try to connect the different conversations together. Slowly, this became a national conversation, with progress reported in media outlets throughout the country and beyond.

One of the first coordinated objectives was to define some shared core values and ideals. When asked in the surveys to come up with a single word for what the country was about, almost half of the respondents said "Freedom."

The next closest was "Opportunity" at 32%. In conversations, too, most people insisted that everyone should have a true and sincere opportunity to succeed and contribute, as well as espouse a belief in the value of having the freedom to express one's own individuality.

But there was a problem with agreeing to the definition of terms. What "opportunity" was being promised to and expected by people in the country? Was it that everyone should have a fair opportunity to comfortably provide for themselves and their family? Would it include the opportunity to be proud of what one was doing, making a real contribution that was well-suited to the passions, interests, and talents of the individual? For many it was also important to be working and making progress toward something. Could this sort of opportunity possibly be provided in a society? Capitalist economists insisted that it was impossible. Despite the mythology that the country was the "Land of Opportunity," the United States struggled to offer everyone a decent opportunity in life. There were simply too many advantages given to people with wealth. Wealth was power, and power brought opportunity. This naturally limited the opportunities for the rest of the country. Most people rejected this idea of success. Success should not be measured relative to others, and success should not be achieved by tearing others down.

"Freedom" was no easier to define than "Opportunity." In his 1940 State of the Union Address, Franklin Roosevelt had an interesting angle on Freedom, one that continued to have meaning in the 1980s. First he offered two conventional freedoms: Freedom of Speech and Freedom of Worship. But then he introduced concepts that were truly innovative for the time, inspired by Depression-era politics and economics. He suggested that people should have Freedom from Want and Freedom from Fear. The latter was particularly relevant in the 1980s, as fear was oftentimes used as a political weapon of manipulation. Roosevelt had combined the traditional concepts of Freedom with the basic precepts of Opportunity. While motivated by a desire to preserve the Capitalist system, Roosevelt had done a convincing job of describing the basic expectations of most people in the United States: Freedom, Opportunity, and a government that didn't resort to manipulation to satisfy the needs of a powerful minority.

The challenge remained: what to do with competing freedoms when the freedoms of one person interfere with the freedoms of others. If everyone were completely free to do whatever they wanted, that would be anarchy. This clearly took the idea of Freedom into sinister territory, where murder, thievery, and survival of the fittest (as defined very narrowly) would be the norms. Such absolute Freedom was not what anyone wanted, despite the stark similarity between this concept and the hard-line Capitalist ideas for an unregulated business environment in which everyone was left to fend for themselves.

Freedom and Opportunity were easy ideals to agree on as general concepts, although the details would continue to prove more difficult. With Christianity once again being used aggressively as a political tool, the issue of whether religion should be part of the country's identity was much cloudier than one would have imagined in a country that claimed to cherish its Freedom of Religion. If decisions about the future form of government, and later the decisions from that government, were not based only on shared secular values but also specific Christian values, then there was a real potential that Freedom and Opportunity would be restricted for a significant portion of the people.

The case for declaring the country a Christian nation was essentially two-fold: history and demographics. There can be little doubt that practically all—if not actually all—of the "Founding Fathers" were Christian. Thomas Jefferson offered perhaps the most difficult case to decide. While his critics portrayed him as an atheist, he often represented himself as a deist, believing in a god but not necessarily the Christian God. In addition to the Founding Fathers, for much of the country's history, the population itself was overwhelmingly Christian, although always with plenty of exceptions. While the country was no longer as homogeneous as it once was, a vast majority of the people in the country still considered themselves Christian, with broad variations on how that identification manifested itself in actions and sincere beliefs.

The US had a long tradition of religious tolerance. It had been with the country from the very beginning, as many of the original colonists fled England to escape religious intolerance. In the few cases where religion was mandated or given special privilege, the colonists responded by demanding more freedom and greater separation between personal beliefs and public governance. It was important for most people to know that their individual right to worship would be protected. If they were Christian, that meant knowing that their denomination would also be respected. The example of the Church of England—which in the 1700s was more of a social and business club for the nobles to manage their privileges than a source of spiritual guidance—loomed large as a cautionary tale, for anyone familiar with that history.

There was also the matter of free will. If religious observance was compelled or provided social, economic, or political advantage, then there were likely to be more "pretenders" engaged in churches. The ministers of a church would be better served helping sincere believers work through spiritual questions. The same free-will issues arose with any attempt to legislate morality. Do church leaders want people avoiding temptation not sanctioned by the church because of fear of being convicted in this lifetime? Such laws would not only make Christianity in the United States look weak but also create additional animosity between Christians and non-Christians.

Furthermore, there were the practical issues raised by differences between denominations of Christianity. Any attempt at the federal level to introduce explicitly Christian concepts into government laws or ceremonies would quickly be confronted with challenges from different denominations. Which Bible should be used? Which prayer? Which symbols should and shouldn't be displayed? In any number of decisions, inevitably one denomination would be favored, even if unintentionally. It was, in fact, these issues that first caused people to question the tradition of prayer in public schools. As early as 1890, a Roman Catholic contested the use of the King James version of the Bible for use in school activity in Wisconsin schools as it appeared to favor a particular denomination of Christianity.

Despite being somewhat counter-intuitive, perhaps the most compelling argument against incorporating Christianity as part of the identity and government of the country was to keep the Christian spirit of the country strong. After all, there was ample evidence to suggest that it was because the United States had such strong religious tolerance that Christianity remained omnipresent. This stood in contrast to Europe, where Christianity was fading. In Europe, wars were fought over religion, and people were compelled into state churches. As a result, people rebelled against the church as they rebelled against the government. They suspected the church just as they suspected the government. In contrast, because people in the US were not mandated to join a church, more people in church were sincere believers, and the faith was stronger.

As the country openly discussed these issues and considered the implications of a government that declared itself Christian, it slowly became clear that what people really feared most was the potential threat of the country becoming less Christian and, accordingly, what that shift would mean for devout believers. But the answer to fear of losing a majority was not to compel more people into the majority belief, but rather to make sure that the majority didn't matter. That way, no matter what other people decided to do, an individual's rights to personal choices would remain secure.

The old political system

"Democracy" was another word that came up often in lists of what the United States stood for. But what did it mean to people? At its core was a government that was held responsible to and worked for the people. But few people wanted a requirement or expectation that everyone be actively engaged in decision making on all issues, so-called "Direct Democracy." Most people didn't have enough interest or knowledge to make a helpful decision on most issues, and there was a rational fear of what an uneducated majority would do with that much responsibility. Instead people wanted someone they could trust to represent them in discussions. The original framers of the Constitution asserted that the elite could be such trustworthy representatives. In practice, however, this was far from true, something the contemporaries of the framers knew from the very beginning.

The government rarely seemed to act as if it represented the people. More perks and rewards in office came by serving the interests of the wealthy minority than those of the majority, so that is where most politicians put their energy. And as campaign funding became critical to election and reelection, the priority further tilted toward policies that favored people and organizations with money to "donate" to a politician's cause. The way the system worked in practice meant that even those who might have entered office to serve the people would need to satisfy upper-class constituents in order to stay in office. The resulting lack of genuine representation was something that frustrated potential voters to the point that many decided to stay home on voting day. They simply didn't see the point in participating in the charade.

In practice, the two political parties put much more effort into fooling the voters than understanding them. Tactics and slogans were tested and explored until the right cocktail of words and imagery was hit upon to sell a candidate to an electorate. Nationalism and fear were some of the more common and destructive tactics, creating and expanding animosities both within and outside of the country, instead of finding ways for different viewpoints to compromise and get along. Fear of Great Britain, France, Spain, Natives, slaves, new immigrants, Mexico, Canada, Germany, farmers, labor, Communists, the Soviet Union, and the poor all took their turns. Candidates who communicated a commitment to a strong defense against these threats to "our way of life" won elections despite the fact that these defenses typically meant denying liberty and opportunity to large swaths of the US population. Time and time again, the people conceded Freedom and Opportunity in exchange for a sense of security from threats that the country's leadership had created or made sound much worse than they actually were.

Despite being such a fundamental requirement, the ideas and logic of representation were poorly formed. It is difficult to imagine that people living in the same geographical area all really held the same basket of ideas and preferences. Yet it was expected that a single representative would represent all the diverse opinions and views of hundreds of thousands (up to millions) of people on all topics. If 51% of the people in a person's district viewed things one way and 49% the opposite way, there was no one who represented the large minority. Worse yet, if 51% of the people thought issue A (social issues, for example) was most important in choosing a representative, then that would drive their voting decision. But the person best suited for that issue would also represent them on issue B (corporate-tax policy perhaps), even though only a tiny minority might share that representative's views on that issue. It was this dynamic that the political parties and ruling powers skillfully exploited to push through policies contrary to the interest of the majority.

Without sincere representation, debates in Congress were often shallow, more for show to appear to be engaged than a real discussion of the needs and interests of different constituencies. It wasn't about how to accommodate different perspectives with a minimum of trouble and compromise for all sides but about how to provide the greatest value to those with the most influence. A Congressperson could "buy" votes on something that was important to his or her wealthy constituents by promising to support a bill or project that was important to another Congressperson's wealthy constituents. If the cotton industry wanted government subsidies to pad their profits and the defense industry wanted increased spending on weapons procurement, they both could take from the people's tax revenues by working together and supporting each other's bill. These were not compromises on the issues between divergent sides on the same debate; these were agreements across multiple issues where the representatives of the wealthy conspired to take as much as they could from the people.

Even if real representation could be achieved, there were issues with democracy in theory that caused difficulty in practice. The guiding principle of democracy is the rule by the majority. Between two different options, the choice that received more than half the votes was the one that was pursued. This, however, could be quite oppressive to those in the minority. In the United States, the Bill of Rights was the primary defense against government abuse and was needed to shield minorities from the worst assaults by the majority. But it could do only so much.

The myth alone that the United States had majority rule created a great deal of animosity and anxiety. Those in the majority were anxious to push through their agenda quickly and forcefully while in power in fear of losing it someday. And the nature of democracy encouraged people to be more aggressive in pursuing their agenda and less considerate of other people's viewpoints. It made everyone more anxious. Furthermore, to secure their position, they often changed the rules in their favor. They found ways to game the electoral system, including limiting voting rights and realigning districts to make sure they retained their power. Such was the fear of democracy. People felt that, in order to avoid being its victim, they had to manipulate it.

Meanwhile, those in the minority felt a sense of helplessness. It made people desperate to find some way to achieve a majority. Ironically, since the system was so poorly representative, even groups clearly in the majority felt that same sense of helplessness, imagining themselves outside of the majority and becoming just as desperate to gain control.

If a group was unable to achieve a national majority, they often attempted to exploit (sometimes even manufacture) state or local majorities and then move decisions to those local jurisdictions. It was a way for local elite or other anxious interest groups not powerful enough to compete on the national stage to exploit the gears of democracy to impose their values and interests on local populations. The call for "states rights" was often used this way. And for most of the history of the United States, there were few protections at the state and local level, since the Bill of Rights in the Constitution did not extend to the action of state governments until 1925. Before then people had to rely on the often weak state constitutions for protection, making them prime targets for exploitation and abuse.

The myth that states made sense as homogenous political districts went back to before the country was founded. The southern slaveholders needed a political jurisdiction where they could continue to impose their will on slaves and other free whites without interference from the federal government. To justify these local jurisdictions and the transfer of decision-making to that level, the ruling elite had to convince everyone that the people in one state had more in common with each other than they did with people in other states. But it wasn't true beyond those at the top in the colonial days, and it wasn't true in the 1980s. Cities versus rural was a stronger predictor of political opinions than New Jersey versus New York, or Oregon versus Washington. The country was diverse.

However, even in the 1980s, some people argued that a majority should be able to impose its way of thinking on a minority in violation of basic rights. For example, it was argued that if a majority in a state, county, or town wished to introduce religious services or iconography into their government institutions, they should have that right. They felt they should be able to ignore the principle of separation of Church and State if a majority agreed. What they were missing in their reasoning was that once such majority rule was allowed complete authority, it could be turned against a group just as readily as used by them. It had happened before. In the first half of the 1800s, the Church of Jesus Christ of Latter Day Saints was growing and chose a Missouri location as their central base. They called for a migration of the faithful, making the locals living there nervous. It looked certain that soon the new immigrants would outnumber the earlier immigrants and be able to impose their religious, moral, social, and legal beliefs onto people outside of their faith. To prevent this outcome, the earlier migrants fought back. They attacked the towns the Church had established and intimidated their residents until they had to flee the state. They felt they had to resort to violence to avoid the implications of democracy.

But despite the tendency of states and "states rights" to be abused, there were a few cases where individual states actually led the federal government in improving human rights and expanding freedom. Women's right to vote, for example, evolved exclusively from state action as western states (starting with Wyoming) started to experiment with offering women the right to vote. Although the states had their detractions, a place to incubate new progressive ideas and to put pressure on the federal government to move forward had tremendous value.

The old economic system

There was skepticism in the community discussions that a better political system could be devised, one that would not be overtaken by an elite anxious to achieve some level of security for themselves in a highly competitive world. Despite the right to vote expanding to people without wealth and property, companies and the wealthy managed to remain in firm control by leveraging increasingly larger sums of money to help their favorite candidates "campaign" and manipulate voters. With more money, politicians could use increasingly sophisticated techniques to convince voters to fear the latest threat or submit blindly to nationalist and patriotic rhetoric. It seemed no form of government could be safe as long as so much economic power was wielded disproportionately. In order to get a real chance at freedom and opportunity, it was clear some sense had to be made of Capitalism.

The basic assumption of Capitalism was that people would pursue their own interests with all their energies at the exclusion of other concerns. The core principle was that humans were fundamentally selfish and greedy. Capitalism, therefore, proposed a system in which everyone was equally empowered to pursue their own personal agenda, with the struggle between competing interests resulting in a fair and balanced outcome. If a buyer and seller were both looking out for their own interests, negotiation between the two of them would be a balance between what the seller wanted for the item and was willing to part with it for and what the buyer was willing to pay for it. The more people who wanted to buy an item (the demand), the higher the price went because the seller had more options. The more of the item that was available (the supply), the lower the price, because the buyer had more options.

These theories in Capitalism fell apart pretty quickly in the real world. It turned out that people were more social and less overwhelmingly selfish than assumed. And both sides of a trade did not all have access to the same set of information as expected for Capitalism to produce a balanced outcome. In a simple example, if one person was buying a car from a classified ad, he'd know the make, model, and year of the car and would be able to compare the price of this car with other similar cars available from other sellers. But the seller might know that the engine was about to give out. Assuming the buyer was no car expert, he'd be dependent on a mechanic to be able to spot a problem with the engine to evaluate any adjustment to the value of the specific car. With this imbalance, Capitalism rewarded—sometimes quite extravagantly—people for their ability to deceive and manipulate others. If someone could be duped into giving up their money, then it was earned by the duper. Far from fostering a sense of collaboration and community, it pitted everyone against their neighbors, making it unsafe to trust anyone.

In order to remain competitive and avoid being swindled at every turn, people needed to be experts in a broad range of topics. This was completely impractical for most, if not all, people. Yet there was typically someone around to exploit anyone's lack of perfect knowledge. Fortunately the government stepped in to bridge some of the gap. If the government hadn't regulated the quality of food or medicine, for example, each citizen would need the ability, knowledge, and the equipment to test quality before they bought in order to ensure they weren't getting tainted product. But the government could do only so much to mitigate the deceptions encouraged by real-world Capitalism, particularly with the Capitalists campaigning heavily to limit the government's regulatory capabilities. Meanwhile the weight of those regulations designed to trap dishonest operators hampered the ability of honest small businesses to operate.

The rules of supply and demand that applied to goods also applied to labor. Capitalists could not affect the demand side much, except for during the occasional economic crisis. But they had several ways to leverage their wealth to increase supply and diminish the negotiating power of labor to get lower wages. Capitalists invested heavily in automation to decrease their reliance on low-in-supply skilled labor and push more people into the unskilled labor pool. The gains from introducing automation went to the Capitalists with lower costs and greater profits, while the costs—which manifested themselves in increased crime of all types, drug use, destruction of families, etc.—were picked up by the society.

In the early days of industrialization in the United States, Capitalists advertised in other countries, spinning incredible stories about opportunities in the United States in order to encourage immigration. The resulting immigration put massive downward pressure on wages and made life miserable for millions. As global transportation improved, companies and Capitalists increasingly shed their loyalty to a specific country and went shopping for the cheapest labor. There were often enough labor savings in moving an entire manufacturing operation to a developing country, where people were willing to live with less (often next to nothing) to cover the costs of the move. For the United States, this meant that after the Capitalists went to all that effort to bring (literally) boatloads of people to the country to lower labor costs, they then abandoned the now-enlarged population, leaving people without any way to make a living. While admittedly making the costs of goods lower, global labor competition dramatically changed the supply-and-demand equations and the balance of negotiating power in the favor of Capitalists.

Countries started competing against each other to persuade Capitalists to set up their businesses and provide jobs for their citizens. For those countries, like the United States, that were not willing to invest in education, it became a bidding war to see which country was willing to provide more tax breaks, lower wages, and, least of all, the best infrastructure. And it wasn't just the countries that would compete. States within the United States also competed with each other, pushing up the profits for Capitalists and the wages for everyone down. It was truly a world for the Capitalists.

On the other side of labor negotiations, employees were almost completely powerless against the oppressive weight of the free labor market. Someone who was living paycheck to paycheck (often just barely) couldn't move and couldn't improve his or her skills, since training costs money. They became slaves to whoever was willing to hire them as unskilled labor at whatever price they were willing to pay. The more people that were desperate for work, the lower the pay. Eventually the pay got so low that families were forced to put their children to work to get by. There was nothing in Capitalism to counter the ever-increasing imbalance between rich and poor and ensure that the basic requirements of the labor force—food, shelter, clothing, health, and a minimum of dignity—were satisfied. Government again eventually was compelled to step in, to subsidize the income paid to the labor pool through support for the poor.

Making matters worse, Capitalism disconnected people from the impact of their decisions. It allowed people to take and take, without considering what all that taking was doing to others, because it was desperate surrogates doing the actual taking. Middle-class managers, on orders to improve profits, pushed labor costs lower, compromised safety, jeopardized quality, and damaged the world's environment. Political operatives needing wealthy support to remain in their positions pushed increasingly extreme measures in support of those with the most money already. Often these measures were taken without the support of the wealthy they were intended for.

To balance the power of employers, the employees tried to unite together in unions and negotiate as a group on wages, working conditions, and layoffs. This proved successful at times but was difficult to sustain when work became extremely scarce during economic downturns. As people became more desperate for work, Capitalists were able to break apart unions and put in protections against their forming again. Always anxious about staying competitive, Capitalists had little choice but to take every opportunity they could find to break up unions and restore their complete control over labor negotiations.

Even consumer purchases, which people felt they had control over, were heavily manipulated by big business through advertising and the cultural pressure to consume that advertising created. It was true that companies looked to develop products and services that they could sell to people. This was how it was possible to argue that Capitalism was democratic. The problem was that it was not a very direct representation of the people's will. It involved a great deal of unnecessary risk for the Capitalists, which is why they demanded high profits when they got it "right." And it created a strong tendency toward products that could be sold at high profit margins, often through deception instead of ones that people genuinely wanted or needed and offered maximum value to them. Often as much or more money was spent on marketing and advertising to convince people that they needed a product than in discovering and addressing real needs. Somehow more money was being spent on making pointless widgets than on making sure everyone had food, water, and shelter. The priorities were completely misaligned.

Capitalists acknowledged that there was no mechanism in the economic system to meet the basic requirements for everyone willing to work. Instead, they argued that churches and charitable organizations would fill the void in order to keep people from being pushed into crime and revolution by starvation and desperation. It was quite an admission, a system that assumed that people were selfish had to rely on people's giving and generous nature to avoid total collapse. It was also an enormous weight that was being placed on churches. While definitely consistent with the image of Christianity as a caring and compassionate faith (an image often tarnished by anxious religious leaders), the reliance on churches to prop up the economic system limited funds for and distracted church leaders from their mission to serve the spiritual needs of their followers. To make matters worse, it was typically the poorest churches hardest hit, not those with wealthy contributors. It was the poor who were asked to dig deeper to help assist the poor.

Under Capitalism, life was tolerable for the poor in good times. For most people there was work to do and money to cover the basics. However, during the regularly recurring economic crises, it could get horrific, completely inhumane. People saw a government bending over backwards to save the bankers while showing no concern for the rest of the country's population. In fact, those in control often blamed the poor and middle class for the crisis even though it was almost always the bankers' desperation and greed that caused the problems.

From a Capitalist point of view, there was nothing undemocratic or elite-dominated about the economic system. In theory, anyone could set up their own business and make the sort of decisions critics said were limited to the elite. Anyone could hire who they wanted at whatever rate they agreed upon. They could put them to work inventing or building whatever product they wanted. They could buy natural resources and use them as they saw fit. They could treat their immediate environment according to their own needs as long as they were within existing laws. And they could use their wealth to pay for lobbyists and buy off politicians to change laws to make their way easier. One of the many problems with this argument was that many people didn't have any money left over to do any of this—they could only just *survive*. And those at the very top had so much more money that they could do many more of these wealth-generating activities, giving them more power, freedom, and opportunity. Capital was the only barrier to entry, but the poor distribution of wealth meant a tiny minority had enormous power, while the majority could do little more than accept it.

Ironically even though the world was run for and by the wealthy, many of them were still miserable. In the United States, they were taught that the secret to happiness was the accumulation of wealth. So they pushed themselves (or were pushed) into often-inhumane careers that did not satisfy or make use of their passions and interests. They, too, were being denied the Opportunity promised by the nation. Even when they got to the point where they could buy anything they wanted—many were so rich that they didn't even have to buy things (companies would gift them things in order to win an implicit endorsement)—they were not happy.

For those thinking back on a life building their wealth from modest beginnings, their happiest days were typically early on, when they were just starting to build their business and still vowed to be different, to care about customers, employees, and the community. They were under constant pressure from competitors, society, and shareholders to exploit more and more. By the time that they reached the peak of their "success," they were riddled with guilt over what they had done to people to get there. Fantastic justifications and rationalizations were devised to help them cope with their guilt, but these could only mask their guilt.

Meanwhile Reagan's trickle-down theories and pro-business policies tied with continued suffering in the country were making the wealthy out to be villains (in movies and television even), vilified by people who were growing fed up by their privilege and sense of entitlement. And to top it all off, there was the anxiety of possibly losing everything on the next venture. In their drive for ever-greater wealth, they took risks with the country's resources and lived in constant fear of potential upstart competition. Many even engaged in illegal action to suppress any competition from rising. This anxiety pushed them to more extreme actions and made it impossible for them to truly enjoy their lives and privileges.

In Capitalism, there was no way for the people to express their will directly or consolidate funds for that effort. Someone was needed to anticipate the market's needs and wants and raise the funds needed to satisfy them. Without direct feedback from the market, however, there was enormous risk for the Capitalist funding a project. Profit was explained as the reward for a person taking on this risk. This was the source of the sense of entitlement Capitalists felt, how they justified taking such a large portion of the wealth created by labor for themselves.

Many saw great potential for improvement, while strong skepticism remained after endless propaganda from Capitalists that Capitalism was as good as society could get, given the greedy human nature. The challenge was to come up with a way for investment decisions to be democratized, eliminating the need for someone to interpret the market and raise the funds based on that speculation. Perhaps, if there were a way to put control of investments more directly in the hands of consumers, it would reduce the risks associated with such ventures. In that way, the risks could then be distributed publicly instead of placed on an anxiety-ridden Capitalist. A more representative model for product-development decisions would certainly produce a more socially and environmentally conscious output.

Without any clear examples of a large civilization operating without privileged and powerful elites, serious questions were raised whether a society without an elite could be developed. But a couple of important questions that would help drive future discussions evolved from the attempt. The first question was whether anyone who enjoyed the public's trust would inevitably try to find ways to exploit that trust. If so, how could the society be structured to limit the impact of that exploitation? Having a small cadre of decision-makers (elites, in a way) who people trusted to make decisions in the best interest of the whole country and not just certain interest groups is fundamentally different from a small cadre of decision-makers who exploited their position to provide advantages to themselves and their friends. The second question was: if the country had to have an elite class and could choose, what type of elite would it choose?

Alternatives

The country's people consider an economic alternative that puts the people in charge of their own lives and the market for goods and services. Even getting the money out of politics does not make the government work for the people, so a new government of the people is devised. Having come up from the people, the new systems have broad appeal, offering something for everyone to be hopeful about.

Economic alternatives

Most people took Capitalism for granted. Communism was the only alternative any one ever talked about, and that concept had been completely corrupted by the Soviet Union, making it a dead issue. So few people in the general public ever really asked what they should expect from an economic system. Whenever the discussion did get started, it typically got mired in a shouting match between the pro-Capitalism and anti-Capitalism camps. The latter would point out all the weaknesses of Capitalism without offering any new and compelling alternatives, while the former pointed out that it was better than Soviet Communism.

To make any progress, something had to be done to break from that pattern where the economic spectrum was viewed solely along an axis between just two of the many potential economic models (most as of yet undiscovered). So a sincere effort was made to center the conversation on the goals without getting mired in the debate between Capitalism and Soviet Communism.

The focus remained on Freedom and Opportunity. And with that focus, one of the baseline requirements that most people agreed upon was that the economic system should be able to satisfy the basic living requirements of people willing (and typically anxious) to work. Few people could challenge that having enough food to eat, water to drink, healthcare against common risks, and shelter from the weather were necessary prerequisites to Freedom and Opportunity.

Another principle discussed was the need to reward and encourage work. After decades of propaganda, there existed an unshakeable belief that people had a natural inclination toward laziness and, therefore, needed a stern push to work. Whether that was true or not in a country that had always put a high value on hard work, it was something that people wanted the economic system to account for. Ironically, despite all its claims to the contrary, Capitalism seemed to provide only a tenuous connection between hard work and compensation. There were some nasty and physically devastating jobs that paid next to nothing, requiring those in them to work vigorously just to get by. And there were plenty of opportunities for the wealthy to make ridiculous sums of money with no work. Capitalism actually discouraged work at both ends of the wealth scale. People born into incredible wealth could afford to live a life of privilege and leisure if they so chose. Profits from investments of their massive fortunes were enough to live on comfortably, so instead of working themselves, they let their money work. On the other end, many people had the will and drive to work entirely beaten out of them. There simply was no hope in it, no opportunity to improve one's lot. In a few cases (far fewer than the wealthy wanted people to believe), some people even gave up looking for work and accepted government support for as long as they could get it. The system stole their self-respect and gave them no reason to care.

Tracking with the themes of Freedom and Opportunity, the next goal was to maximize a person's control over one's own destiny. In Capitalism, too much depended on the family someone was born into and who one knew. Too much of one's life story was written at birth. Another concern was that business ownership was too highly valued, to the exclusion of employees who made businesses successful. Similarly, the ability to sell (ideas, skills, oneself), either honestly or, more commonly, through manipulation and deception, was disproportionately valued. And Capitalism also distorted people's career choices, diverting them away from their passions and toward careers that offered the greatest financial rewards. It was not uncommon for people to become lawyers or doctors for the money and for great teachers to leave their profession because they couldn't afford to keep teaching. The economy motivated people in the wrong direction, something many wanted to see change. If Freedom and Opportunity were to be important, and if the country were to leverage its diverse population for maximum social value, then the economy should account for a large variety of skill sets and specializations. The economy should leverage people's talents, passions, and interests to produce the highest possible benefit for society as a whole. This came back to the notion that if the nation was going to be great, its people had to be great.

And it was demanded that the economic system respond to the will of the people instead of being at the service of any sort of elite. Capitalists argued that the public interest was transmitted through the free market. But looking at the large compensation disparity between bankers and teachers—who were providing an overwhelming social good that required significant specialized education and knowledge—shed light on what the "invisible hand" actually rewarded. It was clear that Capitalism rewarded people who created the most wealth for the most powerful. When people realized this, it really struck at the country's anti-elitism. Here was a small group of people who enjoyed significant advantage in the society at the expense of everyone else.

While people accepted that there were aspects of Capitalism that violated the country's principles of Freedom, Opportunity, and anti-Elitism, they also insisted it did produce a good amount of prosperity (in between the downturns) and created a great deal of prestige for the country (along with a lot of bad will). It was also fairly stable. Even with the regular and excruciatingly painful collapses, the country managed to sustain a dramatic wealth disparity without serious unrest. It was, therefore, hard for many to imagine there would be another alternative compelling enough to risk trying.

Reducing people's receptiveness to alternatives was the fact that there had been some experiments, both in small-scale communities and in whole countries, with discouraging results. Perhaps most damaging were the experiments in the mid-1900s in government-controlled economies. Even though they were ideological enemies (playing off each other for political power), the models used by Fascism and Soviet Communism to control the economy were surprisingly similar. In both cases, it wasn't the invisible hand exploited by the elite but the government that determined what was going to be produced and by whom. The main difference between the two systems was which elite received special privileges, wealth, and (limited) power. In the case of Fascism, the Capitalists continued to receive the profits from manufacturing even though the risks were clearly taken over by the government. In the case of Soviet Communism, it was the bureaucratic elite (Communist Party members) who enjoyed a privileged position in the society that included extra wealth and more freedom.

There can be little doubt that the Soviet regime dramatically improved the country's economic position in the world, driving through an industrialization that would have been much more difficult if a totalitarian regime weren't forcing people to make sacrifices for the "good of the country." The same economic spark could be seen in Fascist Germany and Italy. But both Soviet Communism and Fascism suggested that a strong, totalitarian regime was necessary in order to operate a managed economy. Furthermore, they seemed to prove that such governments could not act in the interests of the people and did not allow for the sort of individuality that was obviously an important objective for the United States. Even though Soviet Communism and Fascism hardly exhausted the possibilities and potential of a managed economy, it was a complete non-starter in the United States. Simply put, the country had invested too much of its psyche into the ideological war with the Soviet Union to even entertain a serious discussion on a managed economy.

Throughout the years, a number of utopian communities had experimented with different social and economic systems, too. Most of them, however, were largely agricultural in their focus and involved—and often demanded—a great deal of uniformity among its members. These experiments, along with the haunting example of uniformity in Soviet Communism, firmly established in people's minds a connection between equal opportunity and mindless, homogeneous drones. No system could be considered that did not allow for maximum expression of personal individuality—this was a higher-level priority than strictly imposed equality of opportunity.

Another radical alternative was considered, although only briefly. With all the trouble and obsession caused by money, some wondered if there was some way to do without it entirely. Could a society in which everything was free work? Consumption would drop dramatically, since there would be no reason to accumulate things as a means to demonstrate success. Everyone would "buy" what they want and need instead of getting obsessed with having more than anyone else. The idea, however, was quickly discarded as too risky and too impractical for people of the time used to a Capitalist society. People's instincts were simply not wired for it. Plus, by the 1980s, there were some resources whose scarcity was obvious. With no structure to the economic sphere to manage the scarce resources, it would be possible for one person to take control of all the resources and essentially hold everyone else hostage while dolling them out to the advantage of a limited segment of the population.

One of the more contentious issues came up when discussing compensation. Could and should it be used to encourage people into different careers? Naturally some people objected loudly to the idea of someone or something pushing people in a particular life direction. Capitalism had claimed that, through the free market of labor, people would be compensated more for careers that provided more value to society. In reality, however, the Capitalist free market was like the political system: it was easily taken over to serve the elite instead of the people. Instead of compensating people doing the most good, it gave the wealthy a plausible cover for taking enormous sums of money for themselves with only a tenuous connection to public good. In theory this myth of Capitalism providing greater rewards to those who provided greater value to the community sounded appealing; in practice, it just invited abuse and caused a great deal of hardship.

The idea of varying compensation based on the value the work provided to society was a demand-side approach to the question of value. The question it tried to answer was what society demanded more. But there was also virtue in exploring the question of value from the supply side: how could a system improve the quantity and quality of effort people put into an economy? It seemed natural to assume that if people were doing what they wanted to do, what they were passionate about, then they would be better at it and put more sincere effort into it. More total value would be created by having people do what they enjoyed, as long as it provided enough value to society to justify the doing in the first place. In fact, any system that didn't deny opportunity to work to people willing and anxious to work would be a significant improvement on the supply side. Instead of aiming (and failing) to maximize public good, a system could maximize personal choice and personal opportunity. This approach would align with the goal of maximizing Freedom and Opportunity, but it was also assumed that it would increase total value of the output. This assumption seemed less tenuous than the assumption in Capitalism that the free market correctly valued work appropriately. If a system made it more likely people would end up doing something they enjoyed for work, then they would be for it. The challenge, then, would be to make sure that what people wanted to do as work actually resulted in a product or outcome that had some value to the public.

Surprising to just about everyone, these ideas of supply-side drivers for value maximization seemed to be pointing to something fairly unsettling for many in the United States: a fixed hourly wage regardless of work. It had instant appeal to humanists, who considered the value of any person was the same by virtue of their humanity. But it was much more difficult for others to accept. A long list of objections had to be overcome before this idea could achieve broad appeal.

For starters, some careers required specialized training. Doctors, for example, had to put themselves through very expensive and time-consuming schooling in order to be able to do their jobs. If there were no financial reward for making that personal investment, then it would put a real strain on the number of people willing to go into those fields. If the driving force behind the economic system was to encourage people to go into fields consistent with their passion and interests, then something would have to be done to balance out this disincentive. The solution was simple enough, however. The cost of education was already factored into the prices paid to doctors. It could be included right from the start instead of asking each individual to advance the money, thereby limiting the people who could and would enter the profession. Studying and learning a profession could become part of the profession, paid for just as any other part of the job would be. People would be paid for the time to increase their value to society, just as they would be paid to make other contributions to society. The advantage of this approach was that it practically guaranteed that people entering professions were doing so out of interest in that career and not for the money. Doctors are a great example for why this is important. After all, who would want to go to a doctor who is in it only for the money? It would be much better to have a doctor who cared about his or her work and sincerely wanted to help.

The next challenge was how to fill particularly unpleasant jobs. If everyone were encouraged to pursue their passions and interests, of course, there would be many jobs that no one would want. There needed to be some way to encourage people to take these least-wanted jobs. In Capitalism, the positions were filled because people needed to work. For not having what it took to fill other jobs, they got stuck in these unpleasant jobs and typically received sub-standard pay as additional punishment. No one could reasonably suggest that everyone would be guaranteed a chance to work in their dream career, even in the new system. The goal was simply to remove obstacles, disincentives, and distorting incentives not intrinsic to the career and to offer a more-level playing field for people on which to compete for jobs. People who could not compete successfully for other jobs would still end up in these jobs. If they did well there, then they could work their way up to something more to their liking. There was no need to pay them less for the work on top of it because the unpleasant jobs would present sufficient incentive for people to work hard. If they were satisfied in the "unpleasant" work, then, even better, they would work contently there.

Another advantage of this proposed plan over the traditional Capitalist system was that paying the same rate for all jobs added urgency to improve working conditions at the least-pleasant jobs. In Capitalism, these jobs and the people who worked in them received little attention. It was more cost effective to ignore complaints of faceless employees whose life issues could be kept out of sight of decision-makers than to "fix" the jobs. If the idea of a single hourly rate went through, then suddenly there would be greater urgency to improve the efficiency of these jobs instead of filling them with desperate workers whose forced silence masked real problems in humane working conditions and inefficient use of human potential. The real costs of the work would surface, costs that were shouldered by the society in Capitalism instead of the employers.

While many people worried that everyone would be competing for prestigious careers that included advanced education, others were convinced the opposite would be true, that simple jobs requiring little attention or exertion would be where the greatest competition would occur. The debate itself revealed the most likely solution to the problem: diversity. Just as different people worried about the two different extremes, the diversity in the population would likely lead to a reasonable distribution of interests in different jobs. The ultimate solution was, of course, competition, for both extremes. Whereas qualifications would drive competition for prestigious careers, people would also compete for "simple" jobs as well. It was expected that, with the greater flexibility in work offered by the new scheme, jobs that required a lot of sitting around waiting for something to happen might be tied together with more rigorous manual-labor jobs. Competition for the simple jobs would be based on who offered the most compelling pairing with another part-time job. Competition would encourage innovation instead of a race to see who, out of desperation, would accept the smallest compensation to do the work.

Obviously the economic system as it was evolving would require a rethink about how people found and were chosen for jobs, particularly if people were going to start offering to pair up different part-time jobs together in creative combinations. The process used to match talented individuals to open positions in the Capitalist United States was woefully inefficient and terribly demoralizing. It seemed less designed to make sure the best person ended up in a job and much more about robbing people of their individuality and making sure anyone looking for work knew it was the corporations that were in charge of the country. With all the efforts Capitalists put into expanding the supply of labor, there were typically scores of applicants, sometimes hundreds, for each open position. This was both dispiriting for candidates and a nightmare for hiring managers. The whole process encouraged candidates to exaggerate and mislead.

Meanwhile employers were skittish about sharing information with candidates lest it land in the hands of competitors or be used in a lawsuit against the employer after hiring someone else. It was made worse by the fact that people desperate for work would apply for anything they could and try as hard as they could to sound like a good fit in order to secure the opportunity. Hundreds of applications were dwindled down to a few candidates on the basis of the applications or resumes, so it was critical to get those just right (often without knowing much about what the job required). Then the hiring manager would have to decide whom to hire, typically based on just a short interview. This usually came down to superficial differences that had little connection with talent for the position. Since the interviews were essentially selling one's talents, disproportionate advantage went to people with selling skills, even for positions that would have no use for such skills. Given the absurdity of the process, many times the whole mess would be bypassed through connections. If a candidate knew someone close to the hiring manager and could make introductions, it would provide a shortcut to hiring that would be impossible for someone who wasn't similarly connected to compete against.

What was needed in the new system to help individuals navigate a complex world of opportunities was someone to serve on the side of candidates, to balance out the human-resource expert operating for the corporations. They could serve as the individual's champion and coach in order for everyone to have the best possible chance at finding the right opportunities. Such an approach would also help facilitate the placement of the best qualified for positions. A network of employment offices designed to actively and aggressively find opportunities for people—and, when appropriate, even engineer them by actively looking for investors for ideas and ambitions—was proposed. They would be empowered to help people discover and pursue their career interests, therefore making them substantially different from the poorly funded (but often equally well-intentioned) programs attempted in the Capitalist United States. The pressure to find matches between people and opportunities would be high, since in a country promising maximum opportunity, something had to be found for anyone willing and interested in working, even if the opportunity offered was only a steppingstone to something better if they worked hard at it. The resources available to these support services would have to be up to the challenge, including intimate connections with investment sources to drive new ventures.

None of this, however, addressed the real engine of the economy: the flow of money. In Capitalism, money typically came from banks and was directed by a tiny segment of the population (the Capitalists) based on their instincts on where the most money could be made for themselves and their investors. To compensate them for this "risk," a large portion of the gains from that investment went back to the Capitalists and banks. The whole banking and investment infrastructure was, therefore, huge and extremely complex. It took a large number of people to make it work, and, since banking was so critical to a working economy, many of them (particularly in the higher echelons) were paid extravagantly. It was an enormous hidden tax just to keep the system working. An alternative to the bankers and investors was needed in the new system. Someone had to make decisions about where money would be spent.

Many of the concepts of the free market and flow of money from Capitalism were brought over, with some critical refinements, of course. Consumers would choose what they buy just as they did before, allowing for the complete expression of personal preferences. Freedom, in fact, would be even greater than in Capitalism, because there would be less incentive for corporations to sell products people didn't want or need, and buying power would be more evenly distributed. Those purchases would sustain manufacturing and services as they did in the old Capitalist model. One of the key differences with Capitalism was that employees would not be punished for being in a job that was no longer necessary. If people stopped buying something, the people who worked in making that product would be relocated, using the services of the employment offices already mentioned. Training, if necessary, would be part of the new job, and every effort would be made to put or keep the person on a career path consistent with their talents and interests.

How decisions about where to allocate limited resources (especially labor) would be made differently than in Capitalism, however. Profit motive would not drive such decisions. It rewarded people too heavily for manipulation and exploitation and was intended as a compensation for individual risk-taking that was targeted for elimination. All that anxiety wasn't necessary or productive. If the problem with Capitalism was that too few people were deciding where to allocate money used for research, development, and community improvement, the solution would be to find some way to distribute investment decision-making among everyone. A "democratic" investment model was called for. It meant taking the investment money typically controlled by a small minority and distributing those decisions among the entire population so that they could make decisions directly instead of having their interests interpreted (and corrupted, not always maliciously) by Capitalists.

The key to the plan was keeping the investment money separate from a person's earned consumer money so that it could be used only for investing. This money wasn't intended as a reward for hard work but instead as a weighted voting mechanism for citizens to provide direct input on how the country's limited resources would be allocated. People would choose how they wanted to use the money, from fixing up the local park to funding research on fuel-efficient cars. Investment capital would then pool until enough was accumulated to work on the project, with any excess left over after completion returned to investors, distributed proportionally according to how much each person contributed—a very simple equation. The days of complex investment schemes involving teams of financial wizards with complex algorithms would be over. If people wanted something, they would and could make it happen on their own.

To many used to Capitalism, this idea sounded like a lot of extra work for the ordinary citizen, distracting people from their lives by transferring responsibility from a few individuals to everyone. Some way was needed that would allow people as much detailed control as they desired without posing a serious burden to those who didn't want to involve themselves too much. Thus reentered the Capitalists, with a twist. Instead of investing in specific projects that may require detailed understanding and a great deal of research to choose between competing options, individuals could instead invest money through new-style Capitalists, each working toward a particular outcome. There may be, for example, Capitalists who focus on improving specific neighborhoods. They would meet with people in the neighborhood and aggregate the wishes of the community to decide how best to direct the money invested with them. There may be Capitalists charged with improving water quality who might, therefore, direct their money toward specific research-and-development projects.

All Capitalists would be answerable directly to the people, however, a dramatic shift from the old Capitalism. Any money they managed would be part of the public record, its purpose clearly stated. If people didn't like how someone was directing the money, the money would simply flow to a different Capitalist who shared more people's vision. The Capitalists would, of course, get paid by the hours they work, just like everyone else, without any extra compensation derived from their position of trust. They were taking no unusual personal risks for which additional compensation could be demanded. And with the Capitalists in place, people could choose to invest with them or directly into projects—the freedom was theirs.

Another challenge to be resolved was how people saved up money in order to afford more expensive items. In the old Capitalist system, people who could afford to put away a portion of their income for later use trusted their money to banks guaranteed by the federal government. They could wait until they had enough money saved up or borrow money from the bank (at substantial profit for the bank) if they couldn't wait. The only substantial difference between how things would operate in the new system would be that interest, in the Capitalist sense, would not be earned, since income was to be derived from work, not from control of money. To save money, one simply would shift money from one's consumer account to one's investment account. When people wanted to make a big purchase, they could reclaim that money from the investment account. When saving, they would have more say on public-investment projects; when spending from the savings, they would have less. This was a new type of Freedom and personal choice.

One of the greatest ironies of Capitalism was that when there was not enough work, it created a very serious crisis. It is difficult to imagine anything more absurd. Imagine in a domestic setting you found yourself with no household chores to do during a long weekend. Would it be a problem? No, you'd enjoy the extra time to relax or otherwise come up with some new way to improve things in your life. It should not be any different in the public arena. With the idea of currency tied almost entirely to labor and practically no way to avoid spending the money (either as a consumer or as an investor), it was essentially impossible for a community to be completely devoid of projects that people interested in working could do. If everyone had the consumer goods they needed, then the money would flow to community projects, or research, or some such investments. It may require some shuffling of people, but that would be easily done when training and education became part of the job. The new free labor market, where everyone chose how much they want to work to earn how much they want to earn, would work out how people wanted to spend the surplus time.

It was a fairly straightforward matter to estimate how much money was spent on research, development, setting up new manufacturing, and community-improvement projects annually in the country to determine how much voting power each person should be provided. Trickier, of course, would be the transition—how to handle all the wealth people had "earned" in the old Capitalist system.

But this was a complication for a later time; first were questions of theory and ideals.

The last major piece that was missing in this new system was determining prices. In Capitalism, pricing was determined by the free market. Sellers would sell only at the price they were willing to part with the item for, and buyers were willing to pay only what they thought the item or service was worth to them. The system not only offered opportunity for manipulation by controlling information, but it also allowed for control over supply to raise prices. An example of this occurred with the robber barons in the second half of the 1800s. Companies gained a monopoly on a valuable resource and leveraged their position to push up the price. The government had to step in and break up companies in order to prevent them from exploiting their position, killing off the potential for positive collaboration in the process.

When you don't have to provide profit incentives for companies to invest in what the people want, pricing can be driven from costs alone, a much simpler model. For most products, the total labor costs required to make an individual unit would make up the bulk of the price. Because research, development, and manufacturing start-up costs would be paid for from the investment funds, the price wouldn't include these factors. One of the advantages of this pricing system—in addition to its simplicity, stability, and predictable nature—was that the pricing could also factor in environmental-impact costs associated with manufacturing and distribution. In traditional Capitalism, it was most commonly just the poorest in society who paid the full environmental and social impact of products. In the new model, those who wanted the products would pay. This extra funding could then be directed toward remediation and research. Likewise, pricing could also reflect scarcity of non-renewable resources like oil, with the extra money going toward research and development for alternatives.

After a seemingly endless array of meetings and town halls, something new was taking shape that was scoring well throughout the country. Many started calling it "Democratic Capitalism," since it maintained so many components of the old system but made it much more democratic in the sense that the people were much more in charge of how things were done. Nationwide, 39% of the population had a favorable impression of it. In some states—particularly in the West—the approval rate reached more than 50%.

The new economic thinking was lauded for its emphasis on free choice: in purchasing, in investing, in how many hours worked, and in what career to pursue. It was also expected that the new system would be more responsive and more efficient, cutting out the hefty "tax" Capitalists took in the way of profits. Many people were excited about the prospect of a system that encouraged collaboration and community instead of competition and manipulation. Everyone had a fair chance at success. Trust could resurface. Anyone walking around with an ostentatious amount of wealth would stand out, making manipulation unrewarding. As an added bonus, the plan also seemed likely to improve the value from the work people wanted to do, taking advantage of people's passions more strategically, to increase the competitiveness of the country.

Political alternatives

Democratic Capitalism would make corruption of the political system much more difficult and the ill-gotten rewards much less attractive. With that said, however, the economic changes didn't address the fact that the current political system was not capable of representing the diverse opinions of the United States or handling compromise sincerely.

The two-party system suggested there were only two types of people, leaving lots of room for manipulation. To end the stranglehold of the two parties and open the door to new parties, proportional representation was considered. Typically in proportional representation, each party submits a list of candidates in an election to fill multiple seats. For example, if a state were to use proportional representation to fill its legislative house, any party could register a list, and voters would vote for the party they preferred. Seats in the legislature would then be apportioned according to the percentage of votes received. So if a pro-environment party got 15% of the vote, they would get 15% of the seats available, taking that many names off the top of their list of names.

This approach had several practical implications and drawbacks. First, people would vote for a party instead of individuals. It would be a significant change for the country, having gotten used to trying to size up the virtue and character of individual candidates. Next, it would be difficult to manage federal elections through the states using proportional representation, particularly for the Senate. With just two seats to fill, the proportional system simply didn't make much sense. Proportional representation also tended to be less stable. Depending on the issue at hand, different alliances needed to be made. Such alliances could be particularly tricky for single-issue parties, like a pro-environment party. Representatives from a pro-environment party would have difficulty deciding how to line up on a social issue that had no environmental impact. Such shifting alliances could cause a change in leadership in the government, creating uncertainty. Proportional representation also would not solve one of the core issues being discussed: voters would still be required to choose a single candidate who best fits their interests on all possible topics. The same person would represent someone for religious-rights issues and for decisions about federal spending and taxes. Proportional representation was, therefore, open to many of the same sorts of abuses that the existing system suffered from.

Fundamentally new ideas were called for, and so, taking a step back, the purpose of government was reevaluated. From Reagan's inaugural speech, the suggestion that government was the problem continued to persist. But it was slowly being replaced by the realization that government itself wasn't the problem. The problem was the way the old style of government worked and how it became corrupted by traditional Capitalism. In 1833, James Madison, writing to an unknown correspondent, might have summed up the matter as well as could be done: "It has been said that all Government is an evil. It would be more proper to say that the necessity of any Government is a misfortune. This necessity however exists; and the problem to be solved is, not what form of Government is perfect, but which of the forms is least imperfect."

Many of the functions of government required in a traditional Capitalist society went away. Restraining and regulating abuse by corporations was hardly an issue when the profit motive for abuse was eliminated. The government would also no longer be needed to fill in the gap between what Capitalism provided and what humans needed in terms of basic living conditions.

Where some form of government was needed was to provide a channel and tools for different interests to resolve differences of opinion. This might include such local decisions as where to put a new park to national issues about how to accommodate diverse views and needs in the education system. Clearly, for this purpose, a strongly representative system reflecting the true interests of the people would be required in order to live up to the demands of the people.

Conventional wisdom suggested that, in order to achieve real representation, a very strong public participation in government would be required. The Constitution set up what Abraham Lincoln later called "government of the people, by the people, for the people." It did eventually give people the ability to operate as a sort of check on the government through elections but only after the right to vote expanded slowly and painfully. It was, however, made intentionally difficult for the people's will for change to be realized, and it did nothing to ensure that the people were properly informed about the issues to make intelligent decisions in their own interest. If economists had difficulty figuring out the best path forward during an economic crisis, it would be practically impossible for ordinary voters to figure out which candidate's plans would serve them best. And the difficulties were much greater for issues that a voter didn't care much about but was still asked to chime in on through voting. That arrangement was taking public participation too far, taking into consideration the opinions of people who had no stake in a topic.

Over time, voter participation declined dramatically, since many people realized they had no real options, with so much of the actual power controlled by the elite regardless of the election results. Those who did vote were easily manipulated by fear and hateful rhetoric to get them to vote against their own best interests.

Ultimately, as the discussion continued, it was revealed that people didn't want to be experts on all matters political any more than they wanted to be experts on all matters related to the things they buy. They didn't want to have to evaluate complex plans for fixing a broken economy any more than they wanted to learn how to test milk or beef to be sure it was safe before buying it. They wanted experts they knew they could trust handling these issues in their interest so that they could focus on what they do and wanted to do. They wanted someone they could trust fighting for them, who could—if asked—explain patiently why what they were doing was going to help them. Those criteria obviously knocked the current representative system out of the running. Representatives in the old model more commonly told voters what they wanted to hear instead of proposing realistic plans and then acted in the best interest of only their wealthy constituents instead of all their constituents.

Searching for new ideas, some looked for inspiration from the old system, asking if there were any examples where people actually were represented faithfully and reliably. The question revealed an interesting, and a bit surprising, answer. It seemed clear that lawyers and lobbyists, two groups with poor popular appeal, actually did typically provide fairly sincere and passionate representation. When someone hired a lawyer, it was very common to have faith that the lawyer would navigate the complicated legal terrain in the client's best interest. The lawyer earned that trust despite typically coming from a completely different background from the client. The reason they got such a bad reputation was that they had become tools of the wealthy, since their advantages were for purchase. If everyone had equal access, maybe the judicial branch and the courts could be the basis for a government. If sufficient power could be given to discontented citizens, it would be a powerful check on government abuses and remove much of the hopelessness people felt about their role in public policy, all without increasing their responsibility or expectations placed on them.

Something new was starting to take shape. If ever anyone had an issue with how things were being run, they could initiate a "reconsideration." If this was meant to be "government by the people," then it should be the people who initiated government. To get things started, a person would hire a "lobbyist." The word seemed a better match than "lawyer," particularly since lawyers would still be needed to handle legal issues between individuals, while the old-style lobbyists would fade. It was expected that a professional pool of lobbyists would develop, with different reputations. People could also appoint someone from their own interest group or even serve themselves if they preferred. When evaluating a lobbyist for the job, however, it wouldn't matter much if a person shared the group's views or not. What would matter most would be if he or she had past experience in learning and respecting other people's views and if the person demonstrated passion in pursuing compromise in the best interest of the group that initiated the action.

To keep the number of frivolous actions to a minimum and in keeping with the "pay-for-what-you-use" philosophy, the person or group of people initiating the reconsideration would be responsible for paying for the time of the lobbyist plus any additional incidental costs. Since it would typically be a public decision that was sought, the funds for the lobbyist would likewise typically come from the person's investment funds, not his earned consumer credits. Unlike the old system, where lobbyists and lawyers worked almost exclusively for the benefit of the wealthy, this would be a level playing field since no one had more investment capital to spend than anyone else to bias the results.

Typically the first step for the lobbyist was to figure out what other interests would be involved in the "case." A permanent third-party service would be set up to analyze the issue to determine what other distinct interests needed to be considered. A provisional lobbyist would be assigned to each of those interests. The nature of the case would determine if these extra lobbyists would be paid for by the interest group that initiated the case or by the additional interests being represented. It wouldn't be right for people to have to defend their interests against random challenges, but if they also had something to gain, they might then be expected to take over the funding. In rare cases, the third-party evaluators might determine that the group that initiated the case was the one who had been wronged and therefore expect the other party to pay for the initiator's case.

Once assigned, the lobbyist next would estimate the number of people included in the interest group. Depending on the interest group, these estimates could come from census reports or may require significantly more creative or elaborate techniques. The idea wasn't to determine who had the largest group and then simply rule in their favor. This wasn't majority rule but instead a search for compromise between competing interests. Having a sense of who was involved in an issue could impact the lobbyist's next steps and ultimately effect the sort of compromises that would be practical and reasonable.

In addition to consulting experts in the topic under discussion, the lobbyists then would go out to talk with a sample of the people they were representing. The purposes of these outings were two-fold. First was to build a portfolio of information about the topic and the interest group. It would be important that the lobbyist fully understand what the group wanted and needed in order to feel treated fairly in the society. Secondly, if the topic struck a chord with the people she encountered, they could contribute to the case funds. If the case ran out of funds, it would be put on hold until new funds were available, so there would be a real incentive for people who cared about the topic to contribute.

The lobbyists would then come together to negotiate a compromise. This type of compromise would be a dramatic change from what passed as compromise in the old system, where elites met with other elites and agreed on how they would exploit the non-elites. At the core of these conversations would stand the basic principles of the country: maximizing individual Freedom and Opportunity for all types of people and views as long as doing so didn't impinge on someone else's freedoms and opportunities. It is from these ideals that the compromise would proceed, with the goal of a fair and balanced decision for all sides and all individuals.

Open to the public and with transparency strongly valued, anyone could attend the meetings of the lobbyists, but only the lobbyists would have a voice in the negotiations.

Throughout the discussions, however, the lobbyists would remain keenly interested in getting all possible insight, so they would be sure to make themselves available to anyone with new ideas or perspectives to share. In the end, all sides would be motivated to find a compromise acceptable to all interest groups in order to avoid having anyone initiate a new reconsideration, a black mark on the record of the lobbyist.

If the lobbyists were unable to agree among themselves, a pair of mediators would be called in to make a decision. These mediators would be chosen at random from a pool of volunteers (like jury duty, but completely optional whether to register for the duty) who all lobbyists must agree are neutral on the case being decided. For a final agreement to take place, both mediators must agree. In the presumably rare case where they could not agree, a new pair would be called up.

Once a decision is made, the decision would be released in a full report proactively to all funders, another benefit of providing funds. The report would also be available to anyone upon request. If any group affected by the decision was unhappy with the final result, they could submit a new reconsideration and start the whole process all over again. The key to this arrangement—and what was substantially missing from the old system—was a clear and direct explanation of the decision and how it met the interests of the groups and honored the core principles. Each year everyone would also receive a report telling them which decisions they were counted in, to close the loop.

The system would provide for a more accurate and realistic representation, by making it representative by topic and tying the responsibility of the lobbyists directly to the people. It also, conveniently, addressed the question of states. Since the geographic scope would be determined on a case-by-case basis, whenever states made sense, they would be used; when they did not, they could be ignored. This new representative model would allow people to become active when they needed to be but otherwise trust that the government—what little there was of it—would not fall into the hands of an elite. The people were firmly and decidedly the check on government abuse.

Something for everyone

Starting out simply as impromptu gatherings of people to discuss first the core values of the country, then how the current systems failed to meet even the basic expectations, and finally some new alternatives, a serious movement and following evolved. The discussions were always intentionally accepting and accommodating to different views and perspectives. By staying away from traditional party and ideological labels and constantly returning to core principles, the movement was able to draw support from diverse populations. What resulted was something that could appeal to different people differently.

For example, the political and economic systems being discussed satisfied both the people arguing for small government (influenced by Reagan) and those who advocated for controls to prevent abuse by elites. Institutions and organizations that would fit the description of previous notions of "government" were difficult to find in the new systems, and what could be found was very close to the people. But this was done without giving the country over to the elite but instead by addressing at the source issues that government was otherwise needed to regulate. The motivations and rewards for corporations and Capitalists to manipulate and exploit people were practically eliminated. This was in response to the sometimes-cited third ideal (dwarfed in significance by Freedom and Opportunity) that the movement was committed to: the long-held anti-Elitism of the country. There may always be groups that might be called "elite," but at least they would not be able to exploit their status to the overwhelming and oppressive extent possible in the old system.

Likewise the new economic model kept many of the concepts and tools that Capitalists believed so firmly in while addressing most of money's corrupting side effects. Money was still at the heart of the economy, the primary tool used to influence decisions of all sorts. The free market concept was expanded and democratized. Individual choice was maximized, while encouraging and motivating people to make individual choices in harmony with a larger community as a way to make their money go further.

The movement also included a peculiar mix of nationalism and anti-nationalism. Much attention was paid to the country's mythology, what people believed about the country, including what people thought made the country great or could make the country great. But an honest reflection on the country's history showed how nationalism and patriotism had been used by the government and the elite to suppress and manipulate people. The mythologies had been developed in the first place in order to convince people the country was already giving people what they wanted. There was, therefore, a commitment to prevent patriotism and nationalism from being used to suppress criticism or frank discussion.

In the social and religious realm, the Christian community took comfort in the fact that their representatives on religious issues would no longer be tied with the party of the exploitative Capitalists. They felt that their voice would be heard more clearly and that more constructive conversations would result. By overturning the principle of majority rule and replacing it with a more complete and sincere respect for different views and faiths, they realized that their freedom to worship would be safe even if there were somehow a major shift in the beliefs of the people from one generation to the next. Among the large number of Christian followers of the movement, there was a strong sense that the change would allow churches to focus on spiritual matters and their followers instead of worrying so much about what the rest of the country was doing. Meanwhile, non-Christians also felt like an oppressive weight would be lifted, since they would no longer be represented on social and religious issues by people advocating a Christian agenda.

Despite decent if not-yet-overwhelming support, optimism that change could be achieved in the United States was still limited. The Constitution was a big obstacle, having been designed to prevent such fundamental change. What drove many people to keep up the fight, however, was the country's mythology, the sense that the country and its people were special and had an important role to play in leading the world to a better form of government and society. It was a notion that went back to the country's original colonists, to the Pilgrims, the Puritans, and the Penns. It was a popular sentiment that got invoked as part of the defense of the Constitution. In *Federalist Papers No. 10,* James Madison wrote:

But why is the experiment of an extended republic to be rejected, merely because it may comprise what is new? Is it not the glory of the people of America, that, whilst they have paid a decent regard to the opinions of former times and other nations, they have not suffered a blind veneration for antiquity, for custom, or for names, to overrule the suggestions of their own good sense, the knowledge of their own situation, and the lessons of their own experience?

The town halls and public meetings continued. There was still plenty of thinking to be worked out. And the hope was that the more people got involved in the conversations about what the country could be, the more support there would be. But if anything was going to happen beyond discussions, the halls of true power would have to be hacked.

To explore different political options, the movement organized what they at first called the "Utopia Party." After all, the goal of the movement was nothing less than to push forward the recurring utopian ambitions of the country. However, the country had changed much since 1891, when Oscar Wilde wrote in his essay *The Soul of Man under Socialism* that "A map of the world that does not include Utopia is not worth glancing at." The Capitalists had worked hard to suppress creative thinking that would challenge their status, a natural defense mechanism for any elite. So by the 1980s, the word "Utopia" (from Greek οὐτόπος, meaning "no place") was being used with a negative connotation, to refer to people's ideas that were outlandish and unattainable, not worth the risk trying. So facing a certain amount of backlash and realizing the enormous expectations they were setting by declaring their interest in jumping directly to a Utopia, it was decided the intent and ambitions needed clarifying.

The goal was to break from the current stagnation imposed on the country by its current form of government, which made change—or even the suggestion that change was necessary—difficult to achieve and sustain. Once freed, it was hoped that the country could continue to move forward in search of the "more perfect union" promised in the preamble to the Constitution. What name could they use to signify that?

The solution eventually hit upon seemed perfectly in fitting with the movement's tendency toward inclusivity. The key was a word that came from the Chinook Natives of Washington and Oregon: *alki,* which means "eventually" or "by and by." The first full colony attempted in the Seattle area in fact was called "New York Alki," demonstrating the colonists' ambitions to create a city that would become as great as New York some day, until the city decided to explore and develop its own path and identity. By pairing *alki* with *Utopia,* a new word, "Utopialki," was coined to express the intent that "someday" the country would become the Utopia it had longed for since the early colonists arrived on the shores of the continent. The new word essentially meant that the people were "on their way to Utopia." The principle repeated the idea expressed by H.G. Wells in his novel *A Modern Utopia* in 1901, in which he wrote that "the Modern Utopia must be not static but kinetic, must shape not as a permanent state but as a hopeful stage leading to a long ascent of stages." It expressed the view that the perfect Utopia was impossible but we should never stop moving closer toward it.

While working toward a goal that inspired much emotion and passion, the new Utopialki Party remained committed to keeping the rhetoric respectful and about systems instead of an attack on individuals. Most important was keeping any form of actual violence completely out of the movement. The movement was about ideas and ideals, not about getting any sort of justice from people who may have benefited from the systems either by luck or even through direct manipulation or exploitation. There would be no gangs going around beating up leaders of the old systems and seizing their "ill-gotten" property. It was about creating new rules to live by, not judging people's past actions by new standards. The worst crime of Capitalist leaders was self-esteem, which was obviously no crime at all. They believed that they deserved just as much privilege and security as any elite did throughout history and then took advantage of the rules of the game to do whatever it took to achieve it.

In most cases, it is safe to imagine people were acting sincerely in ways they thought were best for the country. They believed, as many in the 1980s believed, that power and wealth were genuinely best if limited to a few "worthy" hands. Even Alexander Hamilton, who introduced the tight dependency by the government on the bankers, wasn't acting out of evil intent when he raised the power and influence of them. He acted out of self-interest to some extent (no crime in that) but also in his belief in a strong elite class. As Franklin Roosevelt said in 1932: "It is not necessary for us in any way to discredit the great financial genius of Alexander Hamilton or the school of thought of the early Federalists to point out that they were frank in their belief that certain sections of the nation and certain individuals within those sections were more fitted than others to conduct Government."[47] Thomas Jefferson himself, one of Hamilton's nemeses, acknowledged that slavery was morally wrong and demonstrated himself incapable of ending it not only in the nation he helped form but also in his own personal life. Even great men are powerless sometimes against the forces of their society. There is no reason to punish them or their modern equivalents. It would be better to exert one's energies on reforming the society and its systems that encouraged such thinking and behavior.

Keeping the debate from becoming violent and directed at individuals instead of ideas was something that made the movement stand out from the French Revolution and the Russian Revolution. Restoring order after these movements got out of hand gave a small minority an opening to hijack and pervert the ideals of the people to their own purposes. Everyone knew that, if ever things turned violent, the movement was over, and it would fall prey to the same abuses of those revolutions. Fortunately the movement had a foundation that it could turn to whenever things started to go wrong. Whenever a disagreement started to get heated, people were trained to take a step back and start from the principles. As long as people could agree that the objectives of Freedom and Opportunity were at the heart of anything the country did, then they always had some place to retreat back to. When people did disagree with these foundational principles, the conversation tended to get interesting rather than heated. Many valuable ideas and innovations evolved from these disagreements. They helped anticipate future issues and deal with them in advance.

CHAPTER 3

Transition

A tense election to see if the will of the people can break through to implement real change. Work on a fair and effective economic transition proceeds apace. Employment and consumption are adapted to match the ideals of Freedom and Opportunity for all.

Election of 1984

The new Utopialki Party set about figuring out what it was going to take to push the country out of its current rut and into a new chapter. Even before planning how to advance change politically, the problem they encountered was that most of the country was simply too timid about change. Most people would rather suffer with the system they had than experiment with something new. It didn't look like the movement was going to be able to get ¾ of all states to ratify amendments to the Constitution, assuming it could even pass through Congress. Changing the whole country seemed out of reach. So instead, there was talk of a few states seceding to create their own new country on the new principles. When discussing this idea, it was made very clear from the beginning that this would not be an agreeable arrangement unless the split were managed amicably. The cultural and commercial links between the different states in the United States were too important. Plus there was the fact that the Supreme Court had ruled reasonably clearly that states could not secede from the United States without approval from Congress.

The party first figured out which states it thought could have enough support for secession. They then focused their resources on making sure that support was there and ready to show up at the polls. They also had to make sure there was enough support and good will in Congress to approve the secession. With the old representation model, it was a numbers game, making sure candidates supporting the cause were in the right elections and then driving support to those candidates. Because the question was just a single issue (a big one, but just one), the preferred path for the party was to find a candidate in one or both of the major parties to support in the primaries. In the rare cases, however, where there were no candidates who would support the Utopialki plan, the party ran their own challengers.

Winning enough support for secession from a single election seemed like a long shot, since only one third of the Senate was up for reelection. What brought it within range was the fact that many of the senators whose terms were not ending publicly supported the movement, such was its appeal.

The party secured candidates in as many of the elections as possible and then mobilized voters for the primary elections. The phone center that had been used to coordinate the meetings across the country was repurposed to act also as the hub for a new political action group and as a clearinghouse for information about different candidates in the 1984 elections. They were available to answer which primary candidates in state and federal elections would support moving toward secession so that voters had information they could trust. The day before each of the primary elections, they ran ads in local newspapers highlighting the candidates who supported the movement so everyone had the latest information clear before them. In the final tally, in the cases where a movement candidate was running against a candidate who was opposed to the movement, the candidate in favor of it won 60% of the time. It was enough for most people to consider the primaries a success and give confidence going into the final elections in November.

Not since the fight for approval of the Constitution had a vote held nearly as much significance. But as important as the issue was, it was still only one issue among many that informed people's decisions about candidates. The movement's issue would only become relevant if enough states voted to support the secession referendum. So even though the party once again ran newspaper advertisements listing the supporting candidates, it wasn't always easy for voters to choose that candidate. Never had the representation failures of the old system been so clear. But even with this difficulty, Utopialki-supporting candidates ended up winning 76% of the Congressional elections. With existing support already in the Congress, it was starting to look like there might be a chance.

When it came time to vote on secession in the general election, support was very solid in the western states, where the issue typically came up as a referendum, and in some of the New England states, including New York

State. But it was only in California, Hawaii (the only state where the issue had to pass through the state legislature), Washington, and Oregon that it passed. In the other states, it came down to fear and uncertainty of change, the major campaign message of the opposition. The uncertainty of a new system outweighed the certainty of another depression. With such a small number of states passing the referendum, there was a real risk of failing to meet the minimum population specified by most of the states' referendums. If any of these states had failed to pass, the adventure would have had to wait until another election. But as it turned out, they just squeaked by.

The action next moved to the Congress. The bill that was being considered would sanction the secession of the four states and provide assurances for positive relations with open borders and open trade. It also called for the transfer of national debt proportional to the population being "lost." While this was designed to help achieve positive relations with the parent country, it was also something that most people in the Utopialki Party supported as the "right" thing to do.

With as long as the country had been debating and discussing the issue, the vote proceeded quickly in Congress. But it was still very tense. By Utopialki Party count, the votes were there, but there was no telling whether the politicians would keep their campaign promises. Their past record offered little comfort. In the Senate, the bill passed by a 2-vote margin, meaning that Vice President Bush didn't need to cast the deciding vote. In the House of Representatives, the vote on February 11, 1985, won with just a 5-vote margin. In the end, no one who promised to support the bill voted against it. When the outcome was unclear, they didn't want to be the deciding vote, and, when it became clear it was going to pass, they didn't want to be on the wrong side of history.

It now came down to President Reagan. He had been challenged by Walter Mondale (running with Geraldine Ferraro, the first female nominated for Vice President by a major party), who gained votes by supporting the Utopialki movement. But even with Reagan losing his home state of California, he edged out Mondale. With support for Utopialki below 50% in most states, the Electoral College system worked against the movement, as it always had against third parties and often against the will of the people.

As the latest face of the party pushing fear of change, the threat of a Reagan veto was a real one. It was clear that there were nowhere near enough votes in Congress to override. In the campaign Reagan billed himself as the new Abraham Lincoln, vowing to keep the union together at all costs. It didn't help that Reagan's home state was one where the referendum had passed, a state that would be leaving the cherished union. But fortunately Reagan delayed vetoing the bill, taking time to feel out the wealthy and ruling elite before committing himself to an historical act one way or the other. As it turned out, there were just enough outspoken leaders in the upper classes who were behind the movement to make the decision murky for the President. In the end he decided not to overrule the decision of the states and Congress, thus securing his place in history. He signed the bill on May 1, 1985. This was International Workers Day, which most presidents since 1959 had tried to recognize as Loyalty Day to weaken the recognition of the plight of labor. Some people have suggested he timed it for that day intentionally to foster doubt and raise questions about connections with Soviet Communism.

The referendums spelled out a planned secession by 1990 (5 years from the final passage of the bill), unless all states involved agreed to move earlier. This transition period would be necessary to work out as many of the real-world issues and complications expected in this sort of change and to introduce economic changes gradually.

Despite the fact that Utopialki was designed to be quintessentially "American," with its emphasis on Freedom and the use of the free market and money to drive the political engine, the attack on the movement as a stepping stone to Communism was persistent throughout the debates. Opponents were prepared to declare, "I told you so," when, later in May 1985, Mikhail Gorbachev gave a speech in Leningrad advocating broad reforms in his country. The first leader of the Soviet Union born after the Russian Revolution, Gorbachev announced that the economy had stalled and advocated serious reform. He also urged that economic reform would be meaningless without political reform. Gorbachev's program of *glasnost* (openness), *perestroika* (restructuring), *demokratizatsiya* (democratization), and *uskoreniye* (acceleration of economic development) at a Communist Party meeting in February 1986 sparked a sense of urgency in the Utopialki movement. It looked like the Soviet Union may grab hold of the principles of Utopialki and implement them on their own. In fact, we found out decades later that Soviet diplomats did approach people involved in the Utopialki movement for ideas but were firmly asked to keep their distance.

The movement in the United States felt it was important to implement their system before the Soviet Union had a chance to work out their changes. They didn't want ideological confusion and Cold War nationalism to interfere with the success of the movement. Like the Space Race put pressure on the US to invest in education, pressure from the Soviet Union pushed the states to move the secession date up to February 11, 1990. This new date was chosen to celebrate the final Congress vote instead of the Reagan signing.

Shortly after Reagan signed the bill sanctioning the secession, an independent movement gathered steam in Canada to try to introduce similar economic and political reforms there. As momentum grew and support appeared strong, the Canadian-movement leaders started to show up at Utopialki planning events, suggesting the possibility of the four states joining a reformed Canada. On the surface, it seemed like a reasonable idea. The states could definitely benefit from being part of a larger economic unit. The problem was a matter of national identity. The people in the US states were not prepared to sign up to the identity and history of Canada. Except for confusion on the whole British monarchy being the head of state, few people had any serious issue with Canada. It was just that it wasn't part of their identity. The four seceding states could not merge with a larger entity without losing their own unique historical legacy.

Nations and nationality served many purposes. On a personal level, they were often tied very closely to one's identity. The "nation" was a package of cultural values and ideas passed down through its history and traditions that people who grew up in that environment connected with. Separate and distinct from this cultural meaning, nations were also defined political boundaries with a government and a ruling elite. What a nation's government did and how it behaved were important to people not only because of its impact on them as citizens but also because it impacted the identity of the nation that many relied on to help define themselves. The confusion between these two uses of nationality gave the ruling elite and their governments enormous power to manipulate people.

The answer to questions about national identity raised by Canada's request for integration seemed both obvious and outlandish. The two competing purposes of nationalism (personal identity and government) had to be separated to prevent nationalism and patriotism from being exploited for political expediency. To this end the new government and territory would decline a unified national identity and its associated icons that could be exploited like the US elite and (to a much more sinister degree) Nazi Germany had done. There would be no new national flag. The new country would remain nameless, allowing individuals to take up any cultural identity they chose without confusion, prejudice, or pressure. Canadians could live anywhere and still consider themselves Canadian, without having to append any other national identity or bother others by muddying some other identity with their unique characteristics. This presented some awkwardness in how to refer to the area using the new system. Some still called it Utopialki, others referred to it as the "un-Nation," and still others as the "unincorporated territory." Which term was used really depended on the context and personal preferences.

It was a resolution that made it possible also to accept Mexico into the new un-Nation as well. They had their own movement along the same lines as Canada and had been pressing to join. It was soon decided that Canada and

Mexico would join (or secede from their current countries) together on February 11, 1991—one year after the states seceded from the United States. Tying the entry of these two different economies together would help transition all three regions into a more balanced economy without putting too much burden on the original seceding states.

Economic transition

As soon as the secession bill was signed, work began on the transition plan. While much of the framework had already been worked out, the number of details that remained was staggering. The effort was facilitated immensely by the new political concepts. During all the town halls and public meetings, a good number of potential "lobbyists" rose to the surface. They helped to make the political transition fairly straightforward even without access to most of the "talent" of Washington, DC. Everyone had become accustomed to breaking topics down into different interest groups to approach questions in a balanced manner, so by the time the transition was over, most people were pretty comfortable with the new approach to political decision-making. Predictably, the economic matters were much more difficult. Determining the final state was the easiest part; getting there seemed almost impossible at times. But that is why the transition period was so long—to work out all the details and allow people an opportunity to acclimate to new ways of making decisions.

As expected, there was plenty of historical data to determine what percentage of the economy was committed to the sort of activity now classed as "investment" versus what was used for "consumption." It was also easy to calculate an expected number of available person hours that were to form the basis for the new currencies. More difficult was determining modifiers for scarce resources. In many cases, placeholder estimates were made, fully expecting them to change as a better understanding of scarcity and replacement potential developed.

There was, however, nothing that compared to the headaches of moving from an exploitative economic model with an enormous disparity of wealth between those willing to manipulate and those being manipulated into a model where opportunity was maximized for all citizens. Since there was no interest in punishing "successful" people in the old model, the transition plan had to come up with a fair and responsible way to accommodate pre-existing wealth without perpetuating the disparity in the new system.

The first form of pre-existing wealth confronted was property. The United States had long considered the protection of property as one of its core principles. In fact the inalienable rights of "life, liberty and the pursuit of happiness" in the Declaration of Independence became protections for "life, liberty and property" in the Bill of Rights. Protecting property was something that the wealthy and ruling elite were particularly keen on since they owned an ever-increasing percentage of the country's property. They had often used the defense of "property" as a means to defend their privileges and powers. The most egregious example was the southern landowners' insistence that their right to own, sell, and transport slaves was protected as property. Obviously such extreme concepts of property would not be respected. But the popular and practical aspect of personal property was still valued in the new society. Just as before, the government—such as it was—would not be endowed with any right to seize property except in the cases when property was acquired illegally or with fair compensation as part of a reconsideration settlement.

Personal unfixed property was still completely covered in the normal protections. This was just about anything most people would first think of as property. No one was going to take someone's great-grandfather's watch away from them. Real estate (land, buildings, etc.), on the other hand, was more complicated. Starting with the assumption that ownership of one's own land and home were an important component of Freedom and Opportunity, the challenge was to develop some plan for land ownership that didn't open the whole system up to the formation of a new form of landed elite. Once a family could claim hereditary ownership of land, it could serve as the foundation for empires and a source of power and control over other people's lives. After exhausting countless hours trying to make it work, a retreat was in order to re-evaluate the virtues of home ownership.

For most people, home ownership meant security. The home provided financial security, a store of wealth that could be leveraged later in life, either by selling or simply living rent-free. Home ownership also meant not having to live at the mercy of the whims of a landlord who often had too much control over what someone could do in their home and too much power to evict people from their homes. However, the virtues of home ownership were exaggerated for the benefit of the banks. Mortgages were big business and offered significant profits, allowing banks to score big off the dreams of the middle class. In reality, home ownership could cause as much turmoil as security. If a home owner bought at the wrong time or suffered an uninsured disaster or got into a house that needed a lot of repairs, it could suck the life and savings out of the owner. With banks no longer promoting the idea of home ownership as something more than it was, and with financial security provided for anyone willing to work, the only remaining virtue of home ownership that had to be provided was the sense of permanence and control offered by home ownership. This was an easy matter.

People would "own" their homes (any place of residence) in the sense that they could not be kicked out. There would be no landlords or banks whose rights and interests came ahead of residents'. And they had a high degree of freedom on what enhancements and changes they could make to it. Instead of buying a house outright or having a bank buy the house and then slowly pay the bank several times over for the house, "owners" would commit a fixed amount of their consumer income each month, somewhat like rent in the old economy. Just as before, the amount to be paid would be determined by the free market. It was simply a way for people to decide how to allocate limited resources among themselves that allowed people both flexibility and security. They could move around if they chose and couldn't be forced to move out to suit someone else's interests.

For people who had bought into the propaganda of the banks, it was a difficult change to accept, but, with time, people adjusted. The transition from privately owned real estate to non-ownership had to be resolved, however. Some people had worked hard their entire life to achieve home ownership, and no one wanted to take that away from them. So a plan was designed to "reward" people for home ownership during an extended transition period. The value of the home owned by a person minus any amount still owed on a mortgage was converted to a monthly amount—similar to how a monthly mortgage had been calculated. In the first year after secession, that person got that much extra per month that they could use for paying rent on a property. Typically it was the same property they owned before. Even though the money could be used only on rent, this was an enormous advantage compared to people who owned nothing before the secession since it freed up consumer money for other purposes. Over the next four years, the monthly amount provided for previous ownership would drop by 25% so that by the end of the fourth year, the advantage would have expired. This way, people got payback from their past investments without imposing a long-term advantage that could foster elitism.

Having achieved agreement (or at least acceptance) for transferring home ownership to the non-ownership model, the solution was used for other forms of stored wealth, including most forms of personal savings and even the value of businesses owned. Special, and rather complex, transitions had to be created for investments outside of the unincorporated territory and for foreign-owned companies and resources within the territory. Like just about everything else in the new economic model, however, these arrangements were much less complex than the web of legal agreements required to manage business operations in the Capitalist economy.

Entrepreneurs and business owners enjoyed the same thrills in developing new products and solving business challenges as they did before. Now, however, they received much better feedback and trust from consumers. They were also under no pressure to produce profits, allowing them to focus more sincerely on helping customers and providing real value. In fact, some of the most admired company leaders were those who transitioned a company out of existence, freeing up resources for the country to put elsewhere. But for the most part, businesses were much more stable under the new economy.

Despite these lifestyle enhancements, it was always anticipated that a number of people—particularly those with a great deal of wealth—would not take well to the proposed changes. They had gotten used to being above the rest of society and weren't convinced that the new economy would ultimately produce a more fulfilling and satisfying life. They were fixated on what they thought they were giving up. No attempt was made or even considered to restrain these people or anyone else from leaving the unincorporated territories. The only thing that was asked of people wanting to leave before secession was that they advise the emigration office of their intent and what types of wealth they were taking with them and what they were leaving behind. This was only because the transition involved so many complex movements of wealth that they wanted to be able to adjust to changes.

Immigration was another matter to work through. With the idea of nations and national identity eliminated as a driving force in decision-making, there was little ground to forbid immigration. In fact with the restructuring of the economy, with an emphasis on maximizing individual potential, people were likely to become the most valuable asset. But as Canada and Mexico also illustrated, there was definite potential to expand into new territory. Anyone who was enthusiastic enough about Utopialki to move to the unincorporated territories would make a valuable asset in future voting wherever they may be coming from. For this reason primarily, the "official" message out of the unincorporated territory was an encouragement that interested migrants focus on selling the idea of secession to their friends and neighbors at home instead of unsettling their lives to transfer to a new home. Knowing how important money was in United States politics, this request even extended to the large number of wealthy people who wanted to get in on the Utopialki lifestyle. With all that said, however, if people came anyway, they were welcomed. For example, many people crossed the border into Mexico because of the warm weather and enormous amount of (rather thrilling) development work taking place there.

Another significant change in the new economy for some people was the task of keeping track of hours worked. Soon, however, new technology made it dramatically less obtrusive to the point that most people found the exercise provided vastly more benefit than inconvenience. It helped them make better-informed decisions about how much time they were spending and wanted to spend working versus pursuing other interests. In fact, without the social pressure and the need to deal with financial uncertainty, the decision on how much to work changed dramatically. Most people felt they needed to buy less, since they were no longer bombarded with advertising trying to convince them otherwise; so in many cases, it came down to how much they enjoyed the work and the contributions they were making to society versus the pleasure they could take from other uses of their time.

There were, however, some exceptions made to the hourly wage rule. One of the more interesting exceptions was afforded to farmers. The nature of their work and their independent lifestyle didn't lend itself well to keeping track of hours worked. Instead they would be paid as before, by their output. However, the price paid for their output was calibrated to roughly work out to what they would make if they were paid by the hour. Adjustments were naturally made to account for local weather and for alternative methods used, such as organic farming. The big difference versus before was that the risk would be lifted from them in order to encourage them to keep producing. They didn't have to go into debt in order to plant the seed. They were protected against losses from disaster. And they had access to shared equipment to help ensure that they worked as productively as they could.

Employment and consumption

With the date of secession creeping ever closer, another system that needed to be built out was employment-support services. From the beginning, this was envisioned as a sort of career coach and enabler. They would not only help and encourage people to determine their career goals and interests but also be empowered to help people achieve them, navigating the complex paths and options. This was intended to include helping people secure investment capital and partners to start up new enterprises. In short, it was designed to capture benefits from a more diverse set of skills, interests, and perspectives. Being able to sell an idea and manipulate markets (consumer, labor, capital, etc.) were no longer favored over other skills.

One of the tools the Employment Support Office (ESO) leveraged—as did enterprises and individuals—was flexibility in mixing and matching people to different combinations of positions at different enterprises. In the old system, there had been an attempt to get Capitalists to take some responsibility for the social costs associated with their business, which meant there were a number of fixed costs per employee, including healthcare and several different "taxes." These fixed costs meant two employees combining to work 40 hours cost more than a single employee. But in the new economy, it would cost an enterprise the same for 40 employees working one hour each as it would cost for one employee working 40 hours because there were few fixed costs. There were, of course, training costs, but since it was an advantage to the enterprise to have more people understanding the nature of each role, it was typically not much of an obstacle.

As anticipated, this flexibility allowed for the matching of onerous jobs with more sedentary jobs to help spread out the weight of that burden. It also meant more diversity for other jobs as well. For example, many people involved in research or science started to split their time to include either teaching or some other way to share their knowledge and interests with the public, including serving as tour guides. Walking through an archaeological site is far more interesting when you have the top archaeologist for the project as your guide. His or her passion for the topic is quickly contagious.

There were two very different groups that urgently needed employment-support services ahead of the secession. The first of these were the "unskilled" unemployed. The old economy had beaten the will and hope out of many of them. Working was required in the new economy, since people who were unwilling to work would not get paid. To encourage them to engage again with the world, it was typically just a matter of demonstrating true and sincere care and interest in their case and inspiring them to the new possibilities. Giving hope in the future to someone who had none is hugely motivating.

The other group that needed help from the ESO was former Capitalists, senior management, and people of "independent means." Most of them, of course, stayed in positions of management or successfully transferred into the role of Capitalist in the new democratic sense and, therefore, needed no help. If they didn't make a clean transition, however, they could be quite difficult to work with. In the old economy, opportunities had come easily to them, and they felt entitled to the same sort of special treatment in the new economy. The source of their advantage typically was their connections (who they knew), more than any particularly or unusually demanded skill. Their list of skills were often topped by the ability to convince board members and company owners that they provided high value and warning them how bad things could get without them around. But there were few positions in the new economy where these talents were important. Those who stayed and embraced the new work ethic, however, found an ESO just as anxious and interested in helping them find productive and fulfilling work as they were in helping anyone else. No one looked down on the old wealthy elite. There were definitely positions in the new society for them; it was just a matter of their willingness to be part of society instead of above it, looking down, refusing to work.

The public education system also had to be reformed as part of the transition. In the United States, public school was more about telling children what to think than helping them learn how to think for themselves. It was more about encouraging people to fit in than discovering their own personality and identity. This was because the power and privilege of the elite relied on people's belief in the mythology of the country, and a homogenous population made politics, exploiting labor, and advertising easier. It came at a very high price, however. Innovation and new ideas were limited by the attempts at standardization. And the suppression of personal identity created a great deal of anxiety among young people. It was the same sort of issues adults faced in the 1950s, under pressure to conform to a "normal" that was humanly impossible. The pressure drove increasing numbers of adults of the time to psychiatrists. Like the adults, children felt a great deal of anxiety in public school trying to fit in. It's a wonder more kids didn't lose all hope and lash out violently against such inhumanity. Such actions don't help.

With more resources available and a different desired outcome, the new society could pursue a more diverse approach to teaching. Education shifted its priority away from indoctrination and instead emphasized individuality and the ability to think independently. It was expected—and we've since seen—that focusing on individuality and free thought would take away a lot of the pressure to fit in and the pain of not fitting in. It also became possible to accommodate different learning approaches for different types of learners, to eliminate most long-held biases and further increase the diversity of talent in the population. Most of these changes were designed to help young people explore their interests and, therefore, prepare them to pursue their own path. In most cases, "young adults" started talking with their local ESO in their mid-teens to think about what sort of work they may want to do as adults and how to get there. Gone were the days when it was every man, woman, and child for him or herself.

Advertising, too, experienced a dramatic change. In the old system, most information people received was intended to manipulate them. It was true of political messaging, shockingly true of news outlets, and, of course, particularly true of advertising. The volume of products that people were told were absolutely essential for just about everyone to own was overwhelming. Companies were desperate to sell in order to turn a high profit, and this desperation manifested itself in increasingly aggressive advertising and marketing tactics. With no way to differentiate between honest and sincere advertisers versus desperate advertisers, people were as likely to be duped as to find the right product for them.

The new economy had a real advantage in this respect. Companies were no longer desperate to sell, and the mindless consumption needed to drive the traditional Capitalist economy was no longer a priority. In the new economy, nothing created more excitement than the prospect of eliminating unnecessary work and spending. It no longer created an economic crisis but did free up people and resources for other activity. Creating work was no longer considered a virtue. Meanwhile, with innovation unleashed, there were plenty of new and exciting products that could genuinely improve people's happiness or lives. It was for the purpose of getting the right product in the hands of consumers that the Consumer Support Line (CSL) was started.

The Consumer Support Line was designed to replace most of the functions of marketing and advertising. Essentially, if someone was looking for a specific product, instead of relying on their own memory of conscious and subconscious messaging they might have received from past advertising, people could call (later offered over the Internet as well) the CSL for help deciding on the best product for their needs. CSL agents provided consumers with the vast product expertise that was missing in the traditional Capitalism of the United States. This was, of course, a charged service, but since consumers were not forced to pay for the marketing that was built into the old prices, it was a great bargain. Quite distinct from the never-ending insistence of advertising that people constantly buy new products, the biggest complaint people have had about the CSL has been that, often times, the agents try too hard to convince a caller that he or she wouldn't ever use the item being shopped for.

The CSL, however, could not replace all functions of marketing. If someone didn't know a type of product or service existed, there would be no reason for them to call the CSL about it. The same would apply if there were a dramatic change in a product's price or functionality that opened it up to a new segment of the market. In the old economy, this sort of marketing required an extra dose of attention-getting because it had to awaken people to a new reality—not just help them make decisions based on their current understanding of things. Because people were increasingly skeptical of advertising and most media paid for by advertising, it was extremely difficult for new product information to break through in the old model.

In the new economy, trade and hobby magazines (later also taken to the Internet) could be used much more effectively because they were more trustworthy. The integrity of magazine writers was no longer questioned by their proximity to advertisers. Instead they were paid entirely by consumers interested in receiving reliable information about product trends. These journals could also, therefore, be used to help drive "investment" money into new product ideas. Passions were encouraged and leveraged more than ever before.

Another part of the transition that everyone knew was going to be difficult was the new pricing scheme. It was much more difficult for consumers than from a technical or practical standpoint. To help consumers prepare for the change in pricing, as soon as the new pricing became available, retailers started listing both the current price and the future price on packaging and in price lists. For some people stuck in the thinking of the old economy, this practice did encourage some hoarding until they realized that the new economy would not provide much, if any, return for their troubles.

Seeing the new prices created panic, as people noticed the dramatic increase in the price of many food items. It demonstrated clearly how inefficient much of food harvesting had remained, masked by the availability of low-cost labor. The concern was mitigated by a couple of factors. First, people realized that many other items they were used to buying and paying for were dropping in price significantly. This was mostly because research and development, profit, marketing, and advertising were no longer factored into the price. Second, the "sticker shock" inspired investment in new ways to reduce the labor costs in certain types of farming. It was disturbing how little attention had been paid to these back-breaking jobs, jobs that had been done mostly by low-wage-earning immigrants. As long as corporations were able to take advantage of desperate people, there was little incentive to innovate. That changed with the new economy.

While people had to get used to a new pricing system anyway, it was a good time to reevaluate the use of the English units of measurement. The advantages of the metric system were always clear. At the top of the list was the fact that they were much easier to use. There were no conversions to remember between meters and kilometers like there had been between feet, inches, and miles. When the education system in the United States was in such a bad state, it could be argued that sneaking arithmetic and memory exercises onto people served a purpose. But with education a higher priority, this no longer made sense. There was also no nationalism that needed to be accommodated in keeping with the old units. So along with dual pricing, dual units of measurement started to appear ahead of the secession to allow people to acclimate to the change.

The transition also resolved the financing for a number of "public" services. Fire, police, and emergency rooms were some of the least controversial. In the previous system, taxes were collected to support these services. People had no choice but to pay, and it was difficult to learn and express dissatisfaction with how the money was spent. One option was to make the funding for these services entirely dependent upon the free market for investing. But the risk of not having the funding was simply too high to leave it to chance. It was easy to imagine people opting out of funding these services with the assumption that, as important as they were, someone else surely would feel compelled to step up. To avoid these games with public safety, a new approach was needed.

Eventually a compromise position between the two options was hit upon. To take a simple example, all residents in an area covered by fire protection would contribute to the support of the public fire protection service. In addition to the normal channels to express discontent with something (filing a reconsideration case), people could also simply refuse to make their contribution. They could and would typically be expected to append a statement to their refusal to make clear their dispute. The catch was that money not contributed to the public service would not be available for any other purpose—it simply disappeared. Like most compromises, it was far from ideal but seemed to answer most of the requirements asked of it. It provided reliable funding and allowed for people to communicate their discontent clearly and forcefully by "opting out" of funding when they felt the need for it.

Even the ESO was funded this way, although not without some controversy. In this case it was imagined that even if everyone didn't use the service, everyone benefited from making sure people directed themselves into jobs that best suited their interests and talents. In actual fact, practically everyone used it at some point in their lives, but the public value was evident to most people anyway.

Services like education and roads were handled in a hybrid fashion. A portion of the funds were generated the same way as these other public services. Like the ESO, there was a clear case to be made for the public value of an educated population and reliable roads. Even the rare non-driver would typically receive deliveries and would therefore still benefit from maintained roads. The other part of the funds would come from fees associated with actual use. In the old economy, public school had to be free because otherwise, some people would not be able to afford it. Having solved that problem, it seemed natural that people who choose to have kids would pay more for their support. Of course, enhancements or expansions to these services were funded exclusively through investment funds.

A much more complicated issue was how health-care would be handled in the new economy. For starters, everyone would be covered for risks that everyone faced just by virtue of being human. After all, we are all human and suffer the same unpredictability associated with life. The same thing was true for damage incurred from most disasters. Practically all forms of preventive care were also covered. Anything that helped reduce the chance of more expensive medical treatments benefited the whole society.

What made healthcare complicated in the new economy as much as it was in the old was the lifestyle choices of people that put them at a greater risk of health problems. Smoking is an easy example to take up. Following the Freedom principles, it was impossible to simply ban smoking. And even with effective communication of the health risks associated with smoking and its addictive nature, some people still chose to do it. Steps were taken to limit the effect people's exercising of this freedom could have on other people's health, but there was still the question of healthcare for smokers. Should the public have to share the healthcare bill for extra treatment resulting from smoking? On the surface, the answer seemed to be to simply include an extra charge on cigarettes and other tobacco to cover the health implications.

While this seemed like an obvious solution in the case of smoking, it was less clear when the rule was applied elsewhere. For example, excessive alcohol increases health risks. Eating too much of the "wrong" foods increases health risks. Skiing increases the risks of breaking a leg. It was hard to imagine applying the cigarette rule to all of these (and a million more) cases. It was eventually decided (that may be overstating it since it is still a much-discussed topic) that all health services would be provided and that no additional tax would be applied to these personal choices.

Like other public services, a region's healthcare costs would come from investment contributions with the option to opt out of paying in protest. There remain, however, recurring discussions about offering certain incentives for healthy lifestyle choices.

Like basic healthcare, questions about taking care of people as they aged were easy enough. Everyone expected to grow old, and so there was little resistance to the idea of including provisions for that old age. Healthcare, as already described, was taken care of. A plan to afford people more free time later in life was needed. It was something many people had gotten used to in the old economy and demanded a provision for it in the new economy. At a certain age, people would start to receive compensation for hours beyond what they worked. The exact age would be adjusted regularly based on the current life expectancy. The number of rewarded hours would increase as the person aged, until a number of hours equivalent to the person's adult lifetime average was reached. This approach allowed people to slowly transition into retirement if they so chose. Of course, this meant an adjustment to the total amount of currency available to the population, but it was a compromise most people accepted in exchange for the end-of-life "perk."

After working out these and countless other similar challenges, the date of the secession (February 11, 1990) finally arrived. Although it had been a difficult voyage, very few people even considered the option of pushing it back to its original date. While there was no doubt that the event was going to be a major turning point in history, there was actually discussion as to how much of a big deal to make out of it. A big ceremony with a lot of fireworks, banners, and streamers was just the sort of nationalist propaganda that an exploitative nation would use to brush over discontent. It was not something anyone wanted the new government to get into the habit of doing. The answer was quite simple and completely consistent with the new society: Just let people act on their own and according to their own interests. The new Capitalists served as magnets for investment funds to be used for the public celebrations in different locations. In most areas the celebrations were, in fact, huge. It was clear to everyone that the human race itself was entering into a new stage of its cultural development. If the people had anything to say about it—and, of course, they had everything to say about it—the new economic and political models were going to be a big success.

CHAPTER 4

After the secession

The new market economy brings many compelling economic advantages to the people, lifting everyone. Without elite interests desperate for power and privilege, solving social issues becomes easier. There is truly a sense that the country has fulfilled its age-old promise to introduce something new and good to the world.

Economic implications

After the secession, the states slipped into the new economic system with no more difficulty than you'd expect from such a fundamental change to the economy. In fact, most aspects of the new economy worked very intuitively for a population used to living with a free market. The biggest adjustment was getting used to making decisions on investment funds. But once people realized that it was little different from decisions as a consumer, even that aspect of the new economy settled into the normal order of things. Adjusting to the positive implications of the new economy was even easier.

One of the significant benefits has been the dramatic expansion of innovation in the new economy. This isn't to say that innovation was lacking in the United States. In fact there were few countries that had more new businesses created per capita than the United States. But the United States also had a higher rate of failure of new companies than other top innovating countries. The old Capitalist model encouraged people to "innovate" new ideas to get money from people instead of ways to provide value to people. This stood in stark contrast to some economies in Scandinavia, where taxes were higher, more social services were provided, and, as a result, profits were less extreme. In these countries, innovation was still very strong yet tended to be driven by needs instead of opportunities. And more of their businesses succeeded as a result, often quite handsomely.

But innovation in Utopialki was at a whole different level than anything the old Capitalist model could offer. The economy leveraged the creative energies of a much-larger percentage of the population and provided more support to help people bring their ideas to fruition. The way the new free market operated also meant that innovation was sharply focused where it would have the greatest impact on the quality of life of the greatest number of people. No longer was innovation targeted toward improving the profits and comforts of a tiny wealthy minority.

Perhaps the most dramatic impact of the new economy was seen in industries where the cost of manufacturing was negligible compared to the costs of research and development. One such area was medicine. Once the formula and process have been worked out and the equipment acquired, the cost of manufacturing a pill is tiny. This was the cost people paid for medicines in the new economy, which had a profound impact on the costs of healthcare. This was in stark contrast to the old economy. In the United States, when someone went out to buy a pill, they had to pay for the research and development plus a high profit and marketing for the company that owned the patent for the medicine. Far from limiting funds for research with lower costs of medicine, however, the new economy gushed with funds to combat all sorts of ailments and conditions. Medical research has been a very common outlet for investment funds for anyone who knew someone suffering from a medical condition. The recent medical revolution with all its dramatic breakthroughs is typically attributed to the new economic model and its impact on innovation.

The software industry was another area with tiny manufacturing costs compared to development costs. The impact of the new economy on this industry (and the impact of this industry on the economy) is difficult to over-emphasize. Even without the new economy, the West Coast was poised to revolutionize computing. The region already had Microsoft (founded in 1975) and Apple (1976). They were in a great position to benefit from the take-off of the market for personal computers, which in 1982 was named *TIME Magazine*'s "Man of the Year" as people started to realize their potential. But the availability of practically any software product developed in the unincorporated territories at a negligible cost has led to a dramatic increase in productivity, changing not only how people use personal computers (and more recently other "smart" devices) but, as a result, how they live their lives and interact with other people. Meanwhile, exports of software were at world software prices, not Utopialki prices, and so contributed greatly to the ability to pay off the debt and achieve a strong balance of trade. After all, the region continued to have to interface with the old economy of the rest of the world.

The Internet and the new economy and society of Utopialki grew up on the same principles: freedom of movement, freedom of identity, and a free flow of ideas and technology. They quickly developed a strong symbiotic relationship, with each making the other stronger. Utopialki provided significant new public content and information, giving people a reason to engage with new online tools. Meanwhile the Internet provided Utopialki the perfect platform to manage much of its business and interactions between people. It greatly simplified the flow of information between individuals and the government, therefore expanding transparency.

The arts and entertainment industries experienced a dramatic change in the new economy as well. Music is available at practically no cost since the artists are compensated out of investment funds, and all that has to be covered by consumers of music on media (concerts were a different matter) is the costs of distribution, which became negligible with the Internet. Since the economy provided a renewed sense of community, other arts flourished with community beautification projects occurring all over the place, particularly in the neighborhoods that were the poorest before secession. As long as art was for public display, it could be commissioned from investment funds. Art of all varieties experienced its greatest boost whenever there was a slowdown in demand for consumer goods. In times when people were less inclined to buy personal items, they would shift consumer spending into community spending, and a good portion of that went toward the arts. It's hard to imagine how anyone could deny this was a much better reaction to declines in the consumer economy than how the old economy handled them (depression, recession, layoffs, hunger, suffering on a large scale, etc.).

Since television and movie development costs are now covered entirely by investment funds, they have become completely disconnected from the needs of advertising. This means that content no longer has to appeal to people's lowest instincts or urges in a constant drive for the viewers demanded by advertisers. As a result the occurrence of excessive violence or sexual content just for the purpose of selling an inferior program has declined dramatically. That doesn't mean that violence and sexual content have been eliminated as tools for effective storytelling, however. This was something that some Christian communities first objected to until they realized they could simply sponsor their own content that appealed to their tastes and values. Programming has become more responsive to what people really want to watch, not just what they might be instinctively drawn to. Simply put, if enough investment money can be gathered to develop a film concept (either for television or movies), it is made without much concern for how many viewers would watch it. But far from reducing quality, this direct popular involvement in decisions about what sort of programming is made has produced much more popular and creative entertainment. In the old economy, there was an ever-expanding array of channels but a declining number of unique and innovative programs worth watching. In the new economy, there seems to always be something new coming out that entertains and often expands people's minds as well.

The new economy, however, did pose some unique challenges to the entertainment industry. The most striking, perhaps, was how to find evil villains for stories taking place in the unincorporated territories. Without the profit motive to drive people into crime and without desperate people pushed to desperate acts to exploit and manipulate people, there wasn't anyone left to serve as clearly evil archetypes. In the early days after secession, most studios got around this problem by placing the action outside the unincorporated territories or in an historical context. Slowly, however, the studios have explored new ways to tell stories and establish drama without such clear good versus evil. It has made for much greater suspense, since it isn't clear how the story is going to end (most stories used to end with good defeating evil).

Another significant challenge came to the pornography and prostitution businesses. In the old economy, there was plenty of supply and demand for both pornography and prostitution. Because there was money to be made in it, "Capitalists" were willing to invest in it. And because people were desperate for work, there were people willing to participate. Meanwhile serious self-esteem issues, a by-product of the old economy, also spurred demand for sexual exploitation. With a new economy designed to build people up instead of tear them apart, the demand for pornography and prostitution dropped, but the real problem for these industries was on the supply side. With so many more interesting and rewarding options open to people, few wanted to take part. There was no way for the industry to increase compensation to lure people to the work. Traditional Capitalists would argue this was evidence of the failure of the new free-market economy:

people wanted something that was impossible to produce because no one was willing to work on it. But few people have actually made this argument, perhaps for obvious social reasons.

Another noteworthy development in the new economy was a backlash against disposable items. In the old economy, disposable items offered a level of convenience. Instead of cleaning or maintaining the item, it could simply be tossed away and replaced. They were also cheaper in the short-term than durable alternatives, putting them within reach of people who could not afford more expensive products. Since buying disposables over and over again cost more in the long run, however, it was another way Capitalists took advantage of the difficulties of the poor. But the environmental costs of the products were not incorporated into the prices. Instead, those costs fell on the public-at-large, which had to cover extra landfill costs and cope with the environmental impact. Once the new economy switched over and consumers were expected to pay for the disposal of products, people started looking for ways to reduce waste. People began to favor products that were built to last. They wanted to buy less, and what they bought they wanted to last longer, all without any loss in convenience or functionality. Innovation was demanded, so innovation was funded, and new products quickly emerged that better satisfied consumers.

Even products with regular technical innovations were designed to anticipate and accommodate much of the advances in technology. In the old economy, profits were greater on selling completely new items so products were designed to encourage waste. But now, for example, instead of having to replace the whole computer, people can often replace just a single component to be up to date. The change obviously has dramatically reduced the amount of garbage generated, but it also created many new and highly rewarding careers in servicing and upgrading products to make them last.

The new economy also fulfilled President Reagan's promise of wealth trickling down. In the United States, the theory didn't play out as Reagan had suggested it would. Giving money to the wealthy just increased the wealth gap between rich and poor while painfully increasing the amount of the country's debt. There were some who suggested this was part of a master plan to eventually rack up so much debt that programs designed to protect the people from the abuses of corporations would have to be defunded. But in Utopialki, the economic system worked beautifully to help ensure luxury goods settled where they could provide the greatest satisfaction. As mentioned before, there was no forced transfer of personal, unfixed property. No one came along and tried to take anything away from anyone because of some pre-ordained property limit. Many people actually decided to convert other forms of wealth into personal property *before* secession, because they preferred the flexibility offered by personal property over the benefits offered by other forms of wealth.

The challenge *after* secession, however, was finding a place to store all that "stuff." People had to decide if they wanted to pay for enough space to keep everything. If the stuff was important, people found a place for it. If it wasn't, they got rid of it. Depending on what it was, they gave it to a friend, gave to a community organization, or advertised and gave it to someone who could make use of it. It was the best sort of trickling down of wealth, transferring property that held little value to the original owner to someone who could make better use of it.

Religion and social issues

After secession, there was a brief period of mass migration away from religion. A majority of the people leaving the faith were ones who had identified with and participated sporadically in Christianity because of the social pressure and advantages of doing so instead of sincere belief. In addition there were some who felt spiritually manipulated by the attempts of some of the Christian "leadership" to leverage religious belief for political advantage. But when churches no longer had to fight to bring a nation into alignment with their vision and were no longer distracted by pretenders to the faith, they were able to focus instead on the spiritual needs of their true followers. Churches became a safer place for people to discuss spiritual matters with other members. It was this strong support system that has been credited with the reawakening of religious interest in the mid-1990s.

Without the distraction of church leadership with political aspirations, working through social issues became easier as well. Much of the conflict in the United States over social issues was manufactured and escalated for political purposes. People would create animosity between different groups to win votes and gain the privileges and prestige that went with political leadership. As a result, it was not uncommon to see people preaching certain values publicly to drive political support and then practice the exact opposite in their personal lives, hoping no one would notice. It did significant harm not only to the ability of the country to leverage its incredible diversity but also to

Christianity, making it look more hateful and unaccepting than Jesus would have recognized. Once the political benefits of such manipulation disappeared, both the people and Christianity recovered, making issues that seemed impossible to resolve more manageable.

Abortion is a good example of an issue that the United States seemed incapable of resolving because it kept being framed in religious terms. The debate obscured the fact that, on one part of the issue, everyone agreed: late-term abortions should be kept to a minimum, eliminated entirely if at all medically possible. Ironically attempts to impose the moral view of a minority on the majority often had the effect of increasing abortions. While the issue was significantly complicated by the high incidence of poverty, rape, and cases where there was a choice between the life of the mother and the potential life of the fetus, most of the debate hinged on when to put the beginning of life. Some took the scientific approach and put it late. Others, more philosophical or religious, put it as early as conception. Some on the fringes put it earlier still.

But one's choice of where to place it was not so much a function of science but one's beliefs and values elsewhere, including where one stood on the topic of recreational sex and the responsibility to ensure a child brought into the world would be properly taken care of. Because religious leadership (ironically almost always male) was trying to divide the country to take advantage of fear and hatred to win votes instead of solving the problem, they tended to frame their debate in religious terms instead of terms that the entire population could agree upon. As intended, these religious arguments did not resonate with people who were not Christian and did not share the same interpretation of

Christian principles. To them it seemed like an attempt to force a particular set of Christian principles on an unreceptive nation. The dividing of the country worked, providing some individuals increased political influence at the expense of the country's well-being and cohesion.

With the improved economic situation and better education, the demand and need for abortions dropped dramatically in the new society without any policy changes. Improved availability and understanding the importance and how to use contraceptives helped ensure the situation rarely got to the point where an abortion was called for. At the same time, getting rid of the darkest aspects of Capitalism provided enormous benefits as well. Sexual intercourse had been one of the "remedies" people relied on to feel human again, to escape from the demoralizing "real world" and feel like there was someone who cared, even if it was just an illusion. Others used sex for validation, to silence doubts that what they did to succeed was as "evil" as it sometimes seemed. Sex as a tool to manipulate and conceal bigger problems was expressed in the curse words of the past, most associating having sex with damaging or destroying the partner's life. As sex lost its value as a way to address deficiencies in society, it became less likely to occur outside of relationships, where creating and raising a child would be disturbing, even if unplanned. And since real poverty had been eliminated, there was no fear that a child would be born into desperate financial circumstances. The society had become more child-friendly.

But since people had not given up recreational sex and contraceptives are not infallible, there remained plenty of cases of early-term abortion. And despite science being clear that an early-term abortion is no more an attack on life than cutting one's hair or finger nails, there remained some who objected to it on religious grounds. They were offended, therefore, by any association with it through their taxes and identity with the nation. Both of these objections have been addressed. In the old economy, abortions needed outside funding because it was the poorest people who needed them most. Additional mouths to feed made conditions worse for everyone, including, significantly, the newborn. In the new economy, with poverty eliminated, it was reasonable and just to have those people who wanted an abortion to pay for it themselves. It was certainly within their means. In the rare cases where the pregnancy was a product of forced sex, there was a fund created by interest groups that covered the costs of an abortion. Anyone who objected to abortions in all cases could divorce themselves entirely from it. Neither their pocketbook nor national identity was tied to public policies.

Another issue that the aspiring religious elite enflamed in order to substantiate their claims that the non-Christians were a threat that could be averted only through voting the "right" way was the teaching of evolution in public schools. Before it was seized on as a potential political issue, the idea that there might be a conflict between science and religion in the United States was considered foreign, something out of 1600s Europe. After all, it was the Puritans themselves, some of the most devout Christians in continental history, who established Harvard in 1636 with a balanced curriculum of science and religion. Most church leaders realized their role of helping people resolve spiritual problems did not clash with science and that the Bible was intended as a spiritual book, not a scientific one.

Besides, reconciling the Bible to science was not as difficult as some made it out to be. What started out as a small-scale resistance to Charles Darwin's theories on evolution was eventually seized upon by some church leaders as a potential wedge issue to drive strong political support. It resulted in a curious exchange between a small minority of atheists wishing to "disprove" Christianity with science and a small minority of ambitious "Christians" who saw in the topic a chance to make political points. If it weren't for the latter, the former would have gotten nowhere. The notion that science could be used to disprove religion would have been laughed out of the public sphere. Instead the issue exploded from time to time. It was yet another issue that did damage again to both the country and Christianity, as religious leaders started to demand people choose (odd as it sounds) between science and religion. Many people left religion altogether, believing that it was incompatible with science. Others stayed and turned away (again, odd as it sounds) from science.

Without the political motivations inflaming the issue, the pressure to ban the teaching of evolution in public schools or to teach religious beliefs of creationism alongside evolution in science classes died down as people realized there was no real threat to their freedoms. The debate, however, had revealed just how broken the education system had become. In their argument that creationism should be taught alongside evolution, they expressed a concern that the church was telling children to believe one thing and schools were telling children to believe something that they insisted was inconsistent.

Today the thought that schools would tell students what to believe or think is repugnant. According to the new principles, children should instead be provided an idea to think about and come to their own conclusions about it. "Students, here's a play called *Hamlet*. What do you think Shakespeare was trying to say with it?" Similarly, "Students, here's a theory on how people came about, and here's the scientific history behind the theory. What do you think of the scientific methods and reasoning used?" Different perspectives and skepticism about scientific theories, whether motivated by religious beliefs or not, are extremely valuable in advancing science as long as the skepticism is exercised using the scientific method, an understanding of which education can and should provide.

Religion wasn't the only force trying to impose and manipulate morals and values. So much of the economic, political, and social framework of the United States relied on the idea that some, if not all people, were evil. Capitalism was developed on the assumption that the only thing that could be relied upon was people's individual greed, everyone looking out for their own self-interest in a competitive world. Meanwhile it had to rely on people's charity to keep the bottom of the social hierarchy from revolting. And the political machinery of the United States actively implied that there were threats to the country from evil forces in order to increase obedience and limit protest. To accept the aggressive attack on, imprisonment, and sometimes even killing of the country's citizens accused of crimes, one had to accept the idea that there were people among us who were evil and deserved to be so severely treated. Evil, like nationalism, was a useful tool to manipulate the population.

The old criminal system made it pretty clear that evil individuals must be held accountable for their actions.

Many, presumably, were born evil and would always be evil and so must be eliminated from society, jailed, or executed in the extreme cases. Others, it would seem, could be encouraged to control their evil impulses if punished so severely as to discourage future acts of non-conformity. It was argued that without personal responsibility for actions, lawlessness would take over. People would have no reason to control their anti-social instincts. It was an argument that put the blame on the individuals and a philosophy that served those in power, who didn't want people asking questions about whether the country's economic, political, or social systems were a source of the problem. Fortunately for them, few people bothered to ask why the country was producing so many evil people that it was on track to have a larger percentage of its citizens in prison than any other country.

But the popular view on this issue has shifted since secession. Most people believe that the economic and political systems can have a profound impact on personal behavior. To blame someone for taking desperate action when the economic model provided no means for them to feed their family seems barbaric today. There is even sympathy for people who were engaged in active manipulation in the old economy as they were just responding to social pressures to succeed. Few people have difficultly understanding that a political system that allowed for the active manipulation and exploitation of people for the benefit of a minority at the top would naturally create a sense of hopelessness that could easily lead to attempts to lash out, despite the fact that such actions could possibly make matters even worse. Likewise social values that were intolerant to diverse views and lifestyles offered little outlet for people to express their individuality. In a country that valued freedom, it seemed unjust to insist that they deny or suppress who they were. And if for some reason, the society made such a demand, the forced conformity could not help but affect how those born different or chose to be different interacted with others.

Whether evil existed or not, Utopialki made every attempt to avoid pushing people toward anything resembling it. It was based on the notion that being human itself was not evil. Even if it were (a belief many in the Christian community oddly held to despite the rather notable tolerance and acceptance demonstrated by Jesus), then it surely was an evil condition that we all shared and so should be sympathetic to. It was maintained that every effort should be made to avoid systems that put people in desperate situations. Eliminating poverty went a long way toward this goal, but so did eliminating the pressure to engage in destructive and manipulative competitive practices. And the new political system empowered people to fix things they saw that were broken instead of having little choice but to endure them. A more tolerant environment for individuality now thrives, creating a diversity that has paid huge dividends for everyone.

To further help with that effort, Utopialki combined the principles of personal responsibility with an insistence that the society take responsibility as well. The same argument could be applied: without social responsibility for the actions of people in the society, there would be no reason for the society to reform itself and reduce the pressure on people to behave badly. Since crimes of all types had dramatically diminished after secession, there was strong evidence that society and its systems could and did have a profound impact on people's actions. Now each time a crime is committed, it is seen as an opportunity to determine what caused this person to behave that way. Is the law just? Were there societal causes? Even rarer than crimes are cases where the incident of a crime has not led to some sort of change or at least a serious evaluation of some aspect of the social, political, or economic systems that led to the act. It has been learned that it is possible to hold both the person and the society responsible for acts of crime.

Much of the crime in the United States (or at least many of the criminals) was related one way or another to drugs and alcohol. Many responded to pressures from society by escaping through substance abuse. And in an economy with a "succeed at any cost" mentality, where success was measured by income, there were plenty of people willing to supply them illicitly. In Utopialki, most of the circumstances that drove people to abuse drugs and alcohol have been eliminated. People don't feel nearly as much motivation to escape the "real world" and its problems. They don't need help "letting go," because society doesn't require them to hold back (to act unnaturally in order to appear to be something they are not). And without the profit motive, drug and alcohol sellers are not pushing the stuff on people. While drug use has not ceased and few people have given up alcohol altogether, neither is used in the excessive quantities common in the United States. In a society that cherishes Freedom, however, the only legal restrictions put on drug and alcohol use have been to try to curb and ideally eliminate the opportunity someone might have to harm others while under their influence.

Discussing crime typically led a debate on gun control. From a Constitutional perspective, the "right to bear arms" had been considered necessary in the Bill of Rights as a defense against the government of the elite oppressing too heavily on the people. Curiously it managed to persist even alongside the mythology of the United States being a government of the people and a strong historical preference for people in the United States to resolve domestic matters peacefully. While few people beyond the fringes of society talked about the need for arms to take over the government, gun rights became more about the right to hunt and the right to personal safety in a country that had appeared to become overwhelmed by violent crime, judging by the rhetoric at least of the politicians and the 24-hour news cycle. Ironically both sides used crime in their arguments. Gun-rights advocates argued that the right to own a gun should be maintained so everyone can protect themselves. Organizations committed to reducing gun violence pointed to the increasing amount of gun violence as a reason to restrict access to guns. It was another example of trying to ban the immediate problem without addressing the core issues.

Making conditions worse were the gun-industry lobbyists. Hired by gun manufacturers with the goal of increasing gun sales, it was in their best interest to create and inflame conflict and promote fear, just like the people who preyed on religious issues for power. If their interests were truly to protect and expand the rights of gun owners, they would become the most serious advocates for solutions to end violent crime, leading the charge to end their causes instead of adding fuel to the fire. Their true motivations were laid bare, however, by their advocating for more guns as a defense against violent crime and making them easier for people to get in moments of extreme desperation.

They even advocated for the availability of military-grade weapons that could only escalate violent crime, despite the lack of support among gun owners. These policies were, again, designed to divide the country, not lead to a practical compromise that advanced the interests of all sides. And divide the country they did.

In Utopialki the idea of overthrowing or defending oneself from the government has become completely absurd. So much of the new "political" system is designed to listen to and respond to people's concerns that the need of guns for defense against an oppressive government has become widely discredited. Even non-violent protests have become so rare that if one did take place, it would grab the attention of everyone and not let it go until a resolution had been found. Public-discussion meetings still take place but nothing like the old mob protests seen from time to time in the United States. Such protests are simply unnecessary.

Although the motivations behind much gun crime (poverty and self-esteem issues) have been eliminated, there are still rare cases of gun violence, so this complex issue remains. What is completely beyond debate, however, is any notion of limiting hunting rights. The right to hunt was another cultural legacy of England, where hunting rights were once severely limited based on class. In some parts of the United States, hunting remained a cherished act of defiance against elite privilege and therefore an expression of personal independence and freedom. In the new society, moral objections to hunting, while understandable, were considered personal (much like one's moral view on recreational sex) and so beyond the domain of government. Exceptions, however, are made to protect against true cruelty to animals.

Frankly, in a healthy, mature society, there is, in fact, no reason to ban guns. But the United States (and the rest of the world, in fact) lacked the basic hallmarks of a healthy society. The fact that some still felt they needed guns as a protection against their government was a red flag. But even more so was the sense that people needed guns in order to protect themselves against their neighbors. That there were individuals in the society who were so volatile that one needed a gun to protect oneself indicated very serious shortcomings in that society—and which were only made worse by the easy availability of guns. Just like one would not hand an angry child a deadly weapon, neither can one entrust guns to a society where desperation was commonplace and calm resolutions to differences were not universal.

While difficult to justify for the general public, military-grade weapons would still have a place in the military. But there was a question about whether a military would still be justified for a government no longer responsible for depending and supporting the global Capitalist elite. The unincorporated territories consider war a crime, just as someone beating up someone on the street to "prove" a point is a crime. Seeing how war had been used in the past to advance elite interests at the expense of the security and often the lives of ordinary citizens, there was not much interest in empowering the new "government" to declare wars of aggression. Besides, people found it much more efficient to battle competing ideologies by setting a consistent and positive example instead of trying to prove itself through its military. It was clear this approach was having its impact around the world without having to force anyone to the new systems. So the movement's non-violence has been sustained.

However, even without an interventionist foreign policy, there are still people who are concerned about foreign invasion. They believe that if they are left unprotected, some ambitious foreign or domestic leader would find the land free for the taking and its population perfect for enslavement. In a free society, where different opinions are respected, the fears of this population could not be ignored—the system would not allow them to be ignored. Instead it is handled just like almost anything else. People who feel that a defense force is necessary can contribute investment funds to the cause. These funds can be used to train, arm, and maintain an armed force. This armed force owes its first and only allegiance to the entire population, however, and can be deployed only when people are threatened by a clear and present danger. Just like the abortion issue, it answered the needs of one group without implicating other people who had a moral objection to such things by requiring them to pay or directly sanction a military force.

An answer was needed for the threat of terrorism, too. As the United States became more involved in the internal affairs of other countries, and as Capitalists began to exploit the labor, consumers, and environment of other countries, the threat of terrorism increased.

During the Cold War, many countries, particularly those in the Middle East and North Africa, resented being pawns in a battle between the two superpowers. Meanwhile, the more ambitious US Capitalists became in setting up and enriching global Capitalists, the easier it became for extremist groups in other nations to recruit followers to fight against the expansion of US economic imperialism. The stronger the Capitalists got, the stronger the terrorists got. And the stronger the terrorists got, the more power the government could take to keep the country "safe." It was another symbiotic relationship. There was no reason for either the US government or the terrorist leadership to end the standoff since escalation simply made each side stronger. After all, it was not the leadership on either side that was doing the dying.

In the unincorporated territories, it was realized that terrorism stemmed, ultimately, from hopelessness and desperation. When people feel their lives were being severely impacted by an outside force that they had no control over, they sometimes resorted to terrorism, generally making things worse instead of better for their cause. This was true for both domestic and foreign terrorism, since even domestically, people often felt they had no control over their circumstances. The international community, however, didn't even enjoy the mythology of control offered by Democracy—let alone actual recourse—against the imposition of foreign Capitalists to moderate feelings of despair, so the threat of international terrorism was greater. Since they could not register their complaint in the next US election, they might take out their aggression on the US voters traveling abroad, believing that they were somehow responsible for the actions of the US government. The result, as with other forms of violence, was bad for people on all sides.

Utopialki was committed to avoiding these pitfalls. Domestically the issue had been solved automatically by giving people a clear voice and a simple and very effective channel for raising concerns and complaints. To make sure no external groups felt oppressed by Utopialki policies, they opened channels through which anyone around the world could have a voice in the discussions going on in the unincorporated territories. Knowing if someone was going to go to war or retaliate in any way against the territories based on some decision that was being made was very important information when making that decision. So anyone anywhere in the world could hire a lobbyist. The lobbyist's foreign connections would, of course, be made perfectly transparent and would typically be factored into any decision, but the voice was there. In the United States, only foreign corporations and Capitalists had sufficient resources to influence public policy in this way. With a lower price tag, that voice was much easier to acquire. But the need to buy a voice still left some of the world's most oppressed people with no apparent way to speak out. To be heard, they could get the attention of someone in the unincorporated territories who would be sympathetic to the cause and initiate a reconsideration on their behalf. With the wide distribution of opinions and views in the population, it has never been much of a problem for someone outside of the territories to find a sympathetic party to pick up a worthy cause.

It is not just foreign causes that have benefited from the diversity of opinions, interests, and passions in the unincorporated territories. The greatest beneficiaries are the people themselves. Being able to express oneself openly and live freely has provided much personal satisfaction and provides everyone exposure to a much richer experience in dealing with others. By splitting the idea of nations and nationality from politics, people gained a whole new freedom that was difficult to fully and openly exercise before: Freedom of Identity. In Utopialki, identification with a nation has become much more a personal choice about cultural and ideological identification instead of being imposed on people. It is now a shorthand for people to explain who they are, for people who find such to be helpful. After the original secession, and the later secession of Canada and Mexico, most people have continued to self-identify with their old nations, as part of their cultural identity. Many people still identified themselves as "Americans." Identification of all sorts has become much more useful and productive in helping people make sense of who they are and want to be without making people feel like they needed to impose their values on someone else. As opportunities have expanded and have become almost completely disconnected from a person's family history, identity—national and otherwise—became more of a social tool than an economic or political tool.

On the way to utopia

Despite all the talk of anti-Elitism in the Utopialki movement, a new elite is forming. They aren't elite in the sense that they have special privileges or advantages in life, but they are elite in that they stand out and above from the rest of the population. They are the heroes of the new society, people who are respected and trusted typically more than everyone else. It is a trust they would never risk losing by trying to rig some sort of special advantage for themselves or their friends, even if they could. The elite of the new society, the new heroes, are made up of the superstars from the Employment Support Office, teachers in the public schools, the Capitalists who coordinate the use of investment funds for public projects, and the lobbyists who fight for the interests of diverse groups. These are the individuals who people rely on throughout their lives to pursue their individual dreams and grasp the opportunity provided by the new and more sincere Land of Opportunity.

Meanwhile the "grand utopian experiment" in North America has not gone unnoticed in the rest of the world. Certainly the mythologies written and imagined about the United States had a profound impact on the world back in its day. In his *Common Sense,* Thomas Paine wrote:

> The cause of America is, in a great measure, the cause of all mankind. Many circumstances have, and will arise, which are not local, but universal, and through which the principles of all lovers of mankind are affected, and in the event of which, their affections are interested.

But perhaps the country's greatest contribution was its role as an incubator for the Utopialki movement.

Shortly after the successful "secession" of Canada and Mexico into the unincorporated territories, many of the other states of the United States began to seriously discuss the potential of additional secessions. The remaining western states were impressed with the amount of freedom enjoyed in Utopialki and the strong sense of hope in the future. The strongly religious central and southeastern states were impressed with how Utopialki was addressing religious and social issues, taking concerns of the Christians seriously and respectfully. New England was more difficult to convert. It was in New York City and Boston where most of the real decisions for the economy and government in the United States had been made over the centuries. They had invested much of themselves into the old-style Capitalism and were reluctant to abandon it.

In 1992, referendums in most of the western states passed calling for secession by 1996. The central states and southeast were slower, but, by summer of 1993, they, too, were on board and agreed to the 1996 time frame. Upstate New York almost broke away from New York City in their drive to secede, but the northeast finally all agreed in early 1994. If the unincorporated territories would have them, the rest of the United States was ready to secede.

At the same time, countries in South America also began to approach representatives in the unincorporated territories. Mimicking the decision to tie Canadian and Mexican secession together, it was decided that the secession of the rest of the United States would be tied with the secession of most of the rest of the Americas. The diversity would actually make the transition easier. The date was set for February 11, 1998 in order to give enough time for the economies to acclimate to the new economic systems, which required some investment from the United States into a few of the South American countries. As you can imagine, when the date came, the celebrations were enormous. As reserved as the North Americans are in their celebrating is how animated many of the South Americans cultures were. The elite around the globe could no longer mistake the coming end days; most, in fact, were looking forward to them.

Since secession, the new unincorporated territories have embraced the principles of Freedom and Opportunity as much as the original territories. They have also taken the idea of community to new levels. In Boston, for example, the people decided to invest in an awe-inspiring project—called the Big Dig—to put an extensive private/public transportation system underneath the city. The idea is to connect everyone to the public transportation system.

A person can order a small vehicle that picks them up wherever they may be in the city, hooks into the public transportation system, and takes the passengers to their destination, navigated completely by computer. The system will also be used to deliver packages to any home or office, minimizing human labor in the effort as well as environmental impact. The expectation is that, within 15 years, the only people with cars in Boston will be driving enthusiasts who have a car as a hobby. In another 50 years, the system may be expanded so that someone could travel not only within cities but also between cities at super-high speeds.

With the Americas "united," interest expanded to nations around the globe. There was an ambition to complete practically all of the secessions in rapid succession in a few years. But it was simply too much change to process in too short a time frame. Instead it was decided to release a plan to bring in all countries interested in joining onboard over a longer time frame. The amount of untapped human potential in the new regions staggers the mind. But easing people who have lived with so little into a higher global standard of living will be difficult. This was perhaps the biggest challenge facing the committee trying to plan out the future secessions. Also difficult was the goal to allow anyone to live anywhere. The challenge was to allow them to the same freedoms they enjoyed in the culture with which they most identify without compromising the cultural rights of any population they might move into. It was the combination of allowing maximum freedom of movement and personal liberties with the ideal of respecting local cultural differences. These challenges made clear why the world would always be *on the way* to Utopia without ever fully arriving.

Notes

1. John Ferling, *A Leap in the Dark: The Struggle to Create the American Republic* (New York: Oxford University Press, 2003) 219.

2. Ferling 192.

3. Alexander Keyssar, *The Right to Vote: The Contested History of Democracy in the United States (Revised Ed)* (New York: Basic Books, 2009) 10.

4. Ferling 272.

5. Howard Zinn, *A People's History of the United States* (New York: HarperCollins, 2003) 48–49.

6. Ferling 321.

7. Norman K Risjord, *Jefferson's America: 1760–1815* (Madison: Madison House, 1991) 251.

8. Risjord 259.

9. Daniel Walker Howe, *What Hath God Wrought: The Transformation of America, 1815–1848* (New York: Oxford University Press, 2007) 52.

10. Howe 455.

11. William L. Barney, *The Passage of the Republic: An Interdisciplinary History of Nineteenth-Century America* (Lexington, Mass.: D.C. Heath and Company, 1987) 200

12. Barney 157.

13. Barney 338.

14. Barney 68.

15. Barney 49.

16. Zinn 387.

17. Sean Dennis Cashman, *America in the Gilded Age: From the Death of Lincoln to the Rise of Theodore Roosevelt (3rd edition)* (New York: New York University Press, 1994) 51.

18. Barney 386.

19. Zinn 261.

20. Glen Jeansonne, *A Time of Paradox: America Since 1890* (Lanham, Md.: Rowman & Littlefield, 2006) 143.

21. Robert A. Margo, "Employment and Unemployment in the 1930s," *Journal of Economic Perspectives* (Vol 7, Number 2, Spring 1993) 43.

22. Nell Irvin Painter, *Standing at Armageddon: The United States 1877–1919* (New York: W.W. Norton, 1987) 381.

23. Zinn 568–569.

24. Zinn 569.

25. Gary A. Donaldson, *Abundance and Anxiety: America, 1945–1960* (Westport, Conn.: Praeger, 1997) 78.

26. MJ Heale, *The Sixties in America: History, Politics, and Protest* (Chicago: Fitzroy Dearborn Publishers, 2001) 28.

27. Heale 64.

28. Heale 105.

29. Tom Hayden, *The Long Sixties: From 1960 to Barack Obama* (Boulder: Paradigm Publishers 2009) 76.

30. Zinn 557.

31. Philip Jenkins, *The Decade of Nightmares: The End of the Sixties and the Making of the Eighties America* (New York: Oxford University Press, 2006) 96.

32. Zinn 570.

33. Jenkins 101.

34. Zinn 611.
35. Zinn 576.
36. Jenkins 221.
37. Jenkins 182.
38. Jenkins 212.
39. Zinn 579.
40. Jenkins 137.
41. Jenkins 136.
42. Jenkins 237.
43. Zinn 424–425.
44. Zinn 581.
45. Zinn 605.
46. Zinn 609.
47. Risjord 502.

Works referenced

A History of England, Second Edition, Clayton and David Roberts, 1985.

Mayflower Remembered: A History of the Plymouth Pilgrims, 1970.

Puritanism in America: 1620–1750, Everett Emerson, 1977.

"Between Private and Public Spheres: Liberty as Cultural Property in Eighteenth-Century British America," Michal Jan Rozbicki, in *Cultures and Identities in Colonial British America,* Edited by Robert Olwell and Alan Tully, 2006.

Cities in the Wilderness—The First Century of Urban Life in America 1625–1742, Carl Bridenbaugh, 1938.

Local Government in Early America, Brian P. Janiskee, 2010.

Iroquoia, The Development of a Native World, William Engelbrech, 2003.

The Cherokee Nation, Robert J. Conley, 2005.

Colonial America: From Settlement to the Revolution, Rodgney P. Carlisle and J. Geoffrey Golson, Editors, 2007.

South Carolina, Lewis P. Jones, 1971.

New York: A Bicentennial History, Bruce Bliven, Jr., 1981.

Pennsylvania: A Bicentennial History, Thomas C. Cochran, 1978.

1676: The End of American Independence, Stephen Saunders Webb, 1995.

A Leap in the Dark: The Struggle to Create the American Republic, John Ferling, 2003.

American Creation: Triumphs and Tragedies at the Founding of the Republic, Joseph J Ellis, 2007.

Jefferson's America: 1760–1815, Norman K Risjord, 1991.

Wikipedia.org: Battles of Lexington and Concord.

The Birth of the Bill of Rights, 1776–1791, Robert Allen Rutland, 1955.

What Hath God Wrought: the Transformation of America, 1815–1848, Daniel Walker Howe, 2007.

The Right to Vote: The Contested History of Democracy in the United States (Revised Ed), Alexander Keyssar, 2009.

Exiles in a Land of Liberty: Mormons in America 1830–1846, Kenneth H. Winn, 1989.

Texas: A Contest of Civilizations, George P. Garrison, 1903.

The Causes of the Civil War: The Political, Cultural, Economic, and Territorial Disputes between North and South, Paul Calore, 2008.

America in the Gilded Age: From the Death of Lincoln to the Rise of Theodore Roosevelt (3rd edition), Sean Dennis Cashman, 1994.

The Passage of the Republic: an Interdisciplinary History of Nineteenth-Century America, William L. Barney, 1987.

Harvey Wasserman's History of the United States, 1988.

Standing at Armageddon: The United States 1877–1919, Nell Irvin Painter, 1987.

A Time of Paradox: America Since 1890, Glen Jeansonne, 2006.

"Employment and Unemployment in the 1930s," Robert A. Margo, in *Journal of Economic Perspectives,* Vol 7, Number 2, Spring 1993.

Abundance and Anxiety: America, 1945–1960, Gary A. Donaldson, 1997.

The Sixties in America: History Politics and Protest. MJ Heale, 2001.

"*Civil rights and the Civil War,*" BBC History Magazine, March 2011 pp 34–37.

The Long Sixties: From 1960 to Barack Obama. Tom Hayden. 2009.

The Decade of Nightmares: The End of the Sixties and the Making of the Eighties America. Philip Jenkins. 2006.

Who will tell the People: The Betrayal of American Democracy. William Greider, 1992.

Time for Angels: The Tragicomic History of the League of Nations, Elmer Bendiner, 1975.

that's not in my american history book, Thomas Ayres, 2000.

What Ifs? Of American History, Robert Cowley, 2003.

The Company: A Short History of a Revolutionary Idea, John Micklethwait and Adrian Wooldridge, 2005.

www.ingramcontent.com/pod-product-compliance
Lightning Source LLC
Chambersburg PA
CBHW032101040426
42336CB00040B/629